CHRISTIANITY
THROUGH THE AGES

Harper ▲ ChapelBooks

CHRISTIANITY
THROUGH
THE AGES

By Kenneth Scott Latourette

Sterling Professor of Missions and Oriental History and
Fellow of Berkeley College, Emeritus, in
Yale University

Harper ChapelBooks

HARPER & ROW, PUBLISHERS

New York

CHRISTIANITY THROUGH THE AGES. *Copyright © 1965 by Kenneth Scott Latourette. Printed in the United States of America. All rights reserved. No part of
this book may be used or reproduced in any manner whatsoever without
written permission except in the case of brief quotations embodied in critical
articles and reviews. For information address Harper & Row, Publishers,
Inc., 10 East 53rd Street, New York, N. Y.* 10022

FIRST EDITION *published as a Harper ChapelBook, 1965, by Harper & Row,
Publishers, Incorporated*

LIBRARY OF CONGRESS CATALOG CARD NUMBER: 65-11348
80 81 82 83 10

To Mrs. Charles T. Lincoln

*who for forty years turned into faultless
typescript the manuscripts of most of
the author's successive books and who
has exemplified "the fruits of the Spirit"*

CONTENTS

CONTENTS

PREFACE

Here is an attempt to tell in brief compass the history of Christianity. Christianity is usually called a religion. As a religion it has had a wider geographic spread and is more deeply rooted among more peoples than any other religion in the history of mankind. Both that spread and that rootage have been mounting in the past 150 years and especially in the present century. The history of Christianity, therefore, must be of concern to all who are interested in the record of man and particularly to all who seek to understand the contemporary human scene.

This book is deliberately called a history of Christianity rather than a history of the Church or Church history. These are the usual designations of accounts of the course of the Christian faith. They are focused on the ecclesiastical institutions which are called churches, or, collectively, the Church. Normally they include the story of the development of these institutions, of their reciprocal relations, of the movements associated with these institutions, of the forms of worship which have arisen in them, and of the intellectual formulations of the Christian faith. Both the original records and the studies of these records are prodigious. They have engaged the attention of thousands of scholars and continue to do so. Most of the resulting books and articles are confined to special aspects of the story. Others attempt to cover the story as a whole. Such approaches are legitimate and many of the works which have come out of them are notable and useful.

Here is a different approach. While seeking to utilize much of the vast output in what is generally called Church history, it addresses itself to the story from a more inclusive perspective. It is based upon the conviction that, if the Christian faith is true, the story must have basic significance for the entire course of life and especially of human life on this planet. The significance cannot be confined to this planet. It must embrace the universe, both the small fragments of it known to men and everything thus far beyond the range of human knowledge. It must take into account not only all the history of mankind in its multiform manifestations—political, religious, economic, aesthetic, social, and intellectual—but what to human beings, with their limited outlook and endowments, is the staggering and unimaginably vast cosmos in which they are set.

Such an attempt seems preposterous. How can any man, short-lived as all his race are, hope to compass even such information as is available to men? At most he can know only what has occurred on this planet, and the seventy or eighty years allotted to him are too brief to acquire and digest all that his fellows have accumulated across the centuries and are continuing to amass. He certainly cannot penetrate more than the merest fraction of what has happened and is happening outside the speck of matter he inhabits, a speck that is one of several other fragments moving around one of the several billion suns of a galaxy which is in turn merely one of billions of other galaxies, each with its millions or billions of suns. Moreover, man is dimly aware that his instruments can at best disclose only limited features of what he calls the physical aspects of the cosmos. Beyond these physical aspects and untouched by his instruments is what he regards as the world of the spirit, which impinges upon him in every moment of his life.

Preposterous though the undertaking may be, across the centuries daring souls have essayed it. A few of their efforts have commanded respect. Augustine's *City of God* is one particularly famous. As we are to note in Chapter I, many of the writings embraced in the Christian Scriptures are cognizant of the issues and have an outlook which encompasses all time and the entire cosmos. However, most of the attempts at such a comprehensive survey of the record of mankind from a Christian perspective have been viewed by scholars as naïve and quite untenable. Even some Christians have declared that "salvation history"—the record of God's redemptive dealings with men—cannot be rightly embraced in "world history," including the course of all human activity in its manifold expressions.

Daring though it undoubtedly is, here is an effort to suggest in wide scope what such a history should be. It is offered with an acute awareness of its inescapable limitations. It begins with the Christian view of the cosmos and of the course of life, particularly human life, on this planet. It then goes on to sketch the background, so far as we now know it, of that life before the coming of Him from Whom Christianity takes its name. Next is a brief account of the earthly career of Him from Whom Christianity is historically sprung and of the distinctive features which must be borne in mind as we seek to give the story of Christianity. The major portion of the book will cover the main outlines of that story as the author conceives them.

The story will take account of what is generally included in Church history. But it will repeatedly seek to call attention to the wider setting of that history. The book embodies a profound conviction that the distinction between "salvation history" and "world history" is in contradiction to the central core of the Gospel—the "Good News"—from which Christianity has sprung and which is the source of its continuing vitality. The author recognizes, as will be obvious, that throughout history God has been seeking to save man, and that His effort has centred and been climaxed in "salvation history," as it is sometimes called. But he believes that God has been active in all history, and in ways not inconsistent with "salvation history," properly understood.

To this story the author brings a study of history pursued

over a long life. In the course of his career he has sought through teaching and writing to acquaint himself with what are usually adjudged by scholars to be all phases and all eras of "world history." He has specialized on some aspects of it, notably that of East Asia. But both by interest and from professional duty he has ranged over the rest of pre-history and history. He has written extensively on the history of Christianity and has here taken advantage of what he has sought to put down in two multi-volume and several single-volume works. Yet this is not a mere summary of these works. It is in some ways a fresh approach which has emerged from more than a half-century of research, writing, and meditation.

The author is frankly a Christian. No historian writes with pure objectivity. If he professes to do so he is dishonest or self-deceived. The author has not come easily by his Christian faith. He was reared as a Christian and in his youth made a conscious Christian commitment. Yet he has had to face the questions with which from the beginning that faith has been challenged and in addition has had to wrestle, often agonizingly, with questions which are peculiar to his day and are posed by the natural sciences, psychology, and the threats to the continued existence of the race. Originally trained in the natural sciences, he has endeavoured to keep abreast of the major findings in some of them, chiefly geology and astronomy. He has spent most of his years in a great university where many of the questions which confront a Christian are brought to acute focus. He has also participated actively in much of life outside a university and has been immersed in some of the most potent currents of his day. He has tried to face honestly the facts of the history he seeks to narrate and not to dodge any of the challenges which they present to those who, like himself, dare to call themselves Christian. This book is not an apologetic—an attempt to defend Christianity and to persuade his readers of the truth of what underlies that religion. It is, rather, an effort to put in brief compass the course of that religion, directing attention to the challenges it has met, the failures of many of its most loyal adherents to live up to "the high calling of God in Christ Jesus," as the New Testament calls it, and some of the achievements in seeking to make that calling a reality.

As the author is acutely aware, much that is germane to the story, from the Christian perspective, is not accessible to the historian. For example, the records with which the historian has to deal do not penetrate, except by faith, into that life to which, so the Christian believes, existence on this planet is but a prelude. The historian cannot even know some of the most significant features of the portion of the story which he seeks to narrate. Untold millions of Christians have left no continuing written traces of themselves or their work. Yet, as any one who has lived long in a particular community will gladly testify, what the New Testament calls "the fruits of the Spirit" have been vividly manifest in countless lives which have been rendered radiant and selfless by their Christian faith. The contributions of Christianity to some of the movements that are prominent in the narratives compiled by historians are not always easily detected and, when seen, are not readily given their proportionate credit. Yet these inescapable limitations must not be allowed to discourage the historian from entering upon the task here essayed. He must be cognizant of the limitations—even though at times only dimly—and not profess to more knowledge than is accessible to him. But because, as a believer, he is profoundly convinced of the central importance to all mankind of the record of Christianity, he must embark on what can at best be an incomplete and imperfect summary and interpretation of the history of the faith which has gripped him and on which he has sought to build his life.

CHAPTER I

The Cosmic Setting as Presented
in the Christian Scriptures

The Scriptures which Christians believe to be divinely inspired open with the affirmation "In the beginning God created the heavens and the earth." This includes the entire cosmos—of dimensions far more extensive than the writer could know and presumably larger than even present-day science reveals, breathtaking though that is. Here is the conviction that God was before the creation—"eternal," as Christians and Jews have declared. The opening chapters of the Scriptures state that as the apex of life on the planet God created man in His own image. This means that to man God gave a degree of free will. Freedom was conditioned by man's physical body, heredity, and environment. But with all these limitations, it was real. That free will was demonstrated in the placing of temptation before man with the command not to eat of the fruit of the tree which would give him a knowledge of good and evil, with the disturbing moral conflict to which that awareness would give rise. The account also describes the fashion in which man, seeking in his pride to be equal with God, disobeyed the command.

From there the Scriptures go on to narrate how God sought to save man and bring him into that likeness to Himself for which he had been created. God was seeking to create sons and not robots—automata whose responses were pre-determined by the stimuli playing upon them. Always, in His effort, God respected man's free will. By judgement He endeavoured to restrain man and to bring him to repentance. He strove to bring that purpose to fruition by choosing Abraham with the promise, the Scriptures report, that in him should "all families of the earth be blessed." From Abraham sprang a people, so the story continues, through whom God willed to fulfil His purpose. Only once, and then briefly and in a small segment of the earth's surface, did that people create an important state. Moreover, the vast majority of that people were chronically disloyal to the covenant God had made with them. In that covenant, as in His dealings with the first man, God gave to His "chosen people" sufficient freedom of will to obey or disobey and the overwhelming majority disobeyed. Only a very small minority, led by an even smaller minority in a distinctive succession, the prophets, through whom God was believed to speak, were sufficiently responsive to the impulse coming from God to discern His voice. To these prophets, as our records of their words show, response to that voice was accompanied by intense pain; they were only intermittently able clearly to discern what the voice was saying.

Eventually, from this seemingly unpromising preparation but in reality, as one of the early Christians declared, "when the time had fully come, God sent forth His Son, born of a woman" and "born under the law"—that is, among the people through whom God had sought to make preparation for that sovereign act. In sending His Son God purposed out of the unpromising human material to give birth to sons who would respond to His initiative and cry, "Abba, Father." True to His respect for the degree of man's freedom of choice, limited but still authentic, God's Son came in weakness, cradled in a manger because no inn would make room for the young mother in her hour. He grew to maturity in a small village. Then, after a few months, at best only three years, of a public career in which He was hailed by a crowd which proved fickle and had won the adherence of a coterie of men and women who did not fully understand Him, He ran afoul of the leaders of the organized religion of His people, was accused by them of fomenting rebellion against the civil government, that of Rome, and was crucified by the order of the local representative of that government. But, so the Scriptures narrate, the crucifixion was not the end. The body laid by sorrowing and hopeless hands in a tomb was raised from it and, triumphant, met with the disciples for forty days, "speaking of the Kingdom of God"—His main theme in the brief period of His public career. Even then His disciples did not completely understand Him; they thought of the Kingdom in terms to which their earlier education had conditioned them, the restoration of that realm in which, centuries before, their ancestors had had a few decades of political prominence. Yet, they remembered, they had received the breath-taking command from Him to make disciples of all nations, baptizing them, and teaching them to observe all that He had commanded them. In other words which they recalled as having received from Him, even when they failed to grasp what He meant by the Kingdom of God, He had charged them to be His witnesses in all the earth. They reported that He had calmly assured them that "all authority" had been given to Him "in heaven and on earth," that they would receive power, and that He would be with them always, to the close of the age.

Very shortly, in fulfilment of that promise, so the Scriptures say, power did descend upon them. A little later, we are told, Jesus Himself appeared to one of their persecutors, Saul (Paul), won his allegiance, and from time to time continued to speak to him. Within less than a generation little groups of disciples appeared, not only in Judea and the eastern parts of the Mediterranean basin, but also at least as far west as the Bay of Naples and the city of Rome.

Within a generation, moreover, from several of the disciples who, admittedly, in the days of His flesh had never really understood Jesus and who at the crucifixion were frustrated and discouraged, came insights which, they believed, opened the cosmic significance of what they had seen and experienced. We need re-

mind ourselves of only a few of the most startling insights recorded in the New Testament to give an indication of what a
full survey would reveal. We are told that "in many and various
ways God spoke of old . . . by the prophets, but in these last days
He has spoken to us by a Son, Whom He appointed the heir of
all things, through Whom also He created the world. He reflects
the glory of God and bears the very stamp of His nature, uphold-
ing the universe by His power." Essentially the same is another
passage: "In the beginning was the Word, and the Word was with
God, and the Word was God. He was in the beginning with
God; all things were made through Him, and without Him was
not anything made that was made. In Him was life, and the life
was the light of men. The light shines in the darkness and the
darkness has not overcome it. . . . The true light that enlightens
every man was coming into the world. He was in the world, and
the world was made through Him, yet the world knew Him not.
He came to His own home and His own people received Him
not. But to all who received Him, who believed in His name,
He gave power to become children of God. . . . The Word became flesh and dwelt among us, full of grace and truth. . . . No
one has ever seen God; the only Son, Who is in the bosom of the
Father, He has made Him known."

Here are astounding assertions, all the more so in view of the
earlier disillusionment of the disciples. They declare that He
Who on that first Good Friday seemed to be a discredited and
frustrated dreamer had made known the incomprehensively
great God Who created and infills all that univrese which to
men is immeasurably vast and of which they know only fragments. The more elaborated of the two assertions insists that the
Word which became flesh was "full of grace and truth." By
"truth" is meant at least that in the Word, become flesh in a man
Who was born and lived in a particular time and in a cultural
environment and religious heritage which He reflected, we are
given an authentic and sufficient view of the nature and purpose
of the universe and are enabled to call God "Father." Moreover,
it says that of the essence of "truth" is "grace."

Again and again in the New Testament the changes are rung on "grace." "Grace" expresses the attitude which governs the dealings of the eternal God with man. Although man, using such freedom of will as he has been given, rebels against his Creator and aspires to arrogate to himself the power which characterizes his Creator, God seeks through His self-giving love, which man had forfeited and never had deserved or could deserve, to win him to Himself. "Herein is love not that we loved God but that He loved us, and sent His Son to be the expiation for our sins." "God shows His love for us in that while we were yet sinners Christ died for us." "God so loved the world that He gave His only begotten Son, that whosoever believeth in Him should not perish, but have everlasting life. For God sent not His Son into the world to condemn the world, but that the world through Him might be saved." "Everlasting life" is described not merely as continued existence, for that could be an intolerable burden, but as knowledge of God and of Jesus Christ and "fellowship" with the Father and with His Son, Jesus Christ.

"Grace" is described as shown in ways which human prudence deems foolish. Thus the crucifixion appeared to the Jews to be weakness, for they had conceived of the establishment of God's Kingdom, for which they hoped, by the kind of force employed by David, their king, to whom they looked back with reverence. To the Greeks, the intelligentsia of the Mediterranean world into which Jesus was born, who sought a solution to the riddle of existence through philosophy, the crucifixion was irrational. Yet Paul, the most prominent of the early Christian missionaries, declared the cross to be both the "power of God and the wisdom of God; because the foolishness of God is wiser than men and the weakness of God is stronger than men." In the concluding book the New Testament the risen and glorified Son of God, before Whose overpowering majestic presence the prophet fell down as dead, is described as saying to one of the early churches which, like many of its successors across the centuries, was self-contented, lukewarm, neither cold nor hot, that He stood at the door and knocked, not forcing it, but waiting for it to be unlocked, and promising, if those inside would open it, to come in, eating with them and they with Him.

We shall see, as we proceed with our narrative, that the way the Scriptures picture God as dealing with man characterizes the history of Christianity, not only in the preparation for the coming of His Son in the flesh and in the reception of His Son, but as well in the subsequent record of the religion named after the traditional designation of His Son. Through the long centuries in which God was seeking to prepare the way for the "incarnation"—the coming in human flesh of Himself through the "Word," the self-expression of Himself in the creation of the cosmos—He was seeking men who would willingly respond to "the light which lighteth every man" and slowly was finding some in the small minority of His "chosen people" who were struggling to understand what His Spirit, respecting their free will, was trying to say through them. Then, as might have been expected and as God clearly foresaw, when the Word became flesh the incarnation provoked man to his greatest crime, the crucifixion of the Son of God. But God was not defeated. The resurrection followed. Soon came a fresh outburst of the Spirit which empowered men and women, filled with amazed wonder and transformed by His love. These men and women were still imperfect, but one of the greatest of the early Christians was confident that "He Who began a good work" in them "would bring it to completion." Yet again and again the ecclesiastical institutions springing from the impulse given by Christ and professing loyalty to Him contradicted His Spirit in action. Fully as thought-provoking, as we are to see, has been the fact that some of the chronic evils which have plagued the human race have reached their most colossal dimensions through peoples which have borne the Christian name and have been longest under the influence of Christianity. Yet from men and women inspired by the Christian faith have come efforts, unprecedented and unequalled, to counter the evils, so that where "sin abounded, grace did much more abound."

Those calling themselves Christians, as well as others, have wrestled with the question of why this contradiction should exist, seemingly so strange, in a world in which the opening chapter of the Bible declares that after God had created it "everything" was "very good." Thus, in Paul's words, the "whole creation groaneth and travaileth in pain together until now." As we see it on this planet, nature is red in tooth and claw. But, Paul also affirms, while "the creation was subjected to futility" that was "not of its own will but by the will of Him who subjected it in hope, because the creation . . . will be set free from its bondage to decay "into the glorious liberty of the children of God."

Repeatedly the writers of the New Testament insist that the contradiction is eventually to be overcome. Thus it is confidently said that the "mystery" of the will "of the God and Father of our Lord Jesus Christ" is "in the fulness of time" to "gather together in one all things in Christ, both which are in heaven and which are on earth." Similarly the sweeping assertion is made that in Christ "all the fulness of God was pleased to dwell," and that through Christ God purposed "to reconcile all things unto Himself, whether on earth or in heaven." We also read that God has given to Christ Jesus "a name that is above every name, that at the name of Jesus every knee should bow, of things in heaven, and things in earth, and things under the earth, and that every tongue should confess that Jesus Christ is Lord, to the glory of God the Father."

In both the presence of evil and the eventual triumph over evil the sweep is cosmic. It embraces the entire universe, what to man is both seen and unseen. The victory is to be accomplished through Christ.

Precisely when and exactly through what process this consummation is to be reached the writers of Scripture do not specify in terms which the historian can pin down to exact details. However, they are agreed that it is to be a reality.

Obviously he who would attempt to write the history of Christianity cannot do more than recognize that from the standpoint of the Scriptures the story he essays to write has cosmic significance. The facts at his disposal are only the events on this planet, and this planet is a relatively tiny speck in a physically vast universe. The historian cannot know whether life in physical forms exists elsewhere or, if it exists, what its characteristics are. Nor can he wisely seek to penetrate that, to him, unseen world of spirits, good and bad, which the Scripture writers declare surround and condition man. Neither can he, as an historian, embrace in his narrative what has taken place beyond the physical death of the billions who have inhabited this planet. As a Christian he must believe that he lives in a universe. The natural scientists, he is aware, are confident that the forces which their instruments detect operate uniformly as far as they can glean information in the vast reaches into which they enable them to peer, Presumably, therefore, the God Who created and sustains the universe is everywhere the same. Always, so the New Testament declares, God is creative love. Everywhere His Word operates consistently in the manner in which the Christian believes He has acted and continues to act on this planet. But that the historian cannot prove. Nor can he hope to do more than narrate such fragments of the past on this globe as the records available to him enable him to discern.

CHAPTER II

Pre-Christian History

CHRISTIANITY IN THE HISTORY OF RELIGION

Compared with the thousands of years in which human life has been on this planet, Christianity is a recent development. When contrasted with the much longer time that life has been present, the course of Chirstianity thus far is but a brief moment. Here are profound questions into which, if he is wise, the historian, as historian, does not enter. He simply notes them. If he is a Christian the historian must believe that God has always been active and has been pursuing His purpose of creating sons and not robots. In doing so, God must have been following the procedure which was eventually manifested in the incarnation. Paul declared that "when the time had fully come, God sent forth His Son, born of a woman, born under the law, to redeem those who were under the law, so that we might receive adoption as sons." He viewed the people of Israel and God's covenant with them as a preparation for the incarnation, the cross, and the resurrection. But, when seen against the background of the entire record of mankind, the appearance of Israel was only slightly earlier than that of Christianity. Paul seems to have taken account of that fact where he says that what could be known about God was plain to men, because God had shown it to them. "For the invisible things of Him from the creation of the world are clearly seen, being understood by the things that are seen, namely, His eternal power and Godhead." Presumably God had always been seeking men, but without violating the degree of freedom of will which He had deliberately given them. As Paul is quoted as saying in his address to the students and scholars at Athens, God made of one blood all nations of men, that they should seek Him in the hope that they might feel after Him and find Him.

Certainly, so far as archeology has been able to trace the beginnings of culture, from the first, men have struggled to understand themselves and the world in which they live and have been aware, even if dimly, of a power or powers outside themselves which they have either revered or feared and have endeavoured to find ways of propitiating and of bringing to their assistance.

In the history of religion which has engaged the interest of scholars, especially in the eighteenth, nineteenth, and twentieth centuries, thousands have sought to trace the inception and the development of religion and to describe the myriad forms which religion has taken, both earlier and in the contemporary scene. We need not here go extensively into that history. We must, however, note that what are usually called the high religions made their appearance within about twenty-five hundred years—most of them within fifteen hundred years. The twenty-five centuries are roughly between 1800 B.C. and A.D. 700. These centuries saw the beginnings of Hinduism, Judaism, Greek philosophy, Zoroastrianism, Buddhism, Confucianism, Christianity, and Islam. The fifteen hundred years from 850 B.C. to A.D. 650 spanned the birth of the last five and striking developments in the first three.

BASIC QUESTIONS

Five questions emerge as this long history is faced. (1) What is the reason for this presence of religion as a continuing accompaniment of human history? (2) Is advance seen in the history of religion? (3) Which if any of the high religions most nearly approaches the truth with which religion is concerned? (4) Is religion to continue, or is it a passing phase in mankind's long pilgrimage? (5) If religion is to continue, what form or forms will it take? The historian as historian should not venture on definitive answers to any of these questions. His craft enables him to contribute data to some of them. Even he who approaches them as a Christian must recognize that full agreement is not found among those who share his faith. Indeed, on some issues profound disagreement has existed and still exists.

Possible Answers

As to the first question, many see in the presence of religion as a continuing feature of human experience the efforts of men to give meaning to the unknown of which they are more or less aware as impinging on them. Through religion, so this answer would have it, men have been seeking to promote their own welfare and the welfare of their group by propitiating such elements in the Unknown as seem to them hostile and by enlisting in their behalf potentially friendly elements. Others see in the varied forms of religion man's search for the answers to the Unknown or partially Known which they believe or at least hope exists and in which is the solution of the riddle of their existence and of the world about them. They perceive in these answers gropings which at best result in only partial apprehension of the truth and suggest that progress towards the truth, if truth there be, is in sharing the insights emerging from these quests. Their attitude is akin to that of the scientists who probe through their respective disciplines into aspects of man's environment, but with a difference: the scientists are confident that, if they are persistent and employ the right methods, they can enlarge man's knowledge of what they believe is an orderly universe and open the dangerous possibility to the utilization of the universe by men. The possibility is dangerous because, as in nuclear power, men may employ their knowledge in such fashion that it will harm them and even destroy them. But the possibility is there, so they are assured, that through knowledge man's welfare can be advanced.

Christians may give and indeed have given quite different answers to the question. On the one hand, some have said that aside from the development which issued in the incarnation all the groping is an expression of man's sin. For example, Paul declared that although men knew God through what, it could be clearly seen, He had created, they "glorified Him not as God, neither were thankful, but became vain in their imaginations . . . professing themselves to be wise, they became as fools, and changed the glory of the uncorruptible God into an image made like to corruptible man, and to birds, and fourfooted beasts, and creeping things." On the other hand, and in seeming contradiction to this position, Paul is quoted as having said that the search for God is of His appointment, and as declaring that God had made of one blood all nations of men and had allotted periods and the boundaries of their habitation, that they should seek Him in the hope of finding Him. Again, Paul is reported to have said that God is "not far from every one of us." Related to both views is the conviction that God has always been seeking to make Himself known to men but has respected man's freedom. Man has responded by seeking God but, because of his sin, has reached distorted or completely false views. Christians agree that God did not cease His efforts, and among the people of Israel a few were sufficiently responsive to enable God through them to prepare the way for the incarnation and so reveal Himself fully to man and to act once and for all time for man's redemption and salvation.

The answer to the second question, that of advance in man's religious quest, must depend on the criteria which are judged valid for measuring advance. Unquestionably in the "higher" religions profound and at times sophisticated thought has been displayed; in it many sincere and deeply religious souls have been nourished and to it they have contributed. If dependable criteria are to be found in what Christians believe to be God's act in the incarnation, the answer must be ambiguous. All religions, even the most "primitive," have elements which are in accord with the incarnation. But all display features, including fundamental features, which sharply contradict the incarnation and all that the incarnation entails.

In seeking an answer to the third question, many would say that all religions, especially the "high" ones, have striking likenesses. These are seen, so it is declared, in their ethical teachings. Numbers of those who take that view have advocated syncretism, a religion which would combine the insights of all and a joint search for the ultimate truth, if there be ultimate truth, and which would avail itself of all that man has thus far found in his age-long quest. This answer has appealed to many men of goodwill, particularly in the nineteenth and twentieth centuries, especially to those in the Western world who have come out of a Christian heritage.

Any answer, if it be well informed, must recognize in each of the "high" religions basic convictions that are in fundamental contradiction to the essence of the Christian faith. Judaism, in which Christianity has its historic roots and to which it is deeply indebted, cannot accept what is at the very heart of the Christian faith, that in Jesus of Nazareth God became flesh and fulfilled the Jewish hope. The most that one of Jewish faith can do—and some have gladly done it—is to say that Jesus was the greatest in the long succession of Jewish prophets. None can acknowledge that Jesus was the Messiah without becoming a Christian. Islam, possessing much in apparent accord with Christianity, including a belief in one God and the ascription to God of many characteristics wholeheartedly accepted by the Christian, emphatically insists that God cannot have a son, and that the gulf between God and man cannot be bridged. Thus it denies the central conviction of Christianity, that in Christ, by His initiative, God has bridged the gulf to make Christ "the first born among many brethren." Or, as one early Christian, Athanasius, declared, "God became man that man might become God." Moreover, central in Islam is the conviction, embodied in its daily reiterated proclamation, that Mohammed is *the* prophet of God. Then, too,

Mohammed taught that Christ was not crucified, thus denying another essential tenet of Christianity.

Zoroastrianism, while recognizing the conflict between good and evil discerned also by Christians, cannot admit, without being untrue to itself, that in Christ, God, Who is supreme, revealed His love, and that in the incarnation, the crucifixion, and the resurrection He triumphed over evil.

Hinduism's basic tenet is that many roads exist by which men have pursued and still pursue their quest for the truth and that none has universal validity. In contrast, as the root and source of Christianity is the conviction that Christ is "the way, the truth, and the life"—that in Christ God has revealed Himself and acted for man's salvation in such fashion that no other revelation or act is needed.

Basic in the Buddha's teaching and fundamental in Buddhism is the conviction that life is not worth living and is so inescapably linked with suffering that salvation consists in a self-discipline which ends in *nirvana,* the dissolution of the entity called I, and so in releasing the soul from the endless succession of births and rebirths which to the Buddha was axiomatic. Later forms of Buddhism modified this conviction, spoke of a heaven of happiness and postponed indefinitely the entrance to *nirvana,* but they could not negate *nirvana* without being false to the teaching of the founder. In contrast, Christianity, while acknowledging the presence of suffering, declares that life can be infinitely worth living and opens the way to eternal life in fellowship with God Who so loved the world that He gave Himself in Christ.

Confucianism stresses ethics, human relations, and the competence of reason, but its dominant attitude has made for agnosticism. Here is striking contrast to Christianity's belief in God's action in creation, in history, and in revelation and the incarnation.

Attempts at combining these various approaches have been many but have never had enduring vitality. Essays at syncretism which down-graded the uniqueness of the central core of Christianity—the incarnation, the crucifixion, and the resurrection—and the work of the Holy Spirit, while numerous and recurring, either have been passing phenomena or have failed to enlist large numbers. Such were the Ebionism and the Gnosticism of which we are to say more in another chapter and, latterly, Unitarian humanism and the Brahmo Samaj.

The question of the persistence of religion entails prophecy. On this, if he is wise, the historian does not venture. He can simply point to trends. As we shall see in due course, the nineteenth and twentieth centuries have witnessed a growth of atheistic Communism and of a secularism which is less overtly hostile but is eroding the foundations of all religions. Yet they have also seen revivals in some of the non-Christian religions and a spread of Christianity in geographic extent and in depth of rootage unparalleled in its history or in the history of any other religion.

Similarly, so far as the historian can detect from the mounting trends in the nineteenth and twentieth centuries, here lies the answer to the question of what form or forms, if it persists, religion will take. Zoroastrianism has long been dwindling, is confied to small remnants, and is making no gains. Judaism is making few converts, is ethnic as has always been the case, and is suffering from mounting secularism. Except in some portions of Africa south of the Sahara, for at least five centuries Islam has made no significant geographic gains. In the past two centuries Islam has given birth to few new movements. It owes its persistence partly to its association with nationalism, mainly, as at its outset, Arab ethnicism, but, as well, to other nationalisms and to cultural lag. Hinduism, while vigorous, has lost ground in lands in South-east Asia and Indonesia where it was once influential and is confined almost entirely to India. Buddhism has been waning for over a thousand years; such revivals as it is displaying are associated chiefly with Singhalese and Burman nationalism, and nationalism has been stimulated mainly by resistance to the Occident. The acids of modernity, represented strikingly in Communism, have so weakened Confucianism that only attenuated remnants survive. So far as can be discerned from the history of the past four centuries, the future of religion appears to depend primarily on Christianity. Here many declare the outcome to be ambiguous. On the one hand is the fading of that faith among millions whose ancestors professed it. On the other hand are striking evidences of vitality in the emergence of new movements and, as we have suggested, in geographic spread and in depth of rootage among more peoples than ever before.

THE PRE-CHRISTIAN RELIGION OF ISRAEL

Christianity emerged from the religion of Israel. Or rather, it has as its background a persistent strain in that religion. To that strain Christians have looked back, and rightly, as the preparation in history for their faith.

As we have suggested, only a minority among the people of Israel were loyal to the covenant which, they were taught God had made with Abraham and their ancestors. That minority treasured the writings in which were recorded the teachings of the law-givers, the visions of the prophets, regarded as the authentic spokesmen of God (and again, a minority of those who claimed the role of prophet), and the poetry and hymns that had arisen from their faith.

These writings, Christians have believed and continue to believe, foretold Christ and His work. The Psalms, the anthology of the hymns of Israel, are still used by Christians. Yet one of the early Christians declared that the prophets were enquiring and searching diligently into what the Spirit of Christ was seeking to make known through them: presumably they did not see it clearly nor understand it fully. One of the greatest of the prophets confessed that God was saying: "My thoughts are not your thoughts; neither are your ways my ways. For as the heavens are higher than the earth, so are my ways higher than your ways, and my thoughts than your thoughts."

The prophets and the writers of the Psalms were clear that God was continuing to work in the universe and in all history.

They declared that He had created the universe. They said that the heavens proclaimed His glory and that the earth is His. They perceived Him in the thunder storm. They saw Him making grass grow and giving the beasts and the birds their food. They praised Him for providing plentiful harvests. They saw His acts in making wars cease. They believed that He was interested in all nations, judged some, and called others to do His will. They regarded Him as reigning in all the earth. They held Him to be an enemy to injustice and to the oppression of the poor and humble by the rich and mighty. They were convinced that His compassion is over all that He has made. They held that His love is steadfast and that every individual can call on Him with the assurance that He will hear. They believed that He knows each man better than a man knows himself. They were conscious that their sin was against Him but that He would forgive if they repented and that He would heal their iniquities. They struggled with the problem of evil and suffering. Why is it that the righteous are afflicted? Why do men and women go astray? They wrestled in agony over the spectacle of a mighty, aggressive nation over-running the weak and the innocent. Yet they continued to trust in God when they could not understand. The prophets were well aware that only a minority would heed them and that the majority would hear but would not understand. But they were convinced that in His own way and His own time God would triumph.

The Global Scene on the Eve of the Coming of Christ

As we have said, Christ was born in the Roman Empire. Much in that empire facilitated the spread of religion and favoured the triumph of one faith. Roman rule brought political unity to the lands bordering on the Mediterranean Sea. At the outset Rome was a city-state. The empire which it governed was made up chiefly of city-states and embraced some of the oldest of civilized peoples. It included the Nile Valley, Palestine, the western edge of the Tigris–Euphrates Valley, what was later called Asia Minor,

Greece, and Italy, all of them with civilizations hundreds of years old. Its rule made possible commerce throughout its domains. With commerce went an interchange of ideas and the possibility of a cultural unity. Greek was a kind of *lingua franca,* especially in the cities and among the educated. In the western part of the Empire Latin was coming into wide use.

Religiously the Empire was pluralistic and marked by a search for a faith which would be satisfying intellectually and ethically and would give assurance of immortality. Official cults continued from the days before the formation of the Empire. They were maintained partly because of their utility in preserving traditional ways of life and partly for the purpose of enlisting the support of the gods for the state and for the inherited civilization. To them was added the cult of the Emperor, chiefly as a means of promoting loyalty to the Empire. Philosophies of Greek origin attracted the intelligentsia and many, not among the educated, who sought answers to the riddle of life. Prominent among the philosophies were Platonism, Stoicism, and Epicureanism, and there were in addition the Peripatetics (carrying on the Aristotelean tradition), the Pythagoreans, and the Cynics. Neoplatonism would later seek to combine several of these systems. Common to many of them and to Greek thought was a dualism which regarded matter, including flesh, as evil and sought to emancipate the human soul from it and so to achieve immortality. Mystery religions were widespread and popular. They were largely of Eastern origin—Egyptian, Syrian, Anatolian, and Persian. Since their rites were secret we know them very imperfectly. They borrowed extensively from one another, for the general temper of the age was syncretistic; in the search for truth the assumption was that no one religion or philosophy had all the truth but hopefully each had some of it. Every mystery religion centred in a saviour-god who was supposed to have been slain by his enemies and to have risen from the dead. The adherents of each were believed to share symbolically in the death and resurrection of the god and thus to obtain immortality. Some of the mysteries were built around Dionysus, others about

Orpheus, and still others about Attis and the Great Mother who had loved him, mourned his death, and effected his resurrection. Some had Adonis, some Osiris, and some Mithra as their centre. They not only were believed to insure immortality to their adherents but also created fellowships among those initiated into them. Akin to the mysteries was Hermeticism, which sought emancipation of the spirit from matter. Hermeticism was potent in Gnosticism, a religious strain which took many forms and which was greatly to influence Christianty and threaten it by absorbing it into a syncretism congenial to the age. Judaism was widespread and attracted many by its monotheism and its ethical idealism.

From our mention of the Roman Empire we must immediately go on to note that the Roman domains included only a fraction of civilized mankind and an even smaller proportion of the human race outside the "higher" cultures.

Directly to the east was the Persian Empire. Under the Arsacids, a Parthian dynasty, it embraced most of the Tigris-Euphrates Valley with its early seats of civilized mankind as well as what we now call Iran. In chronic wars it kept Rome out of Mesopotamia. Later, as we are to see, the Sassanian ruling line engaged in wars with Rome which brought both régimes to the edge of exhaustion and so prepared the way for the Arab invasion and the spread of Islam. Zoroastrianism was the official religion under both the Arsacids and the Sassanians and offered more resistance to a new religion than did the state cults of the Roman Empire.

East and south of Persia was India. Although never fully united under one political structure, India was the seat of ancient civilizations and culturally did not rank behind either the Mediterranean world or Persia. For many centuries Hinduism had been strong. Buddhism, older by about five centuries than Christianity, was flourishing and had not yet reached its apex. Jainism, another offshoot of Hinduism but with far fewer adherents, was also part of the Indian religious scene.

Still farther east was China. About the time that Rome was

rising to prominence China was being brought under one ruling family, known in history as the Ch'in Dynasty. The Ch'in Dynasty was short-lived, but it was followed by the Han Dynasty, which with a brief interruption was in power from 206 B.C. to A.D. 214. Although exact statistics cannot be obtained, whether for the Roman Empire or for China, nor are acceptable criteria possible for measuring the relative worth of cultures, under the Han China occupied as many square miles of land territory as did Rome, its population was probably about the same as that of Rome, and its civilization compared favorably in many ways with that of the Mediterranean world. Presumably it was as wealthy as the latter. Under the Han Confucianism had the support of the state. Other religions were present, notably two of indigenous origin, Taoism and Mohism. By the end of the Han, Buddhism had been introduced, but it did not win an extensive following until later.

Of the four high civilizations—Rome, Persia, India, and China —the first afforded the most opportunity for the spread of a new religion. Its state-supported cults could command less respect from men seeking the answers to the riddle of the universe and of human existence than could those of the others. The religious ferment seen in the Mediterranean world when Christ was born was probably no greater than that in the other three areas of high civilization, but the stories of the gods worshipped in the temples maintained by the government had to be allegorized if the thoughtful and morally sensitive were to believe them. Nor were they undergirded as effectively by philosophy as were the popular cults in the other three realms. As we shall see, Christianity did not win the professed allegiance of the Roman Empire without severe persecution, but conditions more nearly facilitated its spread than had it come to its birth in Persia, India, or China.

Although when Christianity appeared the total population of the planet was only a fraction of that of the twentieth century, most of the earth's surface was quite outside the Mediterranean world, Persia, India, and China. Here, too, men had been groping for the knowledge of the unseen forces which they believed surrounded them and had sought ways of enlisting their support. As the event proved, their cults were less resistant to "high" religions, including Christianity, than were these religions to Christianity. But for several centuries Christianity had little contact with them.

This was the setting in which Christianity was born. It came at a time and in a region which was best prepared to receive it. But, semingly weak as it was at the outset, it was threatened by the environment which was part of that region's heritage. Again and again it was apparently about to be denatured and deprived of its very essence.

Here are questions to which the historian, even when he thinks of himself as a Christian, is aware that he does not have the answers. He may agree with Paul that "when the time had fully come, God sent forth His Son." He may see, as we have suggested, that by the long preparation through Israel and the religious hunger in the Roman Empire conditions were more favourable for the reception of the Gospel than they had ever been or than they were in any other segment of mankind. But he must ask: Why did God wait so long? Could He not, even when respecting man's freedom of will, have earlier accomplished the incarnation? What was the fate of the millions who had died before the coming of Christ? If God's love is from everlasting to everlasting, why did He permit these millions to live and die with only such glimpses of Him as could be obtained through the orderly processes of nature? Why did He witness the groping of men for the light—the grace and truth brought in the incarnation—without more clearly revealing Himself? We must recognize the sincerity of the founders of the "higher" religions and of many among the "lower" or "primitive" religions. We may believe that God was always seeking to reveal Himself to men, but because He had created man in His own likeness and so had given him a degree of freedom, limited but still authentic, He could not do so until He found in the succession of the prophets and seers of Israel men sufficiently responsive to Him to prepare the way for His act in the incarnation. But could He allow the millions who had died before the coming of Christ or who lived after that coming to pass through the gate of death into darkness without the opportunity to learn of His love? Here are questions with which Christians as well as critics have continued to wrestle. To us this side the gate of death and with no clear knowledge of what transpires in that "bourne from which no traveller returns" the only honest reply can be that we do not know. The historian as historian has no answer. As a Christian he must believe that God's love will not be defeated. But how and in what fashion God's love will triumph he cannot know. He can simply trust, with the early Christians, that it is the purpose of God to sum up all things in Christ, both in heaven and on earth. In many radiant lives known to him who even now are bearing what Paul called the fruits of the Spirit, in thousands of whom he has read who across the centuries have displayed those fruits, and in the many millions who, passing, have left behind them no written records but presumably have also been characterized by these fruits, the historian sees the beginnings of the fulfilment of that purpose. Here is what the Christian regards as a guarantee or pledge of the realization of the final triumph of God through Christ, not only in history, but also in the entire cosmos.

CHAPTER III

The Earthly Life of Him Through
Whom Christianity Began

Christianity begins with a historical figure in a distinct historical setting. The setting was Palestine at the time when the Roman Empire was in its youth. Palestine had been incorporated into that empire. It was seething with the unrest against Roman rule which within a generation of the crucifixion broke out in a revolt that was crushed by Roman arms. Among the Jewish people were a number of religious currents. A clique of worldly Sadducees controlled the central shrine, the Temple in Jerusalem. They were intent on maintaining their hold and identified it with the welfare of the Jewish people. The Pharisees, spiritual heirs of the movement to preserve the Jewish faith against the compromise with Hellenism which had followed the conquests of Alexander the Great and his successors and which under the Maccabees had become political, were adamant in their efforts to preserve loyalty to what they regarded as the law given through Moses and defended by the great prophets. Minority ascetic movements flourished. Among them were the Essenes and the monastic community, presumably Essene, which was brought to light in the 1940's and 1950's by the discovery of the Dead Sea Scrolls, documents produced by them and preserved in the dry air of caves where their writers lived.

For our first-hand knowledge of the life of Jesus we are dependent chiefly on the Four Gospels which head the New Testament. They arose from the need to instruct inquirers and neophytes in the early Christian communities. Made up predominantly of the remembered sayings and acts of Jesus and of accounts of the crucifixion and resurrection, the Gospels are not formal biographies as the twentieth century understands biography. However, they give a vivid picture of Jesus, of His teachings, and of His death and resurrection. Composed chiefly from the reminiscences of eye-witnesses and intimate companions of Jesus, they enable us to know Him as well as though we had been in the inner circle of His disciples. In addition, in letters of early Christians are fragments of His teachings and especially of impressions which He made on those who knew him best.

We need here to rehearse, and that briefly, only such features of the story as determine the nature and course of Christianity. Jesus was reared in Nazareth, a hill town in Galilee. We know few details of His life before His emergence into the public eye. From His sayings and parables we can be sure that He was a keen observer of the life around Him and of the beauties of the rural scene that lay spread below Him on the plain of Esdraelon. He had learned to read, was a diligent student of the sacred books of His people, and worshipped regularly in the local synagogue. Presumably Joseph, the husband of Mary, died before her son began His public career, for we never hear of him after the childhood of Jesus—except that fellow townsmen remembered him as the supposed father. Obviously the nativity story as told in Matthew's Gospel could have come only from Joseph, just as that in Luke's Gospel bears all the marks of having Mary as its source—and, incidentally, provides a most illuminating picture of Mary's characteristics. The home in which Jesus was reared was deeply religious. As we gather from the names of those who are called His brothers, it was in the Maccabean tradition of loyalty to the traditions of His people. The one concrete glimpse which we are given of His childhood discloses a highly intelligent lad who was already beginning to be aware of His mission.

We must remember that across the centuries the relation of the divine and the human in Jesus has been a mystery which Christians have sought to penetrate. They were early convinced that He was God incarnate, that in Him the eternal Word had become flesh. They were also certain that He was fully human. Thus the Epistle to the Hebrews, which begins by declaring that the Son was appointed by God to be the heir of all things, was the express image of God, and upholds the universe by His word of power, also insists that in every respect He was made like His brethren, that He suffered, was tempted as men are tempted, and "learned obedience by the things that He suffered." As we shall see later, a formula, that of Chalcedon, which the majority of Christians have accepted declares that Jesus Christ was "perfect in Godhead and perfect in manhood, truly God and truly man," in whom the two natures, divine and human, were not "separated into two persons" but were preserved and concurred in one person.

What has been called the public ministry began dramatically. John the Baptist, who we are told was related by blood to Jesus, was preaching the impending judgement of God, urging repentance and moral reform, and baptizing in the Jordan River those who responded. Jesus, then about thirty years of age, was baptized. Presumably He sought the rite as an act of dedication, not of repentance, for, significantly, although He had a keenly sensitive conscience and urged his followers to repent, we have only one slight hint, and that capable of another interpretation, that He thought of Himself as less than perfect. The baptism was accompanied by a sudden and profound conviction of His peculiar relation to God. As a boy He had been partly aware of it, but now it came upon Him with such force that He was impelled to seek solitude to discern its meaning. Deep inner struggle followed and from it came a clear conviction about what that relation entailed. He won through to the knowledge that the relation did not exempt Him from the limitations common to mankind, that He must not compromise with evil to achieve worthy objectives, and that His reliance must always be entirely on God.

From His experience in the wilderness Jesus emerged, we are told, so matured that those with whom He had grown up in Nazareth could not believe He was the one whom they had known. He began preaching and teaching. His theme was the Kingdom of God. He announced that the Kingdom of God was at hand and, indeed, already present, although not as yet consummated. As He saw it, this was good news, news so wonderful that those who were gripped by it would give up all that they had to enter the Kingdom. Membership in the Kingdom demanded a complete shifting of values. Even to recognize the Kingdom what amounted to a new birth was essential—entrance to it could be only by a change in perspective and purpose which could best be described as being born anew. That new birth was wrought by the Spirit, Who had come upon Jesus at His baptism. To prepare for it repentance, "a complete change of mind," was an inescapable prerequisite. Entrance must be by striving which might have in it agony. But it meant eternal life, life with God in fellowship with Christ. That life was marked by attainment to high ethical standards—among them complete purity of heart, unswerving honesty, outgoing love, even for one's enemies, and being perfect as God is perfect.

Yet Jesus was not a legalist. As He saw it, the kind of life demanded by the Kingdom is not a meticulous observance of set rules. That may lead to pride and self-righteousness, and Jesus had nothing but scorn for the self-righteous. He would not let rules, such as the strict observance of the Sabbath which had been one of the marks of those who had resisted Hellenizing tendencies, stand in the way of the welfare of individuals.

Jesus had a great yearning for the sick, the consciously unrighteous, and the underprivileged. He possessed remarkable powers of physical healing, the exercise of which was to Him one indication that the Kingdom of God was arriving. So far as our records enable us to know Him, He was at times physically weary but was never ill. He sought the wayward and those whom He described as lost. Through Him moral and spiritual transformation was wrought in harlots and gouging tax-collectors.

Jesus did not dodge evil. He recognized it and fought it, especially as it injured individuals. He advanced no philosophic or theological reason for its existence. One of His parables, that of the field planted with good seed and in which an enemy sowed weeds, seems to indicate His belief that both good and evil would continue to the end of time, both growing and reaching larger dimensions. Yet Jesus had no doubt of the ultimate triumph of good and the destruction of evil.

Jesus did not actively engage in the political struggles of his day. That is all the more significant in view of the seething currents which were soon to break out in futile resistance to the rule of Rome. Jesus clearly foresaw that disaster—as any level-headed resident of Palestine should have done. By a tragic irony He was crucified on the charge, palpably false, that He had sought to stir up revolt.

What Jesus did, rather, was to offer His people another way, the only possible one consistent with His convictions; if followed, it would have averted the fateful outcome of the Roman-Jewish tensions. He offered it with the full realization that it would not be followed.

The way which Jesus offered to the Jews arose from His conception of His mission, reached only after intense thought and prayer and with much inward struggle. The title given to Him was Christ, the anointed of the Lord, or, in Aramaic and Hebrew, the Messiah. Various meanings had been given the term by Jewish leaders and in popular Jewish thought. In general, they included the reëstablishment of the kingdom which had had David as its most revered monarch, and through that kingdom a world-embracing régime of righteousness and peace. In the day in which Jesus lived, among the devout Jews the hope of the early appearance of the Messiah was widespread. Jesus was affected by that hope, especially since in His infancy, so we are told, He was greeted as the instrument for the establishment of the kingdom, and in His public ministry His healings and His teaching, given with a sense of authority, stimulated many to hail Him as the Messiah. Precisely what went on in His mind we can probably never know fully. From the records, we can be confident that Jesus refused to fit into any of the stereotypes which contemporaries had of the Messiah. He had come to the conviction that the mission given Him by His Father differed basically from the popular conceptions—even those held by His immediate disciples. He saw that the road assigned him led inevitably to the cross and to apparent complete frustration. Here seems to have been a conclusion first reached in the temptations which followed His baptism. We have a hint of it—and of the continuing inner struggle by which it was confirmed—in the reported sharp rebuke to Peter when that bewildered and loyal friend expressed his horror that the role of the Messiah must be climaxed by the cross. Here may be the reason for the fashion which Jesus chose for His final entry into the city, humble and without an armed company to support Him. Here, too, may be a clue to the report that when He approached Jerusalem on that fateful visit Jesus wept over it, saying that even then it might know what made for peace, but that it was blind and was faced with complete destruction. Jesus was well aware that the response which greeted Him could only be the prelude to His seeming failure. Possibly this is part of the reason for His agony in Gethsemane. He knew that He had failed in His appeal. But He could even then have escaped and, accompanied by the eleven, have gone to the other side of the Jordan to the hills, which were clearly seen in the light of the full Pascal moon. There, temporarily relieved of his enemies, He might teach until at least some would understand Him. Should He do so, and there continue His mission? On Him, too, rested the burden of man's sin and the tragedy which that entailed for mankind. The conviction He had previously reached was reaffirmed, perhaps because when He saw the approach of the lights of the soldiers brought by his betrayer He knew that escape was impossible.

At His crucifixion, we are told, Jesus prayed: "Father forgive them, for they know not what they do." He was stating a fact, for the priests, Pilate, the multitude, and the soldiers were not aware that they were committing man's greatest crime, the crucifixion of the Son of God. Yet in His plea for their forgiveness Jesus was exemplifying the love of God which had expressed itself in the incarnation. Here, too, is much of the history of Christianity. Man has been blindly and tragically misusing God's greatest gift. That gift had come through the self-giving love of the infinite God. Through misusing it men have brought on themselves the judgement of God.

The issue is made the more poignant because Jesus had not taken the steps which human wisdom would have dictated to give permanence to His mission. He had written no book in which to record His teachings. So far as our records permit us to know, He had given little or no thought to a continuing organization. He had chosen twelve to be with Him, seemingly symbolic of the twelve tribes of Israel and with the hint that here was to be a new Israel. But, if so, none of the twelve really understood Him. When one of the eleven impulsively sought to fight to prevent His arrest, Jesus commanded him to put up his sword. All our records unite in saying that the friends of Jesus were completely discouraged and felt themselves impotent to prevent the tragedy. We read that two of the wealthy and deeply religious intelligentsia who had hoped that in Jesus might be fulfilled the dream long cherished by the devout in Israel could do no more than ask for His dead body and give it decent burial.

Yet the records also agree that seeming failure was what to the faithful became thrilling triumph. The faithful were assured that the crucifixion, far from ending all, was the necessary preliminary to the resurrection. Here was not the end of the life they had known but a radiant life, a continuation of Him Whom they had known and loved, with the assurance that through faith in Him all men might have the victorious, self-giving life which they saw in Him. Soon, fulfilling the promise which Jesus is said to have given them, the Spirit took possession of them, sent by Jesus and the Father, Who began to bring the fruits in them which they had already seen in Jesus.

In the life, teachings, seeming frustration by the cross, resurrection, and transforming power of the Spirit is the epitome of the history which is to be our theme in the chapters that follow. Here, as the Christian sees it, is the fashion in which God has dealt with men and continues to deal with them. Here, if he is correct, is the clue to the history not only of Christianity but of all mankind as well. Again and again we will see God's good gifts perverted by men's blindness and sin to work incalculable harm in individuals, in groups, and in entire peoples and nations. Repeatedly we shall see issuing from the Spirit Who is inseparably related to the Father and the Son healing for individuals, for segments of mankind, and for mankind as a whole.

CHAPTER IV

The Initial Five Centuries of Christianity:
Professed Allegiance of the Roman World; Influence of That World; Birth of the Catholic Church; Definition of Christian Beliefs

In the five centuries after the death and resurrection of Jesus the religion which had Him as its centre took form, won the professed allegiance of the large majority of the peoples of the Roman Empire, and spilled over beyond the boundaries of that realm. Here is one of the most surprising developments in history. As we have suggested, from one whose public career was no more than three years, who wrote no book, who seemingly gave little thought to a continuing organization, and who died in apparent frustration emerged a religion that captured one of the major centres of civilization, developed an organization whose main features have been perpetuated into the twentieth century, gave definitions to its basic convictions which have continued to be normative, and modified substantially the culture which was its environment.

PROFESSED ALLEGIANCE OF THE ROMAN EMPIRE TO CHRISTIANITY; SPREAD OF CHRISTIANITY BEYOND ROMAN BORDERS

How was it that Christianity became the professed faith of the Roman Empire and began to spread beyond its borders? By what steps did it win against its admittedly formidable rivals? Those rivals were the state cults, Judaism, the many philosophies which developed in the Hellenistic world, the numerous mystery cults, and the closely associated Hermeticism and Gnosticism. Against these competitors Christianity seemed to have little chance. The state cults had the support of the government and the latter sought to stamp out any serious dissent. To its mind dissent was seditious and threatened the existing way of life. Judaism was well rooted in a widespread continuing community. Although the Romans crushed efforts at political independence, they tolerated Judaism so long as it did not incite to revolt. The numerous philosophies did not contend with the imperial power. Adherents of the mysteries saw no inconsistency between their membership in these brotherhoods and loyalty to the Emperors and participation in the rites of the state cults. Hermeticism and Gnosticism in their various forms seemed not to threaten the state. Yet, while protesting their loyalty to the Emperor and insisting that they prayed for him, the Christians would not participate in the worship in the temples of the gods and were accused of being atheists. Their intransigence invited persecution, both by imperial officials and by the populace.

We know something of the history of the spread of Christianity, but much passed from recorded memory and much was transmitted by tradition whose accuracy has been repeatedly questioned.

The company of the followers of Jesus who, inspired by the resurrection and the coming of the Spirit at Pentecost, continued in Jerusalem were, on the whole, loyal Jews. They worshipped in the temple and observed the Jewish customs, including the dietary restrictions. To the casual observer they seemed to constitute one of the many sects characteristic of the Judaism of the day.

Some early realized that their faith had a universality which could not be bound by these integuments. This appears to have been the conviction and teaching of Stephen which brought about his martyrdom at the hands of orthodox Jews. Saul, better known by his non-Jewish name of Paul, was impressed both by the message of Stephen and by the radiant joy of the victim at the time of his death and his prayer, reminiscent of that of the crucified Jesus, for the forgiveness of the men who were stoning him. On his way to Damascus to continue the persecution of the Christians Saul was torn by the inner conflict between his strict Jewish rearing and what he had seen in the face of Stephen— a triumphant peace to which he was a stranger and which his moral rectitude had failed to give him. Just before Saul's arrival at Damascus, where he would have to carry out his errand, the conflict was unexpectedly resolved by a vision of Christ. The conviction came that the Gospel was for all men, and that the struggle for conformity to the Jewish law, which had failed to give him what he longed for and what he saw in the followers of Jesus, was not only unnecessary but a handicap to entering the life made possible by Christ. Paul became the great missionary to the Gentiles. He was by no means the only such missionary, but we hear more of him than of any of the others. We know that through him the faith was planted in several cities in present-day Turkey and in Greece. We are given glimpses of communities of Christians which had arisen quite independently of Paul, notably in Antioch, on the Bay of Naples, and in Rome. The early churches were chiefly in the cities and among Greek-speaking elements. The one in Alexandria has traditionally been ascribed to Mark, once a travelling companion of Paul and declared by early report to have been with Peter in Rome and to have written down the memoirs constituting the body of the teaching of that Apostle, which we have as the Gospel of Mark. Another of the original Twelve is said to have planted the faith in India. That has not been proved, but it is entirely possible in view of the fact that trade flourished between India and the Mediterranean world and that merchants from Roman domains established themselves in several places on the south coast of India and in Ceylon. We know, too, that the faith had an early spread among Syriac-speaking peoples in Syria and Mesopotamia. In the second century Christians were numerous, especially in Asia Minor. By the middle of the second century churches existed in the Greek-speaking populations in Lyons and Vienne in Gaul.

In the third century after Christ the faith continued to spread. It had a following among the Latin-speaking elements on the northern shores of Africa. There, indeed, the earliest Latin Christian literature was written. In North Africa it penetrated, but more slowly, the non-Latin-speaking population. By the second half of the third century Italy appears to have had about a hundred bishoprics—but this does not mean that Christians were more than a minority. A little earlier in the century more than twenty bishoprics were found in the Tigris-Euphrates Valley. The third century witnessed the mass conversion of the Armenians, a people who inhabited a buffer state between the Roman and Persian empires. The major agent was Gregory "the Illuminator," of the Armenian aristocracy, who had become a Christian while in exile in Caesarea in Cappadocia and, returning to his native land, won the king to his faith. The bulk of the population followed the king, and numbers of the pagan priests and their sons became clergymen in the newly created church. By the middle of the third century Christianity had reached most of the provinces of the Roman Empire and had been planted outside the borders of that realm.

The spread of the faith met with persistent and chronic persecution which in mid-third century and at the beginning of the fourth century on three occasions was vigorously pressed on an empire-wide scale. The persecution in the first century by Nero is famous, but apparently it was confined chiefly to Rome. Presumably adherence to Christianity was chronically proscribed. But until the second half of the third century persecutions were mainly local. Some of the educated scorned Christianity as a superstition and as untenable by intelligent men. More widespread was popular antagonism. Christians were regarded as separated from society and therefore destructive of the Greco-Roman way of life. Because, to avoid publicity, much of Christian worship was in secret and the non-baptized were not permitted to be present at the celebration of the Lord's Supper, the report was current that in their conventicles Christians engaged in sexual promiscuity.

By the second half of the third century the Roman Empire was palpably in decline. Many held that the decay was due to the neglect of the gods who had made Rome strong. In 249, to counteract this neglect the Emperor Decius commanded all his subjects to sacrifice to the state gods. The edict bore especially hard on the Christians. Although in 251 Decius fell in battle with the Goths, his successor continued his programme. That programme soon lapsed, but in 257 the Emperor Valerian renewed the persecution. Valerian adopted even more vigorous measures, directing them in particular against the clergy and adherents of the faith who were in government positions. He also threatened with death all who attended meetings or services of the Church. In 260 Valerian was captured by the Persians and the persecution ceased. During the following four decades the Church flourished and became the strongest congeries of institutions in the Empire with the exception of the state. How large a proportion of the population professed the faith by the end of the third century we do not know. Estimates vary from five in a hundred to fifty in a hundred. In 303 the Emperor Diocletian instituted the most drastic persecution with which Christians had thus far been visited. It was most severe in the East. Hundreds, perhaps thousands of Christians perished. Not until 323 did the persecution die down.

The turn of the tide came in 312, when Constantine, an aspirant to the imperial purple, adhered to the faith. He did so just before a successful battle with one of his rivals, being impelled to the step, so he later said, by the vision of a cross of light in the sky with the inscription "Conquer by this." In 313 Constantine and his chief remaining rival, Licinius, entered into an agreement at Milan which contributed to the toleration of Christianity.

The acceptance of Christianity by Constantine was followed by its augmented spread. Constantine did not forbid the continuation of the non-Christian religions but he removed the disabilities under which Christians had suffered and encouraged the erection of churches. In Byzantium, which he made his capital and renamed Constantinople, he built many churches and forbade the repair of pagan temples. His three sons, who followed him on the imperial throne, patronized Christianity, placing restrictions on non-Christian cults. Under imperial favour the Church experienced a rapid growth. Many who thronged into it did so from expediency rather than deep religious conviction, and the moral and spiritual quality of the Christian community suffered.

In spite of the friendly imperial policies, non-Christian cults only slowly dwindled. During his brief reign (361-363) Julian, a member of the Constantinian family, called "the apostate" because he repudiated the faith in which he had been unwillingly reared, sought to revive and purify the worship of the old gods. But he instituted no persecution of Christianity, and his early death in war against the Persians was followed by the elevation of a Christian to the imperial throne. The pagan cults long had the adherence of the aristocracy of Rome. They persisted in remote valleys and were late in being supplanted in the western part of the Empire—especially Italy, Gaul, and Spain. To the adherents of the traditional paganism the fall of Rome to the Goths (410) seemed positive proof that the growing weakness of the Empire was due to neglect of the gods who had made Rome great.

New religions entered and were a threat to Christianity. Prominent among them were Neoplatonism and Manichaeism. As its name suggests, Neoplatonism was an outgrowth of Platonism. It had its main creative figures, Ammonias Saccas and Plotinus, in the third century. Mani, the founder of Manichaeism, lived in the third century too, was reared in Mesopotamia, and, convinced that he was divinely commissioned to be a prophet and the creator of the true religion, developed a strongly dualistic faith which had elements from Zoroastrianism, Judaism, Christianity, and the ancient Babylonian beliefs. Manichaeism spread widely—across the Mediterranean world and Central Asia and into China. In the West it stressed features derived from Christianity. An indication of the popularity of Manichaeism and Neoplatonism was the fact that Augustine of Hippo (354-430), who was reared by a Christian mother, was attracted first by one and then by the other until the conversion which made him one of the outstanding Christians of all time.

The mounting invasions of "barbarians" from the North brought in additional pagan groups. The non-Christian philosophies persisted in their traditional stronghold in Athens; not until 529 did an imperial order close the schools where they were taught.

But the progress of the faith continued, both within and outside the Empire. In the fourth century the converted soldier Martin of Tours, a pioneer of monasticism in the West, as bishop led his monks in destroying temples and in baptizing their former adherents. Ambrose (c. 340-397), the great bishop of Milan, by his eloquence and force of character won not only Augustine but also many other pagans in his diocese and encouraged missionaries in the Tyrol. John Chrysostom (c. 345-407), a contemporary of Ambrose, was baptized in his mid-twenties, became a noted preacher in his native Antioch, and as Bishop of Constantinople sent missionaries to the Goths. In the fourth century many Goths were converted to the faith, with one of their own number, Ulfilas (c. 311-c. 380), as the leading missionary.

In the fifth century Christianity was planted in Ireland. The most famous of the missionaries to the Irish was Patrick. Reared as a Christian in Britain, Patrick was captured in his youth by raiders from Ireland and for some time was a slave in that island. Escaping, he eventually felt constrained to carry the Gospel to his former masters. With other missionaries he helped to make Ireland a Christian outpost when non-Christian Germanic peoples were overrunning Great Britain and much of the neighbouring continent. In the fifth century also the Burgundians, moving south from the Rhine region, adopted the faith which they found dominant among the Gallo-Roman population in what was the later France. In 496 Clovis, the leader of another Germanic people, the Franks, was baptized, thus furthering the conversion of those who were soon to dominate most of what had been Roman territory between the Rhine and the Pyrenees. In the East Christianity was firmly planted in the Persian realms, in Central Asia, in Arabia, and on the African coast of the Red Sea, but only among minorities.

Inevitably the question arises: Why, from being the faith of a small, persecuted minority in competition with other religions which appeared to have better prospects of success, did Christianity eventually enroll the large majority of the population of the Roman Empire? To that outcome several factors contributed. In the disintegration of the existing order which by the end of the second century was becoming obvious many individuals were seeking spiritual and material security and believed that they could find it in the Christian faith. By the end of the third century, while enlisting only a minority, the Church was Empire-wide, was more comprehensive than any institution except the state, and gave to its members a sense of brotherhood and solidarity. Christianity assured its adherents what many in the ancient world were craving—high ethical standards, a spiritual dynamic in which was power to approximate to those standards, and immortality. The Church was inclusive: its brotherhood included both sexes, rich and poor, intelligentsia and men and women of no intellectual attainments. Many intellectuals, including Augustine, found in the faith not only moral power but also, in the incarnation, the Word become flesh, what was absent in the highest philosophies of the time. The constancy of the martyrs awakened the admiration of thousands. So did the fact that Christianity was uncompromising in its demands. One modern scholar, T. R. Glover of Cambridge University declared that the Christians out-thought, out-lived, and out-died the adherents of the non-Christian religions.

The primary source of the appeal of Christianity was Jesus—His incarnation, His life, His crucifixion, and His resurrection. Here was the sense of security and of meaning in a perplexing universe and in a society whose foundations were crumbling. Here were the command for and, although imperfect, the realization of a comprehensive fellowship. Here were high and exacting ethical commands and the proved power to approximate to them. Here was victory through apparent defeat. Here was the certainty of immortality in ever-growing and never-ending fellowship with the eternal God Who so loved that He had given Himself in His Son.

Although by the end of the fifth century after Christ to be a Roman and a Christian were seemingly identical, we must not forget that the other great cultural centres were almost untouched by the faith. The Persian Empire and India had a few Christians, but as small and culturally alien minorities. So far as we know China had none. Except for a few of the "barbarians" on the fringes of the Roman Empire and a few peoples in Central Asia, the vast majority of "uncivilized" mankind was untouched.

BIRTH OF THE CATHOLIC CHURCH, WITH FEATURES WHICH HAVE CONTINUED TO CHARACTERIZE MUCH OF ECCLESIASTICAL CHRISTIANITY

In the first five centuries of its history Christianity gave rise to the Catholic Church. The Catholic Church bore the imprint of the Roman environment. The several ecclesiastical bodies which emerged from it and, although divided, were its continuation have ever since enrolled the majority of those bearing the Christian name. They have perpetuated the main features of their parent body.

The Catholic Church sprang from the profound conviction that all Christians should be in one body. The first disciples remembered that Jesus had commanded them to love one another as He had loved them; all men would know that they were His disciples if they loved one another. He had prayed, they recalled, that all who believed in Him might be one, as He and the Father are one, that the world might believe that the Father had sent Him. The fulfilment of that command and the realization of that dream were not easy and have never become total actuality. But they have continued to inspire and rebuke Christians.

An early form of organization developed by Christians, suggested by what they had seen in the Jewish synagogues, had as one of its features elders, or, to give them their Greek name, presbyters, from which the word "priest" is derived. Paul appointed them for the churches he organized. During the first century much variety was seen in the many congregations. Early in the second century a structure was in evidence which, at first not universal, eventually became normal for ecclesiastical Christianity. The church in Antioch had at least one bishop, Ignatius, who acted as though he had the acknowledged right to address himself with authority to other churches. On his way under guard to Rome for martyrdom, Ignatius wrote letters to several churches. He commanded that nothing be done without the bishop and declared that the Eucharist, or Lord's Supper, was to be administered either by the bishop or by some one delegated by him. Ignatius also spoke of presbyters and deacons as officers of the Church. Eventually, and perhaps at that time, a city customarily had only one bishop. Ignatius spoke of the "Catholic Church," saying that "wherever Jesus Christ is, there is the Catholic Church." By the end of the second century the term "Catholic" was increasingly applied to the Church, with the sense that the Catholic Church was both universal and orthodox. In the course of time the district over which the bishop presided became known as a diocese. The term was borrowed from the civil administration of the Roman Empire, especially as it was organized in the fourth century. To this day the majority of Christians are in churches in which the three major ranks of the clergy are bishops, priests, and deacons, and organized by dioceses presided over by a bishop.

Well before the end of the second century the Church of Rome was being accorded an outstanding place in the Catholic Church, partly because Rome was the capital of the Empire.

As such, until Constantine placed his capital at the former Byzantium, it was regarded as the chief (although it was not necessarily the largest) city in the Empire. Even after the main centre of administration was transferred to Constantinople, Rome continued to be esteemed as the symbol of the Empire and the focus of what the people of the Empire regarded as the civilized world. Paul treated the Church of Rome with great respect. Both Peter, whom the Catholic Church reveres as the Prince of the Apostles, and Paul were in Rome and persistent tradition has it that both were martyred there. In the third quarter of the second century, Irenaeus, Bishop of Lyons, in Gaul, and of Asian not Roman origin, declared that "it is a matter of necessity that every church should agree with this church [i.e., of Rome] on account of its prëeminent authority."

The Struggle to Arrive at a Consensus on the Beliefs, Expressions, and Structure of Christianity

Christians were early confronted with the problem of determining precisely what is essential in the faith they professed. They were also troubled by what should properly be their relations to contemporary religious movements, practices, and beliefs, what structure they should devise for their fellowship, what forms of worship they should develop or adopt, and what methods they should use to be true to what had come to them from Christ. The task was rendered the more difficult by the fact that Jesus had written no book, had not put His teachings in an orderly intellectual structure, and at best had given only a few hints about the form which the fellowship of His followers should take.

Christians agreed from the very first that Jesus is central. They soon began to formulate what they believed to be His relation to God. This entailed an enlargement of their conception of God. As good Jews, the first Christians had as a major feature of their confession of faith the affirmation that God is one. As the first disciples lived with Jesus and meditated upon what they had seen of Him and His resurrection, they became convinced that here, too, is God. Seeing the power of the Holy Spirit manifested in fresh and potent ways after the resurrection, they came to believe that here also is God. They were still convinced that God is one, but they now viewed God as Father (the designation given Him by Jesus and not unfamiliar in the Jewish Scriptures), Son, and Holy Spirit.

The relation of Jesus to God and the place of Jesus in God's plan for men's salvation were not easily determined. Christians struggled with them for many centuries and continue to do so. Within the first five centuries conclusions were reached to which the Catholic Church and the majority of Christians assented and still assent.

THE JEWISH CHALLENGE

Groups who thought of themselves as followers of Jesus but who sought to confine Him to Judaism continued for several generations. Some, called Ebionites, held that Jesus was a prophet, a spokesman for God, but a man. They differed among themselves but united in condemning Paul and his insistence on breaking the integuments of Judaism. The large majority of Christians rejected Ebionism.

THE GNOSTIC CHALLENGE

A more serious challenge came from Gnosticism. As we have suggested, Gnosticism was of pre-Christian pagan origin. It took many forms and when Christianity appeared was widely popular in the Mediterranean world. In general it accepted the sharp disjunction between matter, identified with evil, and spirit, regarded as good, which was axiomatic in much of popular thought and Hellenistic philosophy. The Gnostics taught what they held to be a *Gnosis,* a knowledge which had been revealed and was transmitted to initiates. In accord with the current dualism, they said that pure spirit is good but has been imprisoned in corrupt matter. Salvation, they believed, is the freeing of spirit from matter. This they promised to bring to the believer. Gnostics who professed to be Christians held that they had sayings of Jesus which had not been committed to writing but had been handed down secretly. Although they varied greatly among themselves, in general they taught that a first Principle exists, the All-Father, unknowable, Who is love. Since love abhors dwelling alone, the first Principle created other beings, aeons. This present world was created by one of the aeons, who, moved by pride, sought to do what the All-Father had done. That aeon was associated with a subordinate being, the Demiurge, who, the Gnostics declared, was the God of the Old Testament. The present world, of which men are a part, they went on, is compounded of spirit and matter, and salvation, the freeing of spirit from matter, was accomplished by Christ. Various accounts were given of Christ. Some Gnostics held that He was an aeon which had never ceased to be spirit but merely seemed to be man. Many men, the Gnostics said, have little or nothing of spirit and in due time will be destroyed. The others, with a portion of spirit in them, can be saved through being taught the hidden knowledge, the *Gnosts*.

For a time in the second century the Gnostics who thought of themselves as Christians may have been more numerous than the members of the Catholic Church. They had special rites, some of which resembled those of the mystery religions, but no central organization. In general they tended to minimize the historical elements in Christianity. They sought to acclimatize Christianity to a popular religious trend.

THE MYSTERIES

Within the last few decades some scholars have declared that Christianity conformed to the religious environment of the early centuries by becoming a mystery religion. They have called attention to the resemblance to the mystery cults in the Christian teaching of salvation in union with one who had been killed by his enemies and had been raised to life, of Christian practices of baptism in which the old nature was washed away, and of a meal in which believers participated in the body and blood of the crucified and so shared in his resurrection. The superficial resemblance is striking, but no clear evidence exists of a connexion between the mystery religions and the faith as taught by the Catholic Church. An essential contrast is the fact that no saviour god of a mystery religion had historical existence, whereas Jesus Christ was clearly an historical person whose life, teachings, deeds, crucifixion, and resurrection are supported by well-authenticated documents.

The Marcionites

Resembling Gnosticism, but not a phase of it, was a movement begun by Marcion. Said to have been the son of a Christian bishop and to have been reared a Christian, Marcion came to Rome in the first half of the second century. Like the Gnostics, he held to a sharp distinction between spirit and matter and maintained that the former is good and the latter bad. Unlike them, he laid no claim to a distinct and secret *Gnosis.* He taught that the world, with its wickedness and suffering, was the creation of an evil god, whom he called the Demiurge. That god, he said, is the one described in the Old Testament as rejoicing in battles and bloodshed and as vindictive. In striking contrast with this god, Marcion insisted, is a second God Who remained hidden until out of pure love He revealed Himself in Christ. Christ, so Marcion believed, was not man but only appeared to be a man. He proclaimed a new kingdom and deliverance from the Demiurge. Those loyal to the Demiurge crucified Christ, but in doing so they contributed to the defeat of the Demiurge, for the death of Christ was the price paid by the good God to the Demiurge for the release of men from the latter's dominion and so enabled them to escape into the kingdom of the good God. Marcion said that Christ also rescued from the underworld those who had previously died but in their lifetime had not submitted to the Demiurge.

All that the good God asks of men, Marcion taught, is faith in response to His love. Marcion believed that Paul understood the Gospel but that the Catholic Church had obscured it. To support his views he made a collection of the letters of Paul and the Gospel of Luke but expurgated all that seemed to him contrary to the Gospel. In the churches organized by Marcion chastity and celibacy were enjoined on all the members, for sexual union perpetuated the flesh, which Marcion said was evil. Churches embodying his teachings persisted into the fifth century, especially in the eastern part of the Empire.

MONTANISM

Another movement, quite distinct from Gnosticism, the mysteries, and Marcionism, was Montanism. It arose in Asia Minor and flourished in the latter half of the second century. Montanus, its founder, "spoke with tongues" at his baptism, declared that the Holy Spirit had utterance through him, and taught that the Holy Spirit had revealed to him that the end of the world was at hand and that the New Jerusalem would "come down out of heaven from God." Montanism spread widely and persisted into the fifth century. While prizing the records of the teachings of Christ and His Apostles, it held that the Holy Spirit continued to speak through prophets and that some of the latter were women. In the second century others than Montanists, including two bishops, taught that the end of the world was imminent. To prepare for it Christians were urged to be celibate, to fast, and to hold martyrs in high honour.

ATTEMPTS TO CONSERVE THE FAITH: THE APOSTOLIC SUCCESSION

To meet divergences from the faith taught by Christ and His Apostles the leaders of the Catholic Church stressed what to them were its distinguishing marks. They did not create them, but they emphasized them. The three marks, or guarantees, were the apostolic succession of the episcopate, the New Testament, and the Apostles' Creed.

By the apostolic succession was meant that bishops who had followed in unbroken line from the Apostles had transmitted what Christ had entrusted to the Apostles and the Apostles had handed it on to the bishops they had appointed. One of the earliest to apply this test was Irenaeus, bishop in Lyons, who gave the succession of the bishops of the Church of Rome as he understood it. These bishops continued, he said, what Peter and Paul, the organizers of that church, had conveyed to Linus. Linus, he insisted, had headship which had begun with Peter. Irenaeus hints that he could, if he wished, give similar lists for other churches. Early in the fourth century Eusebius, the most famous of the early historians of the Church, gave lists for several other churches. As time passed, the bishops who were held to preserve the apostolic succession met locally and regionally to consult on issues which concerned the Catholic Church.

ATTEMPTS TO CONSERVE THE FAITH: THE NEW TESTAMENT

Christians early began inquiring as to what documents preserved the faith as taught by Christ and His Apostles. Several of the letters of Paul were regarded as doing so and were read extensively in the churches. Irenaeus declared that there must be four Gospels, no more and no less. Gradually consensus was developed as to which additional documents should have a place in what came to be called the New Testament. Some were at first included and then rejected. Assent to several others came slowly. By the end of the second century common accord had been given to most of the twenty-seven now in the New Testament. The first complete list of the twenty-seven which we have dates from 367.

ATTEMPTS TO CONSERVE THE FAITH: THE APOSTLES' CREED

The present form of the Apostles' Creed dates from the sixth century. It was a development of the formula for baptism—"in the name of the Father, and of the Son and of the Holy Spirit"

—which had as its authority the closing verses of Matthew's Gospel and was an amplification of that formula intended to explicate it. An early form was in use in the Church of Rome at least as far back as the fourth century. With the exception of two or three phrases it was known to Irenaeus. That form, as well as its later amplification, could be used against the Marcionites and may have owed some of its phraseology to a desire to make clear the repudiation by the Catholic Church of some of the tenets of those dissidents. The opening phrases, "I believe in God the Father almighty, Maker of heaven and earth," rule out the Marcionite contention that the world is the creation of the Demiurge and not of the loving Father. The following "and in Jesus Christ His only Son, our Lord, who was conceived by the Holy Ghost, born of the Virgin Mary, suffered under Pontius Pilate, was crucified, dead and buried. On the third day He rose again from the dead" clearly insists that Christ was born of flesh and was the son not of a previously unknown God but of God the Father Who is also Creator and was fully human and not a phantom.

The Treatment of Repentant Sinners

Sharp differences developed over the treatment of Christians who were guilty of sins which the Church had said, if committed after baptism, were unforgivable. The issue became especially acute in connexion with those who had lapsed under persecution and then, the persecution over, had sought restoration. The majority opinion in the Catholic Church permitted restoration after assured repentance and strict penance. However, after the Decian persecution, when many who had defected were seeking, with tears, for readmittance to the Eucharist, and Cornelius, the Bishop of Rome, was disposed to concur if the sinner was genuinely contrite, Novatian, a presbyter in the Church of Rome, an able theologian and of unchallengeable orthodoxy, emphatically dissented. He was chosen bishop by his sympathizers and appointed other bishops. Novatianism spread widely in both East and West and partly coalesced with Montanism. Those who came from the Catholic Church were re-baptized. Novatian churches persisted into the fifth century. After the Diocletian persecution a similar movement arose in North Africa when a bishop was elected to the see of Carthage who was said to have weakened under the persecution. It was led by Donatus, a bishop, and at one time was reported to have 270 bishops. Donatism continued into the fifth and possibly into the seventh century. Countering the position of the Donatists, councils of the Catholic Church declared that the validity of baptism and ordination was not dependent on the moral character of the persons through whose hands they were administered. It may be that these controversies led to the addition to the Apostles' Creed of the phrase "[I believe in] the forgiveness of sins."

THE RELATION OF THE SON TO THE FATHER: MONARCHIANISM

Within the Catholic Church men continued to wrestle with the problem of the relation of Christ to God. They endeavoured to preserve a belief in the unity of God and yet to find a place for the unique role of Jesus of Nazareth.

Some called Monarchians put forward a variety of views. Dynamistic Monarchians held that Jesus was a man born of the Virgin Mary and that in Him an impersonal power resided which issued from God. A view widely held among them was that this power came upon Jesus at his baptism or, some said, at his resurrection. This was called Adoptionism. Others, Modalistic Monarchians, maintained that the Father was born as Jesus Christ and that He died and raised Himself from the dead. This view was also called Patripassianism, for it taught that the Father suffered. Monarchianism was condemned by the Catholic Church and its proponents were excommunicated.

THE RELATION OF THE SON TO THE FATHER: TERTULLIAN

Tertullian (c. 155-c. 222), a North African of Latin stock and a lawyer by profession, in his maturity was converted while in

Rome. A pioneer Latin theologian, he brought to his writing a legal mind. His view of the Trinity proved highly influential in Catholic thought. He believed that God is one in His *substantia,* or substance, but that in God are three personae (a Latin legal term), Father, Son, and Holy Spirit. He held that in Jesus Christ, one of the *personae,* the Word (Greek *Logos*) was incarnate, that Jesus Christ was both divine and human, but that the two natures did not fuse.

THE RELATION OF THE SON TO THE FATHER: CLEMENT AND ORIGEN

Contemporary with Tertullian, who did his writing in Carthage, were Clement (his precise dates are uncertain) and Origen (c. 185-c. 254), younger than Clement but like him reared in Hellenistic thought and succeeding him as head of the catechetical school in Alexandria. Clement was a convert; Origen was born of Christian parents. In his teens Origen wished to follow his father in martyrdom but was deterred by his mother. Clement taught that God is one and that the Word, or *Logos,* always existed—as the "face" of God—and in Jesus was made flesh and shed His blood to save humanity. Origen, devout, a first-class mind, an indefatigable student, and an inspiring teacher, spent much of his life in exile in Caesarea in Palestine. Origen held that God is one, and is the Father, that Jesus Christ is the *Logos* become flesh, is co-eternal with the Father but subordinate to Him, and that the Holy Spirit is uncreated and is associated in honour and dignity with the Son.

THE RELATION OF THE SON TO THE FATHER: THE STRUGGLE OVER ARIANISM

A view which led to a sharp division in the Catholic Church was associated with Arius, a presbyter in the Church of Alexandria. Arianism, which took its name from him, taught that God is without beginning but that the Son had a beginning and is not a part of God. Arian views were influential in the eastern part of the Empire.

The controversy became so severe that the newly converted Emperor Constantine, fearing that it might divide the realm which he had so painfully united, called a council of the Catholic Church to deal with the issue. It was the first of what are known as Ecumenical Councils. It met in Nicaea, not far from Constantinople, in 325, and Constantine presided. Feelings ran high. As in many ecclesiastical assemblies, the love which Christ had enjoined on His disciples seemed conspicuous by its absence. In the end a creed was adopted and in its main features has been perpetuated as the Nicene Creed. It rejected the Arian position. As framed at Nicaea it read:

"We believe in one God, the Father Almighty, maker of all things visible and invisible, and in one Lord, Jesus Christ, the Son of God, the only-begotten of the Father, that is, of the substance (*ousias*) of the Father, God from God, light from light, true God from true God, begotten, not made, of one substance (*homoousion*) with the Father, through Whom all things were made, those things which are in the heaven and those things which are on earth, Who for us men and our salvation came down and was made flesh, suffered, rose again on the third day, ascended to the heavens, and will come to judge the living and the dead."

Essential in countering Arianism were the affirmations that Christ was "true God from true God, begotten, not made" and that He "was made flesh" (the phrase was later altered to read "was made man"). The Arian contention was emphatically denied that Christ was a lesser being than the Father and had been created. *Homoousion* ("of one substance") with the Father further stressed that He was "true God from true God" and was equal with the Father. "Was made man" sought to make clear the belief that Christ was "true man" as well as "true God."

The Council of Nicaea did not heal the doctrinal rift in the Catholic Church. Although the council anathematized—cursed—those who held to the Arian position, and Constantine banished Arius, ordered the death penalty for those who did not conform, and commanded the burning of the books composed by

Arius, Arianism persisted and for a time appeared about to prevail. Within a few years Arius was permitted to return from exile and before his death was restored to communion. The animus of the Arians was directed chiefly against Athanasius. Like Arius, Athanasius was prominent in the Church of Alexandria. In time he became its bishop. He had been carefully trained in Greek philosophy as well as Christian theology. Still young and a deacon, he was present at Nicaea but, not being a bishop, could not engage in the public debates. As bishop in the see of Alexandria, the most important in Egypt and in a city prominent as a commercial and intellectual centre, Athanasius attracted attention because of his firmness against the Arians and another group which made common cause with the Arians. In general, the Arians were influential in the eastern part of the Empire and the Nicene views prevailed in the West, with the Bishop of Rome as their chief protagonist. In an attempt to settle the issue, several councils were held, not recognized as speaking for the entire Catholic Church. Constantius, a son of Constantine, who for a time was sole ruler of the Empire, gave his support to the Arians. An effort to bring the two wings together took place through the adoption of the term *homoiousion* (of "similar substance") not *homoousion* (the "same substance") in describing the relation of the Son to the Father. Athanasius would not agree. In the ebb and flow of the controversy he was five times exiled from his see and each time, after longer or shorter periods, was permitted to return. He died in office (373). His firmness was due in part to his insistence on what he regarded as at the heart of the Gospel and in part to his conviction that the state should not be allowed to dictate to the Church.

Arianism eventually died out. It persisted for several centuries, but chiefly among Germanic peoples who had been won to that form of the faith when it was prominent in the Empire and who in the fourth and fifth centuries were invading the Empire and establishing themselves within its borders. Its Adherents regarded themselves as the true Catholic Church, but the overwhelming majority of the Roman citizens eventually rejected it. In the course of time the Germanic peoples conformed.

The triumph of the Nicene views was aided by the contributions of three men known as the great Cappadocians: Gregory of Nazianzus, Basil of Caesarea, and Gregory of Nyssa. Gregory of Nazianzus, the son of a bishop, was familiar with Greek philosophy and the thought of Origen. He was a pioneer in the monastic movement and for a brief time was Bishop of Constantinople. Basil of Caesarea and Gregory of Nyssa were brothers. Basil, a jurist and an eager student of philosophy, had joined with Gregory Nazianzus in compiling a selection of the writings of Origen. In middle life he was ordained a priest and in time became Bishop of Caesarea in Cappadocia. Gregory of Nyssa, somewhat younger, was Bishop of Nyssa, a small town near Caesarea. He, too, was greatly influenced by Origen. The three Cappadocians helped to call attention to the distinction betwen *ousia* (equivalent to the Latin *substantia*, put into English as "substance") and *hypostasis* (translated into Latin as *persona*, put into English as "person"). They held that in God is only one *ousia,* in which Father, Son, and Holy Spirit share, but there are three *hypostases*—Father, Son, and Holy Spirit.

The Emperor Theodosius, born in Spain and reared by parents who were attached to the Nicene convictions prevailing in the West, was vigorously anti-Arian. He called a gathering which met in Constantinople in 381 and is commonly regarded as the Second Ecumenical Council. Although not adopted by it, what is generally called the Nicene Creed has usually been associated with it. That creed was based on a fourth-century creed in use in Jerusalem and influenced by the one adopted at Nicaea. The major change from the latter were additions at the end in words made familiar by the translation in the Book of Common Prayer: "I believe in the Holy Ghost, the Lord, the Giver of Life, Who proceedeth from the Father ['and the Son,' a later Western addition] Who with the Father and the Son together is worshipped and glorified: Who spake by the prophets. I acknowledge one baptism for the remission of sins. And I look for the resurrection of the dead and the life of the world to come." In this creed the majority of Christians have concurred.

THE RELATION OF THE DIVINE AND HUMAN IN JESUS

The Nicene Creed left an important problem unsolved. What was the relation of the divine and human in Jesus? Prolonged controversies arose on this issue; indeed, they have continued to the present day. They were often punctuated, as were those over the relation of the Father and the Son, by recriminations and lack of brotherliness which were in sharp contrast with the love enjoined by Jesus. In them, too, political factors entered. On the one hand were human pride and sin. On the other hand were an earnest search into the mystery entailed by the incarnation and a desire to preserve both the unity of love and the integrity of the Gospel.

In the debates over the relation of the divine and human in Jesus most of the participants held to the Nicene formula. They agreed that "the only begotten Son of God . . . very God of very God . . . being of one substance with the Father . . . came down from heaven . . . and was made flesh." But in what fashion were the Son of God and the human found in Jesus of Nazareth? Apollinaris, a younger friend of Athanasius, held that in Jesus the *Logos* was the rational element. That position left the divine nature complete but made Christ less than human, for a human being, it was held, had body, soul, and reason. The Cappadocians declared that Apollinaris was in error and that in Jesus both the divine and the human natures were complete. The general trend in Antioch, a major city and important in the life of the Catholic Church agreed with them. Several synods, including the Ecumenical Council of Constantinople (381) condemned the views of Apollinaris.

The debate continued. In it were involved Cyril, Bishop of Alexandria, and Nestorius, Bishop of Constantinople, and rivalries over the relative dignity of the sees of Antioch, Alexandria, and Constantinople. Cyril rejected the views of Apollinaris. He maintained that in Christ the divine and human elements were both complete and that in the human element reason was present. But he held that, while the *Logos* became incarnate in Christ, the humanity of Christ was that of mankind in general and so belittled the historical character and individuality of Christ. This view was in contrast with that in Antioch, where the full historical character of Jesus Christ was upheld. Nestorius tended to agree with Antioch and preferred for Mary the title of *Christotokos* ("Christ-bearing" or "Mother of Christ") to the term *Theotokos* ("Mother of God"), employed by Cyril. Both men appealed to Rome. The Bishop of Rome opposed Nestorius.

The controversy developed unseemly features. In 431 a council, usually called the third in the succession of Ecumenical Councils, assembled in Ephesus. Chaired by Cyril, it condemned and deposed Nestorius before the latter's friends appeared. After a few days the supporters of Nestorius arrived. Headed by the Bishop of Antioch, they declared themselves to be the true council and condemned and deposed Cyril. However, they were outnumbered by the other faction. When the representatives of the Bishop of Rome arrived, the majority reconvened and excommunicated the Bishop of Antioch and his adherents. Both parties appealed to the Emperor, who confirmed the deposition of both Cyril and Nestorius and commanded the latter to live in a monastery. The Bishop of Antioch sent a creed to Cyril declaring Christ to be "true God and true man, consisting of a reasonable soul and body" and spoke of Mary as *Theotokos*. To this Cyril assented and was restored to office. Nestorius remained in the monastery to which he had been confined.

Some clergy, including bishops, who sided with Nestorius were exiled and took refuge in Nisibis, a trading centre near the border between the Roman and the Persian empires but within the latter's domains. There some of them taught in the school in which clergy were trained for the Church in the Persian Empire. How far they adhered to the views ascribed to Nestorius is not clear. Rightly or wrongly, eventually the Church in the Persian realms was known as Nestorian.

Within the Roman Empire the discussion continued. A monk, Eutyches, declared that the two natures in Christ were so blended that there was only one, and that was fully divine. The bishop who succeeded Cyril in the see of Alexandria sided with Eutyches, but a council convened in Constantinople in 448 by the bishop of that city condemned Eutyches. The following year a council called by the Emperor met in Ephesus. The Bishop of Alexandria presided. By a large majority it restored Eutyches to communion and deposed the Bishop of Constantinople.

In 451 a council summoned by the Emperor met in Chalcedon, across the Bosporus from Constantinople. It adopted a creed which was based upon the *tome* of Leo, a document prepared by the then Bishop of Rome. Leo, usually referred to as Leo the Great, was one of the strongest pontiffs ever to hold that post. The creed of Chalcedon declared Christ to be "perfect in Godhead and perfect in manhood, truly God and truly man, of rational soul and body, *homoousion* with the Father according to the Godhead, and *homoousion* with us according to the manhood, like us in all respects, without sin, begotten of the Father before all time according to the Godhead, in these latter days, for us men and for our salvation, born of the Virgin Mary, *Theotokos* according to the manhood, one and the same Christ, Son, Lord, Only-begotten, in two natures, inconfusedly, immutably, indivisibly, inseparately, the distinction of natures by no means taken away by the union, but rather the peculiarity of each nature being preserved and concurring in one *persona* and one *hypostasis,* not parted or separated into two persons." Thus the distinctive views associated with Apollonaris, Eutyches, and those ascribed to Nestorius were condemned.

By another act of the Council of Chalcedon the Bishop of Rome was recognized as having priority in the Catholic Church and the Bishop of Constantinople was placed second to him. Thus the latter had precedence over the Bishops of Antioch, Alexandria, and Jerusalem.

The creed of Chalcedon remained the Catholic Church's official statement of the relation of the divine and human in Christ. It has been followed by the Roman Catholic Church, by most of the bodies emerging from that Church from the Protestant Reformation onward, and by the Orthodox Churches. The position accorded the Bishop of Constantinople, later called the Ecumenical Patriarch, has remained that in the family of Orthodox Churches.

The struggles over the relation of the human and divine in Christ, and those concerning the relation of Christ with the Father were associated with striking disharmony. Some have seen in them the victory of Greek philosophy over the Gospel. However, while Greek and Latin terms were employed, they did not necessarily distort or negate the Gospel. Christians were groping towards an understanding of something quite new in human experience. They were under the necessity of employing terms which were available and which approximated as nearly as possible to what they were striving to put into words. They gave to these terms meanings derived from what they had seen in Christ but alien to the contexts from which they were drawn. Christians were dealing with profound and unique mysteries presented by God's act in Christ. The large majority of thoughtful Christians who have since wrestled with the issues have been convinced that the creed of Chalcedon comes as near to an elucidation of the mysteries as the possible for creatures limited by the use of words.

THE SEPARATION OF VARIOUS NATIONAL BODIES FROM THE CATHOLIC CHURCH

The decisions formulated in the creed of Chalcedon hastened and crystallized divisions in the Catholic Church which were already under way. On the one hand most of the members of the Catholic Church, East and West, adhered to it. They included the large majority in the West, mainly Latin-speaking Roman citizens, who looked to the Bishop of Rome as the head of the Catholic Church. The Germanic invaders, not yet fully assimilated to Roman culture, and some non-Latin elements in North Africa, largely Berber, remained outside the Catholic Church—the Germanic peoples as Arians. In succeeding centuries the completion of the assimilation was marked by submission to the Catholic Church. In the East the Greek-speaking majority submitted to the continuation of the Roman Empire with its capital in Constantinople and looked to the bishop of that city as representing that rule. In contrast were elements, chiefly in the East, who either rejected Roman rule or were restive under it as symbolized by Constantinople. Most of them professed acceptance of the decisions reached at Nicaea in 325 but rejected the definition in the creed of Chalcedon of the relation of the divine and human in Christ. Since they tended to stress the divine in Christ, those who held to Chalcedon labelled them Monophysites, with the implication that they regarded Christ as wholly divine and not human. The dissenters from Chalcedon repudiated the term Monophysite, insisting that they recognized both the divine and the human in Christ but maintaining that the relationship was not as described by Chalcedon.

The Church in Armenia did not conform to Chalcedon. From the beginning it had been identified with the Armenian state and people. Occupying highlands between the Roman and Persian empires, the Armenians sought to maintain their independence of both realms, but not always with success. At times each powerful neighbour sought to establish a sphere of influence in the portion which bordered its realms. It was natural, therefore, that the Armenian Church endeavoured to maintain its autonomy as against the Catholic Church, for the latter was closely related to the Roman Empire.

Similarly the Egyptians were ill content with the rule of Constantinople, more and more associated with the Greeks.

The majority rejected Chalcedon, regarding it as Greek. Their ecclesiastical language was the Egyptian vernacular of the day, now known as Coptic.

The Syriac-speaking peoples in Syria were also restive under Greek rule issuing from Constantinople. Many of them broke from the Catholic Church, giving Chalcedon as a reason. In the sixth century they were drawn into a degree of unity by an ascetic bishop, Jacob Baradaeus. Well-educated, completely devoted, Jacob Baradaeus traveled widely among his fellow Syrians, usually on foot and garbed in a ragged horsecloth, consecrating bishops and ordaining priests. Syrian Christians were eventually known as Jacobites, whether from him or because they claimed to be the custodians of the true faith transmitted by James, or Jacob, the brother of Jesus. Attempts to bring them into unity with the Copts failed.

The Christians in the Persian Empire were chronically subject to persecution by the state, partly because they dissented from the official religion, Zoroastrianism, and partly because they were suspected of being potential and perhaps actual supporters of Persia's inveterate foe, the Roman Empire, by the fifth century officially Christian. Most of the Christians in Persia, a small minority of the population, through clergy trained in Nisibis in a view of the relation of the divine and human in Christ associated, probably mistakenly, with the teaching of Nestorius, claimed that theirs was the true Catholic faith and regarded the Church of the Roman Empire as heretical. They could therefore insist that they were not in any way under the protection of the Roman Empire and so were not a menace to Persian rule.

All these dissenters from Chalcedon persisted into the twentieth century. They were subject to repeated persecutions by powerful neighbours and conquerors. They dwindled in numbers. In the twentieth century their losses continued, but when these lines were written they were still very much a part of the Christian scene.

Across the years attempts were made to heal the breach between those who conformed to Chalcedon and those who rejected the findings of that council. For example, later in the fifth century one Emperor condemned the findings of Chalcedon and another issued a statement which he hoped would be palatable to both sides. The latter won some of the more moderate anti-Chalcedonians, but it was rejected by the Bishop of Rome.

POTENCY OF AUGUSTINE IN THE THEOLOGY OF THE LATIN WEST AND HIS STRUGGLES WITH PELAGIANISM

Augustine of Hippo (354-430) was potent in shaping the theology of the Latin-speaking portion of the Catholic Church. His influence was felt not in defining the relation of the Father and the Son or the relation of the divine and human in Christ, for on these issues the Catholic Church in the Latin-speaking part of the Roman Empire was agreed and he was a loyal son of that church. His special contribution arose out of his own experience, part of it personal and part gained from the decline of the Roman Empire, made especially vivid by the capture and sack of Rome by Alaric and his Goths in 410.

Augustine was converted in 385 under the preaching of Ambrose, the great Bishop of Milan. After his conversion he returned to his native North Africa, lived in community with close friends, and eventually, after long hesitation on his part, was made Bishop of Hippo Regius, a port about two hundred miles west of Carthage. There he lived until his death. Both before and during his episcopate he wrote prodigiously and maintained an extensive correspondence. Many of his convictions he put succinctly in his *Confessions,* a moving and intimate autobiography which across the centuries has had an extensive reading.

From his experience of prolonged inability to control his sexual passions and then the coming of victory through what he regarded as an act of God which he had done nothing to deserve, Augustine arrived at convictions about man's moral impotence and salvation through the grace of God. In this he found support in the writings of Paul and the teachings of Ambrose and some other Latin theologians.

A diligent student of the Scriptures, Augustine maintained that they taught that God had created Adam and had given him freedom of moral choice. But, he insisted, in sinning Adam lost his freedom and was free only to sin. All men, as Adam's descendants, have inherited "original sin" from their forefather and in themselves cannot turn to God in faith. All efforts to do so, Augustine declared, arise from self-interest and mire those who make them ever more deeply in the morass of sin. But God, so Augustine taught, of His great love became incarnate in Christ, fully God and yet fully man, but not stained by original sin. Through faith in Him salvation comes, but that faith cannot be achieved by man's unaided act. Augustine said that of His great mercy God had chosen ("elected" or "predestined") some men to repent and reach out in faith to accept God's gift in Christ. If an individual is among the elect, God's love will pursue him until he repents and turns in faith to God. After having accepted God's grace, an individual may sin, but God will win him back. To put the doctrine in the terms which have been widely used by Protestants in the Augustinian tradition, here are "irresistible grace" and the "perseverance of the saints." Augustine held that this side of the grave a man cannot be certain that he is among the elect. If he could, he would be tempted to pride, the basic sin.

Augustine's views of original sin, predestination, irresistible grace, and the perseverance of the saints did not win universal acceptance. They were much more influential in the West than in the East. In his own day they were challenged by Pelagius and the latter's supporters. Pelagius was a British monk, learned, austere, and ascetic. Arriving in Rome, he was scandalized by the loose living of many who bore the Christian name. He sought to persuade them to reform their manner of life, palpably contradictory to their profession, and said that they could do so if they really wished. One of his close friends who sought ordination in North Africa was refused on the charge of heresy. He had maintained that Adam's sin injured himself only and not his descendants and that every child is as free to obey God as Adam had been before his fall. Pelagianism, as it was called, met with a mixed reception in both East and West. While Nestorius was Bishop of Constantinople he supported it. In 431 the Council of Ephesus which condemned Nestorius anathematized Pelagianism. In 416 synods in North Africa and Rome acted against Pelagianism and the Bishop of Rome supported them. The latter's successor first approved Pelagianism and later rejected it. In 529 a synod in Orange, in Gaul, affirmed original sin, declared that man had lost all power to turn to God, said that turning to God is wholly through God's grace, and condemned those who said that by our will we can anticipate God's action. Yet it said nothing about irresistible grace, affirmed that the beginning of faith and the desire to believe can come apart from the free gift of grace, and condemned the position that some are predestined to evil.

The fall and sack of Rome in 410 stimulated Augustine to write *The City of God (De Civitate Dei)*, which set forth his understanding of history. For centuries it was very influential, especially in Western Europe. Intending it as an answer to the pagans who maintained that the disaster was attributable to the Christian defection from the gods under whom Rome had become great, Augustine did more than make a rebuttal. He set forth what he believed that the Scriptures teach about the entire course of history. In contrast with the prevailing Greek view that history is a succession of cycles, endlessly repeated, Augustine held that history has a beginning and a culmination. He maintained that from the time of man's first rebellion against God two cities have existed, one earthly and the other heavenly. The earthly is the creation of pride and love of self. It is not entirely bad, for from self-interest Babylon and Rome as well as other governments had brought peace and order. The heavenly city is dominated by "the love of God and even to the contempt of self." Men enter it here and now and it is represented by the Church, although not all within the Church are its citizens. As Augustine viewed it, from its beginning all history has been directed and governed by God and moves to a climax in which God's will is perfectly to be accomplished.

In his emphasis upon man in history, as in *The City of God*, Augustine was typical of a major trend in the western portion of the Catholic Church. Here was a characteristic of Rome in the days of its glory and prominent in the Roman Catholic Church and in many of the forms of Christianity which have sprung from that Church. Western Christianity has by no means been oblivious to life beyond the grave, but it has sought to bring all human society to conform to the will of God. In contrast, Eastern Christianity, while not ignoring human society, has been keenly aware of life beyond the grave, but it has sought to bring men into life with God and growth in that life.

Augustine did not confine his writings to the problems of free will and predestination. As a corollary, he addressed himself to the problem of evil. He also wrote on the Trinity and gave form to convictions which were in accord with those of the majority in the Catholic Church and which have continued to contribute to the thought of Christians on that subject, chiefly among Western Europeans and the nations created by them in the Americas and Australasia.

ADMISSION TO THE CHURCH

In the centuries while the attempts at the clarification of Christian belief were being made—a process which has never ceased—the customs of the ecclesiastical bodies to which the faith was giving rise were developing.

Admission to these bodies was by baptism. The customs in the Catholic Church which accompanied baptism displayed many variations. Initially all that was required was an expression of belief in the "Lord Jesus Christ." An early baptismal formula which became standard was "in the name of the Father, and of the Son, and of the Holy Spirit." This, as we have seen, was eventually enlarged into the Apostles' Creed. Baptism was by water. The chronic debate as to whether at the outset this was always by immersion has never been decisively resolved. Paul's image of being buried with Christ in baptism and being raised with Him in newness of life seems to support this form. In practice, by the end of the first five centuries there were several methods of baptism. It was often by immersion, frequently in running water. Sometimes it was by thrice-repeated immersion, the first preceded by a confession of faith in the Father, the second by a confession of faith in the Son, and the third by a confession of faith in the Holy Spirit. In some baptisms water was poured on the head three times. Often baptism was preceded and followed by anointing with oil. For at least a time, in baptism by immersion the candidate was naked; as a symbol that the new birth was a complete break with the past, no one was to take anything into the water but his body. Immediately after baptism the bishop laid his hands on the head of the candidate. Thus, it was believed, the Holy Spirit was received. By the end of the second century the baptism of infants appears to have been common. Since baptism was believed to wash away the original sin inherited from Adam, some advocated its administration as soon after birth as possible, so that if the infant died before being guilty of conscious sin it would be immediately ushered into heaven. However, since baptism could not be repeated and was regarded as cleansing from all sins committed before its administration, some postponed the rite until their death bed. For converts, baptism was often given at Easter or fifty days after Easter. Candidates were customarily to prepare for baptism by fasting, prayer, vigils through entire nights, and the confession of sins. Baptism was preceded by a catechumenate in which instruction was given the neophytes. In some places its length was three years. Catechumens were counted as Christians and were admitted to the services of the Church, but were required to leave at a certain point in the liturgy, before the celebration of the Eucharist.

The Developing Christian Worship

During the first five centuries Christian worship was evolving. In one of Paul's letters we read of the practice in the church in Corinth. Both men and women spoke. Some spoke with tongues, presumably as had been done at the Day of Pentecost. Paul said that he himself spoke with tongues. Some interpreted in the vernacular what was being said in the tongues. Some prophesied. All shared in a common meal, and in conjunction with it the Lord's Supper was celebrated. Paul viewed the Lord's Supper as the participation in the body and blood of Christ and held that it must be observed with dignity and reverence.

From the beginning, Christian worship took over some of the features of the worship in Jewish synagogues. The fact that many of the early converts were Jews made the procedure natural.

By the second century Christian worship centred in the Lord's Supper, which came to be known as the Eucharist, from a Greek word meaning the giving of thanks. Normally it was observed on the first day of the week, "the Lord's Day," because it was then that Christ had been raised from the dead (although for centuries many, even among the Gentile Christians, also observed the seventh day, or Sabbath, held sacred by the Jews). The Eucharist was not confined to the Lord's Day. No one order prevailed. Normally the ritual included readings from the Old Testament and from the letters or other writings of the Apostles, a sermon or discourse by whoever was presiding, offerings to be used for the sick, widows, orphans, prisoners, and others in need, the giving of thanks, and the sharing by all in the bread and the wine. Eventually the bishop or one of the clergy delegated by him presided. The Communion table became an altar on which the bloodless sacrifice was celebrated. Elaborate liturgies were developed, especially after imperial toleration made public celebrations possible. Liturgies of the chief churches, as at Rome and Alexandria, spread widely in the districts surrounding these centres. The liturgies in use in churches which in the twentieth century contain the large majority of those who bear the Christian name preserve many of the features of the ones developed in the first five centuries. They are thus a link which helps to give a sense of fellowship with the Christians of all ages.

In addition to the Eucharist were other forms of worship. Wednesdays and Fridays were observed by fasting, prayer, and readings from the Scriptures as well as the Eucharist. Special days in what became the "Christian Year" were honoured. Easter had the chief place and with it were associated Maundy Thursday, on which the Lord's Supper was instituted, and Friday, the day of the crucifixion. Epiphany, when the mornings begin to lengthen, and the twenty-fifth of December, associated with the winter solstice, were given Christian significance. Epiphany was used to commemorate the birth of Jesus, the coming of the wise men, and the baptism of Jesus. Christmas, celebrated on the twenty-fifth of December, seems to have had its origin in Rome.

In the second century custom enjoined prayers of all the faithful at daybreak, mid-forenoon, noon, mid-afternoon, and nightfall. In some places Sunday worship began before dawn, followed by the Eucharist in the early morning hours. In public prayer one either stood with arms outstretched or lay prone, face downwards.

For hymns, the Psalms were used. But very early, certainly in the first century, distinctly Christian hymns were composed. As the years passed they multiplied. The *Te Deum*, one of the most widely sung across the years, dates from the fourth century. Its author and place of origin are not certainly known. The great Archbishop of Milan, Ambrose, composed many hymns and taught them to his flock.

As persecution ended, buildings were erected for public worship. Some were very large. An early form was that of the basilica, an oblong hall with a double colonnade and apse, which had been used for law courts and assemblies.

Private devotion was common. For it many books existed. The Scriptures were widely employed and translations were made into several vernaculars. Writings traditionally but wrongly ascribed to Dionysius the Areopagite, a convert of Paul, seem to have been composed in the fifth or sixth century. Their content was largely Neoplatonic, with some Christian terminology.

Various cults arose within the Catholic Church. The martyrs were revered, their relics were cherished, their tombs became the goals of pilgrimages, they were believed to work miracles, they were esteemed as guardians of cities and patrons of trades, and they were asked to intercede with God on behalf of their votaries. To the martyrs were added Christians of exemplary lives and angels, especially Michael. The reverence for the Virgin Mary rapidly mounted.

The Developement of a Hierarchical Clergy

A professional clergy early developed. Its main grades, as we have seen, were bishops, priests, and deacons. To these others were added. Ordination was by the bishop. The bishop was supposed to be the choice of his flock including the clergy, and in his consecration both laity and clergy were recognized. Consecration was generally by three bishops, but in emergencies, such as times of persecution, one was sufficient. Bishops of prominent cities were accorded special honour. Outstanding were those of Rome, Constantinople, Antioch, Alexandria, and Jerusalem. The first four cities, with Carthage, were traditionally the major centres of population, government, and commerce in the Empire. Jerusalem was included because of its role in the origin of the faith. In time these sees were thought of as patriarchates. Into the twentieth century the ecclesiastical bodies sprung from the Catholic Church continued to pay them honour, and some of the several bodies which claimed to represent that church—as Rome (through the Uniates, the Eastern bodies in its communion), the (Greek) Orthodox, and the Syrian (Jacobite)—continued to name incumbents, even when, as in the case of Antioch, no city survived, and, as in Constantinople and Alexandria, because of the numerical dominance of Islam Christians were dwindling minorities and Moslems were in the overwhelming majority. The Copts have claimed only one patriarchate, that of Alexandria. Armenians and Nestorians never counted any of the five cities of the Catholic Church as major centres but called their administrative heads patriarchs. Divided into rival jurisdictions, the Armenians have had more than one patriarch. The Nestorian patriarch had his title from Baghdad, long a major city in the area where his flock were numerous.

Episcopal sees were grouped by provinces, usually according to the civil administrative units of the Roman Empire. Ecclesiastical provinces first developed in the eastern part of the Empire, for in the early centuries Christians were more numerous here than in the West. In time the bishop in the chief city of a province was called metropolitan, had a degree of authority over the bishops in his province, including a voice in their selection, and called synods to act on common interests. The Bishop of Rome was the only patriarch in the West. Because Rome was long the political capital of the Empire which was called by its name, and since Peter and Paul were believed to have died there and the former was said to have been given by Christ authority over His Church, the Bishop of Rome, considered to be the successor of Peter and to be entrusted by Christ with the powers of the Prince of the Apostles, claimed jurisdiction over the entire Catholic Church. The Catholic Church in the West acquiesced, but the majority of the Catholic Church in the East, while usually conceding that the Bishop of Rome was *primus inter pares,* did not give him the unique position that was conceded to him in the West. In the fourth century, Cyprian, Bishop of Carthage, although his see was in the West, refused to accord to the Bishop of Rome more than the deference due to "the first among equals."

From early days the bishops corresponded with one another on matters of common concern or on issues within their respective jurisdictions of which they wished to apprise their colleagues or on which they desired their counsel. They aided one another in times of persecution and sought unity on debated questions of discipline and doctrine. Although they did not always agree and in fact frequently vigorously differed, through them the Catholic Church had most of such cohesion as it possessed.

From the beginning the leaders in the Christian communities endeavoured to bring the body of believers to the high ethical standards enjoined by Christ. The remembered commission to the Apostles to make disciples of all nations, baptizing them and teaching them to observe all that He had commanded them, might well seem impossible of fulfilment, especially since it entailed bringing all mankind to conformity to the ideal set forth in the Sermon on the Mount. Yet the fact that the commission was embodied in one of the Four Gospels recognized as canonical served to set it as the goal which Christians could not disavow without disloyalty to their Lord. In letters of the Apostles preserved in the New Testament the objective was reaffirmed, even though in not precisely the same words. From the first, Christians were aware of their failure fully to reach the ideal, but their leaders, undiscouraged, pressed on, as Paul said, "toward the mark for the prize of the high calling of God in Christ Jesus."

Since the conviction was early held that baptism washed away all sins committed before its administration and that baptism could not be repeated, the question arose as to what was to be the attitude of the Church towards sins committed after baptism. Some sins were believed to be especially serious, notably denial of the faith, murder, and gross sexual offenses. Up to the fourth century an official view maintained that one post-baptismal repentance was permissible, but ruled out more than one. The strict application of this rule entailed the danger of legalism (an attitude quite contrary to the Gospel)—that God's favor could be earned by good works rather than dependence solely on God's grace. Grace, as the New Testament writers were aware, was beyond human capacity to merit but was the "free gift of God" and arose from His limitless love. Moreover, since what from Christ's teachings were the most serious sins, pride and the failure to respond to God's love, were less easily detected than the more overt offenses, how could any officer of the Church or any Christian community be always aware of their presence?

As we have seen, some movements, especially Montanism, Novatianism, and Donatism, were adamant in refusing renewal of fellowship to extreme sinners, particularly those who had apostatized under the pressure of persecution.

In contrast, the majority maintained that if repentance was genuine the offender could be restored to fellowship and the Communion, but only after severe discipline to ensure contrition and to guard against a repetition of sin. For public offenses confession was required before the entire congregation. Restoration and discipline were entrusted to the bishop. In the West, especially in Rome, the penitent was required to throw himself on the ground and weep, and the bishop would weep with him. The congregation would also weep and groan. In the East it became the custom for the bishop to entrust the discipline to a priest. This practice gave rise to so much scandal that it was allowed to lapse and the judgment of whether the offender could partake of the Communion was left to the conscience of the sinner. As might have been expected, laxity ensued and the level of morality in the Christian community was seriously lowered.

THE RISE OF MONASTICISM

By the end of the fifth century monasticism had begun the development which was to make it a continuing feature of Christian churches. Christian monasticism seems to have begun in Egypt, where climate and geography favoured it. A narrow strip of fertile land watered by the Nile is bordered by a desert on which rain is infrequent. Hermits could find in the desert the solitude for which they longed and yet be near enough to human habitation to obtain the spare nourishment permitted by their austere discipline. Before the end of the third century they had begun to appear.

Several factors contributed to the rise of monasticism. One was an ascetic tradition which had emerged very early. Jesus Himself was not an ascetic. He lived as a self-confessed homeless wandering teacher, but He went to dinners and said that He came "eating and drinking"—in contrast with John the Baptist, who was rudely clothed and whose food was said to have been the desert fare of locusts and wild honey. Jesus did not marry, but He did not forbid His disciples to do so. Paul was a celibate, but he knew of no command of Jesus which enjoined that state for believers and he advised young widows to marry. Within the first century some widows did not remarry but pledged themselves to remain unmarried, gave themselves to prayer and to the service of others, and were formally recognized as having adopted that way of life. Before the end of the fourth century at least one synod and one regional council had commanded celibacy for bishops, priests, and deacons, one Pope had made chastity obligatory on priests, and another, Leo the Great, had extended the injunction to sub-deacons. In the East the practice became established that sub-deacons, deacons, and priests might marry before ordination, but that a bishop must be unmarried and if raised to the episcopate in the married state must separate from his wife and place her in a monastery. Contributory impulses towards monasticism may have come from Gnosticism, Neoplatonism, and Indian influences. A major source was a reaction against the decline in the ethical practices of many who bore the Christian name, especially as membership in the Catholic Church mounted.

In Egypt the monastic life took three forms. The first two were represented by Anthony (c. 250-356), the most famous of the early monks. The son of well-to-do Christian parents, he heard in a church service the reading from the Gospel in which Jesus said to the rich young ruler: "If thou wilt be perfect, go and sell all that thou hast and give to the poor." He took the injunction to heart and obeyed it. He sought instruction from men who had already adopted the hermit existence, and learned from them graciousness, love, kindness, meekness, endurance, and freedom from anger. For about twenty years he dwelt in solitude. In time his fame attracted others and with them he formed a kind of community, each member dwelling alone but sufficiently near the others to have fellowship with them. In the third form of monasticism the monks lived in community in a monastery. Rules were developed. Their chief early formulator was Pachomius (c. 285 or c. 292-346), a younger contemporary of Anthony. Over each monastery was a head. Labour and prayer were required, strict obedience to the superiors was commanded, but extreme asceticism was discouraged. Monasticism remained a feature of the life of the Church in Egypt and in the twentieth century it still is a dominant characteristic of the Coptic Church. For example, the Patriarch elected in 1959, after some years in business had spent five years as an anchorite and had then returned to Cairo, rented an abandoned mill, and begun preaching.

Monasticism rapidly spread in both the eastern and western portions of the Roman Empire. Two of the Cappadocian champions of Nicene orthodoxy, Basil of Caesarea and Gregory Nazianzus, joined for a time in the ascetic life. Basil's mother, a sister, Macrina, and a younger brother joined in founding a monastic community. Macrina was later esteemed as the foundress of the monastic life for women in the Greek portion of the Catholic Church. Basil had visited Egypt and had been profoundly impressed by what he had seen of the Pachomian monasteries. He worked out a set of rules which helped to shape monasticism in the Catholic Church. Like those of Pachomius, they discouraged extreme asceticism and emphasized work, especially the study of the Scriptures, frequent confession of sins, and complete obedience to the superior officer. The pioneer of monasticism in the West, and especially in Gaul, was Martin of Tours. An older contemporary of Basil, as a catechumen Martin had entered the army in fulfilment of the law which made such service obligatory upon him as the son of a military officer. A story associated with his military service tells us that on a cold winter day he divided his coat with a beggar and that night, in a dream, saw Christ clothed in the half which he had given away and saying that it was He with Whom Martin had shared his coat. Baptized and resigning from the army, Martin became a hermit. By his example he attracted others, who joined with him in founding a monastery. As we have seen, he was eventually Bishop of Tours. A younger contemporary said of Martin that "he judged none and condemned none and never returned evil for evil. No one ever saw him angry, or annoyed, or mournful. . . . He presented to every one a joy of countenance and manner which seemed to those who saw it beyond the nature of man. Nothing was in his mouth but Christ and nothing in his heart but piety, peace, and joy."

Another quite different pioneer of monasticism was Eusebius Hieronimus Sophronius, better known as Jerome (c. 342-420). Enormously erudite, Jerome early was attracted to the ascetic life, lived for a while as a hermit near Antioch, was more than once in Rome, for a time was secretary to a Pope, advocated self-denial, and excoriated the luxury of many of the clergy. Ultimately he made his home in a monastery which he built in Bethlehem. There he engaged in literary work and theological controversy and made a fresh translation of the Bible into Latin from the original tongues. That translation became the basis for the Vulgate, the standard translation of the Scriptures into the Latin vernacular. In Bethlehem his friend Paula, who had followed him from Rome, erected convents and a hospice for pilgrims.

That was a remarkable generation. It included, among others, such outstanding Christians as Ambrose of Milan, Augustine of Hippo, Martin of Tours, the great Cappadocians, Jerome—all of them in that small segment of the globe which was embraced by the Roman Empire.

A bizarre form of asceticism appeared among the "pillar saints," each of whom spent a solitary life for years on the top of a pillar. The most famous was Simeon Stylites, who lived thirty-six years on a pillar east of Antioch and died in 459. The extreme ascetics were revered as "athletes of God" and were said to work miracles of healing.

A majority of the monks were laymen. At first they were looked at somewhat askance by many of the officials of the Catholic

Church, but before long monasticism became a recognized feature of the Catholic Church. In an age when the majority in that church were conforming less and less to Christian standards, monks represented a surge of life which endeavoured in a nominally Christian but essentially non-Christian society to realize fully Christian, community living. The extreme ascetics in their solitary existence sought to separate themselves completely from a world which they regarded as basically hostile to Christ.

THE EFFECTS OF CHRISTIANITY IN ITS FIRST FIVE CENTURIES

What can be said of the effects of Christianity during its first five centuries? What can be learned from them of the fashion in which the Gospel operates in the life of mankind and of the way God works through it? Here was remarkable achievement. But, from the standpoint of the commission which the first Christians remembered as having been entrusted to the Apostles by the risen Lord, to make disciples of all nations, baptizing them, and teaching them to observe all that He had commanded them, the achievement fell far short of full obedience.

The nominal allegiance of the majority of the peoples of the Roman Empire had been won. The state itself, which once had persecuted the faith, was now supporting it. In a civilization in which the creative impulse was waning and little new in art, philosophy, literature, government, and economic life was appearing, the Gospel had given rise to a new religion, Christianity. From it had sprung an ecclesiastical institution, the Catholic Church, which was almost as inclusive as the Empire and was bringing into its ample fold an increasing proportion of the pagan barbarians who were pressing into the Empire. Partly within and partly outside the Empire other ecclesiastical structures claiming to be Christian had emerged. Within the Empire the human intellect, jaded by the philosophical discussions which had seemed to issue in blind alleys or in a syncretism that left some of the best minds unsatisfied, had been stimulated to wrestle with the cosmic issues presented by the Gospel, and theologies had emerged which for centuries were to grip much of the human race. Thousands of lives, most of them obscure and leaving behind them no written records, had been given moral victory and had become radiant and self-giving embodiments of the faith, hope, and love which Paul declared were lasting. They had borne what Paul described as the fruits of the Spirit—love, joy, peace, longsuffering, gentleness, goodness, faith, meekness, and temperance. Constantine had forbidden gladiatorial contests in his "new Rome" and these bloody spectacles were dwindling. Efforts, in part successful, had been made to cleanse the theatre of pornographic features. Church discipline had addressed itself to lifting sex relations and marriage to the high level set by Christ.

Notable as were these results, if an accurate appraisal is to be made, contrasting aspects of the record must be faced. Only a minority of civilized mankind had been reached. The Roman Empire was now ostensibly Christian, but the Persian Empire and India had barely been touched and so far as we know none in the Chinese Empire had so much as heard the name of Christ. The Catholic Church had been torn by dissensions. Although the sense of brotherhood had been in part realized in aid to the poor, the sick, and the captives, the love enjoined by Christ was far from being attained. Most of the early Christians had regarded participation in war as contrary to the faith. Now that the Empire had made its peace with the Church, Christians were confronted with the apparent necessity of defending civilization by armed force, and Augustine had formulated the characteristics of what he deemed just wars as against unjust wars. Although Augustine declared that God did not create man to lord it over his rational fellows and helped to prepare the way for later attacks on slavery, that institution had not disappeared. The presence of monasticism was a tacit confession that the large majority who bore the Christian name had not achieved Christian standards. In the Roman Empire society as a whole was so far from conforming to the teachings of Christ that the best hope of obeying them seemed to be withdrawal from society in order, either by solitary effort or in minority communities, to seek to attain to Christ's commands.

Many in the Roman Empire were realizing that theirs was a sick society. Potent though it was, Christianity was not preventing the decay eroding the foundations of the Mediterranean world. In spite of such great souls as Ambrose, Augustine, Basil of Caesarea, Athanasius, Martin of Tours, and Pope Leo "the Great," twilight was settling over that world. In the next few centuries twilight was to become darkness. For about five centuries not only Greco-Roman civilization but Christianity as well seemed to be disappearing. Occasional gleams lightened the darkness, but the world as Augustine and his contemporaries knew it was disintegrating. From the standpoint of the onlooker the City of God appeared to be a mirage or something to be postponed until after this mortal life. Yet in these dark centuries the light did not go out. Here and there it was manifest. Later it was to shine more brightly and more widely, with mounting contrasts between it and the darkness but never overcome by the darkness.

CHAPTER V

Deepening Twilight, A.D. 500-950

For the four and a half centuries which spanned the years from A.D. 500 to A.D. 950 Christianity seemed to be fading from the world scene. The dates are only approximate. Twilight had begun before the end of the fifth century. Occasionally it appeared to brighten, but it continued to deepen. By A.D. 950 the worst was over, but losses as well as gains were registered after that year. Had a man from Mars been able to pay periodic visits to the earth during these centuries, he would probably have said that Christianity was doomed. In A.D. 500 Christendom was almost completely identified with the Roman Empire. The winning of the allegiance of that realm by Christianity and the growth of the Catholic Church and the bodies which dissented from it had been two of the most remarkable developments in the history of religion. But by that time several other religions rivalled Christianity in geographic expansion and inner vitality. Manichaeism, younger than Christianity, was more widely spread, for by that year or soon thereafter its adherents were scattered across Eurasia from the Western Mediterranean into China. Buddhism, between five and six centuries older than Christianity, was making what looked like a triumphal march across South and East Asia and by A.D. 500 was potent not only in the land

of its birth but also in Ceylon, Burma, Siam, Cambodia, Central
Asia, China, Korea, and Japan. Hinduism was vigorous in India
and Confucianism flourished in China. Manichaeism, Buddhism,
and Hinduism continued to enlarge their geographic boundaries.
After a period when it seemed to be eclipsed by Buddhism, Confucianism enjoyed a marked revival; even more firmly established than before in China, its native habitat, it was spreading
in Korea and Japan. As we are to see in a moment, a new
religion, Islam, was capturing much of the Mediterranean basin,
was displacing Zoroastrianism in the erstwhile Persian Empire,
and was gaining footholds in Central Asia. Of the religions with
major followings among civilized peoples, only Christianity appeared to be waning.

The decline of Christianity between A.D. 500 and A.D. 950 can
be ascribed to at least three factors. First and foremost was
the progressive weakening of the Roman Empire. In the generation which saw the birth of Jesus Augustus Caesar, climaxing
his predecessors' accomplishments, gave to the Roman Empire a
unity which was to persist. During most of the first two centuries
of that unity prosperity mounted but was deceptive. In the
third century illness was already painfully apparent. No one
date can be given for its fatal termination. Long after A.D. 500
the Empire continued, with Constantinople as its centre, and
with a gradual transition to what is called sometimes the Eastern Roman Empire and sometimes the Byzantine Empire. Not
until A.D. 1453 was the Byzantine Empire ended by the fall of
Constantinople to the Ottoman Turks. In the West the attenuated shadow of the Roman Empire endured until 1806.

A second factor was the inroads of barbarians from the North.
Pressure had long existed, as was seen in the capture of Rome
by the Gauls in 390 B.C. It again became acute in the third and
fourth centuries of the Christian era. Many of the barbarians,
mostly Germanic, were permitted to settle within the borders
of the Empire and were not easily or quickly assimilated. In
A.D. 378 the Goths defeated and slew the Emperor Valens in the
Battle of Adrianople, slightly west of Constantinople. In the

fifth century the West Goths (Visigoths) established themselves in Spain; the Vandals, defeated by the West Goths in Spain, moved into North Africa and with their fleets ravaged the Western Mediterranean; the East Goths (Ostrogoths) made themselves masters of Pannonia on the upper Danube; the Burgundians moved into Gaul; the Franks began that conquest of Gaul which in succeeding centuries made them the dominant Germanic power in Western Europe; and Anglo-Saxons moved into Britain. Also in the fifth century the Huns, an Asiatic people, were a destructive scourge. The sixth century saw the creation of the Ostrogothic kingdom with headquarters in Ravenna and the attempt of its great monarch, Theodoric, to create a constructive working arrangement between his people and the Roman citizens. But no sooner was one group of barbarians partly assimilated than a fresh horde appeared and for a time disorder again mounted. The last of the northern peoples to ravage the civilized South were the Scandinavians. Late in the eighth century they began raiding the coasts of Ireland and Great Britain. In succeeding centuries they repeatedly plundered the coasts of Western Europe and Italy, established themselves in England, Normany (named from the "Northmen"), and Sicily, attacked Constantinople, and swarmed along the rivers of Russia, with centres in Novgorod and Kiev. At the outset most of the barbarians were pagans. As we have seen and will remind ourselves a little later, on entering the Empire many of the Germanic peoples were Arian Christians, and were separated from the Roman population, which was Catholic.

The third factor was the conquests of the Arabs, the bearers of a new religion, Islam. The Arabs took advantage of the near-exhaustion of the Roman and Persian empires. For centuries the two realms had been chronic enemies. The borders between them were mastered now by one of the rivals and now by the other. Early in the seventh century the Persians took Antioch, Damascus, Jerusalem, and Egypt. Under an able Emperor, Heraclius, the Romans drove the Persians back and moved into Mesopotamia. At that juncture the Arabs, inspired and united by Islam, moved out of their native peninsula and by the middle of the eighth century overran Syria, Palestine, Egypt, most of the Iberian Peninsula, Sicily, Sardinia, Corsica, and Crete, erased the Persian Empire, and established their capital at Baghdad. Thus within a little more than a century about half of Christendom came under the rule of zealous adherents of the faith taught by the Arab prophet.

In their conquests the Arabs were helped by divisions among the Christians. Some of the dissidents from the Catholic Church were inclined to welcome the new masters, for in them they hopefully saw protectors against the church which had the support of the Roman Empire. In the lands under Arab rule Christianity did not immediately disappear. Some conversions to Islam were forced, but in general the Arabs tolerated Christianity. However, they put its adherents under discriminatory disabilities: they did not allow Christians to serve in the Arab armies, they required them to wear a distinguishing garb, they placed on them a special tax, and they forbade them to give such public expressions to their faith as religious processions or the ringing of loud bells. In consequence, many Christians became Moslems. In most of the Arab lands the churches survived. But they were on the defensive and in many places developed the characteristics of ghetto communities. In North Africa they eventually disappeared. In the advance of Islam Christianity suffered proportionately the greatest numerical losses in its history. Not even Communism was to master so substantial a percentage of the earth's surface in which Christians were a majority of the population.

PERSISTENCE IN THE DWINDLING ROMAN EMPIRE

Christianity persisted in the remnants of the Roman Empire. For a time under Justinian, who reigned from 527 to 565, that realm had a brief revival. North Africa and parts of Italy and Spain were retaken from the Germanic invaders. Justinian was a great builder: his most notable architectural achievement was

St. Sophia, the cathedral church of Constantinople and the most noble example of a new kind of Christian art. Justinian was deeply religious and interested himself in theology. He was an orthodox adherent of the Chalcedonian creed, but in this he differed from his Empress, Theodora, who was an ardent advocate of the non-Chalcedonians. He sought to compose the differences on the issues discussed at Chalcedon. Under him what has been called the Fifth Ecumenical Council of the Catholic Church was convened (553) and made official an interpretation of Chalcedon which, Justinian hoped, would reconcile the Chalcedonians and the moderate anti-Chalcedonians. At first the Bishop of Rome dissented and was held in exile in Constantinople, but he later declared the Council legitimate and was permitted to return to his see. Justinian's effort did not win all the anti-Chalcedonians and caused unhappiness in much of the Catholic West. Justinian sought to eradicate the remains of paganism, persecuted the Manichaeans, and took vigorous measures against the Montanists and other Christians whom he regarded as heretics. He also anacted legislation to regulate the life of the Catholic Church. Among other measures, he prohibited the purchase and sale of ecclesiastical offices and the attendance of clergy at the theatre and horse races and increased the functions of bishops in their respective dioceses, giving them the oversight of some public works and the enforcement of legislation against gambling.

The active concern of Justinian in ecclesiastical affairs accelerated a trend towards the control of the Church by the State. What was called caesaropapism usually characterized the relations of Church and State in those branches of Christianity which stemmed from Constantinople. By tradition, the Roman Emperors had made the control of religion one of their functions. Among their titles had been *pontifex maximus* ("chief priest") of the official cults. The Christian Emperors were not priests, but they too believed the regulation of religious affairs to be one of their prerogatives. This was the case under the continuation of the Roman Empire in the East and has been characteristic of Russia and the Balkan countries whether under Christian,

Moslem, or Communist regimes. As a consequence in the East the Church centred its efforts on worship and did not seek to control the State or to make its voice heard in the ranges of collective life outside the sacraments and individual morals. Yet the Church was not as subservient to the State as the pre-Christian official cults had been. It developed a measure of autonomy, even though limited. A phase of the other-worldly emphasis of the Eastern wing of the Catholic Church was the prominence of monasticism. In general that monasticism proved to be more contemplative than monasticism in the West; the latter was more activistic.

In contrast, in the West, where the Empire disintegrated much earlier than in the East and was followed by governments without the prestige which accrued to the Empire, the Catholic Church was much less controlled by the State and a conflict of functions was chronic. From time to time the State succeeded in mastering the Church. But the Church struggled to effect its independence and sought to bring conformity to its standards in what might be called "secular" issues.

Under Justinian's successors questions of doctrine continued to vex the Catholic Church and to attract the attention of the Emperors. The coming of the Arab menace made desirable united resistance by Christians and the attempt to rise above the traditional controversies. The issue most debated was the relation of the divine and human in the will of Jesus. For a time the Bishop of Rome supported the thesis that in Christ only one will (*thelema*) existed. But later Roman Pontiffs affirmed that in Christ were two wills, human and divine; since Christ was both divine and human, to say that He had only one will, and that divine, would place a limitation on His full humanity. In 680 and 681 the so-called Sixth Ecumenical Council was convened in Constantinople by the Emperor. It affirmed that Christ had two wills, the divine and the human, but held that the two were always in harmony. This continued to be the position of the Catholic Church, both East and West. In the eighth century an Emperor revived the issue. In the Lebanon a substantial number of Christians, usually called Maronites, adhered to monotheletism—the theory of only one will in Christ —and held to it until in the twelfth century they made their peace with Rome.

Theological activity continued in the Eastern wing of the Catholic Church. He who is regarded as the last great theologian of the East was John of Damascus, of the first half of the eighth century, but his chief contribution was not in fresh areas but in a comprehensive systematization of orthodox views.

The major dispute in the Catholic Church in the decades following the Sixth Ecumenical Council was what is known as the Iconoclastic Controversy. That controversy began in 726 and raged, at intervals, until 843. It had to do with the use of images, or icons, in worship. The practice had long been common but from time to time opposition arose. Was the employment of images idolatry or a non-idolatrous aid to worship? The Emperor Leo the Isaurian opened the campaign forbidding their use. Several factors added to the bitterness engendered by his act, among them resentment against the attempt of the Emperor to control the Church. Women and monks were particularly vehement in their advocacy of the icons. John of Damascus vigorously supported them. Theodore of Studius, one of the most influential figures in the monasticism of the Eastern branch of the Catholic Church, was also emphatic in his advocacy. The Western wing of the Catholic Church was not as much disturbed by the controversy as was the East but participated in it. In 787 the Seventh Ecumenical Council met, holding the majority of its sessions in Nicaea. The Council approved the use of icons but regulated the manner in which they were to be honoured. At least two synods in the West denounced the findings of Nicaea. Not until the eleventh century did Northern Europe recognize the Nicaean gathering as an Ecumenical Council. As evidence that the Church wished to assert its independence of the State, we may note that the Seventh Ecumenical Council forbade the appointment of bishops by the lay power and ordered that in each ecclesiastical province an annual synod be held.

From Constantinople as a radiating centre, Christianity spread on the geographic periphery of the Eastern portion of the Empire and among some of the barbarians who had occupied territories formerly within its borders. For example, during the reign of Justinian missionaries carried the faith up the Nile Valley into Nubia, and much of that area became Christian. In North Africa, after the re-conquest of the region from the Vandals by Justinian's armies, many Berbers accepted the faith. Much of Central Europe and the Balkan Peninsula had been occupied by Slavs. Constantine (also known as Cyril) and Methodius, both from Greece and so under Constantinople, were prominent in winning many of them to the faith. Constantine devised a written form of their language and began the translation of the Gospels. In the seventh century the Bulgars, an Asiatic folk of Turkish or Hunnic stock, occupied territory north of Constantinople. In the latter part of the ninth century their monarch, Boris, was baptized and many of his people followed him. Missionaries came from both East and West to instruct them. The church which arose among the Bulgars conformed to Chalcedonian orthodoxy, but in administration it was independent of both Rome and Constantinople.

The Widening Rift Between the Western and Eastern Wings of the Catholic Church

In theory, until well beyond the tenth century the Eastern and Western wings of the Catholic Church remained one. Supposedly the imperial administration and the Catholic Church were respectively the civil and the religious aspects of the Christian commonwealth, the Roman Empire. But by the middle of the tenth century East and West were drifting apart. The Latins were increasingly distrustful of the Greeks. In most of the West the Emperors ruling from Constantinople had little or no authority. The coronation of Charlemagne as Roman Emperor in 800, of which we are to speak, did not constitute a formal breach, for the Emperor in Constantinople recognized him as a colleague, and a long-standing tradition sanctioned the division of the imperial administration between the East and the West. Some of Charlemagne's successors also were crowned as Roman Emperors, but the Roman Empire was still regarded as one realm which ideally embraced all Christians regarded as orthodox by the Catholic Church. However, in actuality in the West the civil administration of what was called the Roman Empire had long ceased to include any but fragments of its former territories.

The waning of Roman imperial authority in the West was accompanied by other contrasts between the Western and Eastern wings of the Catholic Church. Rivalries existed between the Bishops of Rome and the Bishops of Constantinople. In the West the term *filioque* was added to the Nicene Creed. That creed had originally said that the Holy Spirit proceeds from the Father. The West added "and from the Son." The change seems first to have been made in Spain as an attempt of the Catholics to counter the Arianism which flourished among the West Goths and to emphasize the Nicene contention that the Son was of "the same substance with the Father, begotten and not made." *Filioque* spread slowly in the West, but the Bishop of Rome early accepted it. Differences in ecclesiastical customs developed. The Latin priests were celibate and confirmation was only by a bishop. The Greek priests were married and confirmation was by a priest. However, no persistent overt break occurred until later.

SMALLER EASTERN CHURCHES CURBED BY MOSLEM ARAB CONQUESTS

The Eastern churches which separated from the Catholic Church continued through the four and a half centuries covered by this chapter. As we have noted, their refusal to remain in the Catholic Church stemmed ostensibly from their rejection of the Chalcedonian creed, but it was also and chiefly due to ethnic particularism and to unwillingness to be dominated by the Greeks and the Byzantine ecclesiastical structure which predominated in the Eastern wing of the Catholic Church. In theory they adhered to Nicaea but protested that Chalcedon was an heretical departure from it. All resembled the Catholic Church in having bishops and monasteries. The chief anti-Chalcedonian schisms from the Catholic Church were the Copts, the Armenians, the Syrians (or Jacobites), and the Nestorians. On all of them the Moslem Arab conquests brought restrictions.

By the time of the Arab domination of Egypt the Coptic form of Christianity had become the national religion of Egypt and the liturgy and other religious literature had been put into Coptic, the vernacular. The Ethiopian (Abyssinian) Church was in communion with the Copts. The introduction of the faith to Ethiopia had taken place before the sixth century. Secure in its mountain strongholds, Ethiopia was not overrun by the Arabs. But within a generation of the Arab conquest a large proportion of the Copts accepted Islam. Many remained true to the faith, however, and numbers, highly educated, were given official posts by their Moslem masters. Some so employed may have been responsible for the creation of what is called Arab architecture. In the eighth century the Arabs added to the restrictions on the Christians and instituted persecutions which augmented conversions to Islam.

The Armenian Christians were seldom entirely free from persecution. The Sassanid rulers of Persia succeeded in extending their suzerainty over Armenia and as a symbol of acquiescence to their rule endeavoured to force their official faith, Zoroastrianism, on the Christians. They met with such stubborn resistance that in time they granted religious liberty. Late in the sixth century Persia was constrained to cede part of Armenia to the Byzantine Emperor. The latter managed to bring the Church in his sphere to conform to Chalcedon, and a schism in the Armenian majority anathematized Chalcedon. After they had subdued Persia, the Arabs deemed wise the continuation of the toleration of Armenian Christianity which had been granted by the Sassanids. Late in the seventh and in the eighth century Constantinople, presumably as a phase of its imperialism, attempted to bring all the Armenian Church to conform to

Chalcedon. However, in 719 a synod re-affirmed the opposition of that church. Then, as later, many Armenians were merchants in other lands, notably in Mesopotamia, Persia, and Central Asia. Frequently they held to their faith and in the cities of their sojourn established congregations of their church.

Syrian Jacobites also engaged in trade and industry in other lands. From them Christian minorities arose in Mesopotamia and farther east. For example, they had an ecclesiastical structure in Persia.

Nestorians were the chief representatives of Christianity in Central and East Asia. Nestorian merchants and missionaries lived in several of the main caravan centres in Central Asia. Before the coming of the Arabs they won many converts, chiefly among the Turks and the Hephthalite Huns. Their major rival was Manichaeism. In 635 they planted the faith in Ch'ang-an, the capital of China. China was then ruled by the second and most powerful Emperor of the T'ang Dynasty and was the strongest realm on the planet. Ch'ang-an was the largest city in the world and attracted foreigners from many parts of Asia. Nestorianism spread widely in T'ang China, but only among minorities; Central Asians were usually at the heart of its communities. It suffered from the restrictions placed on Buddhism and other foreign faiths in the ninth century, and in 980 monks sent to strengthen their fellow believers in China could find none of the latter. Both the Zoroastrian Abbasids and the Moslem Arabs persecuted the Nestorians, but the Arabs employed many of them as physicians, accountants, astrologers, and philosophers. Nestorians made the early Arabic translations of the Greek philosophers.

INVADING BARBARIANS GRADUALLY WON BY THE CATHOLIC CHURCH IN WESTERN EUROPE

From the perspective of later centuries, the most significant developments in the history of Christianity from A.D. 500 to A.D. 950 were in Western Europe. At first sight this is surprising.

The inroads of the northern barbarians overwhelmed the western portion of the Roman Empire and in that region threatened to eradicate civilization and the faith. During at least eight centuries wave after wave of invasion menaced such recovery as had been achieved in the interval between the successive incursions, and the prospects both of a high culture and of Christianity seemed grim. The invaders were most unpromising material for the Gospel. They were vigorous and possessed native ability, but they admired the warrior, were hard-fighting and hard-drinking, and seemed to despise the Christian virtues as the traits of weaklings and to view with scorn the story of a crucified Saviour.

Yet in retrospect the outcome is understandable. In the East Christianity was handicapped by its close association with the Roman (later Byzantine) Empire. There the Church, while not as fully subservient to the State as its pagan predecessors had been, was often a tool of a nominally Christian but essentially non-Christian régime. Moreover, from the seventh century onward that régime was confronted by aggressive Moslem enemies and with difficulty maintained a slowly losing rear-guard defense against them.

In contrast, in Western Europe the Catholic Church was more nearly independent of the State than in the Byzantine realms. It was, therefore, less handicapped in giving expression to the Gospel than in the East. The independence was not complete. As Christianity was adopted the rulers attempted to use the Church for their purposes. But many of the leaders of the Church were not happy with that control and from time to time escaped from it. Although the Church, even when emancipated from the State, only partially embodied the Gospel, on the whole it more nearly shaped the civilization which emerged among the former barbarians in the West than it did in the East. In the disorder accompanying the break-down in Western Europe of the Roman Empire and the associated culture the Catholic Church became the tutor of the invaders. It stood for law and order. Such education in letters and arts as survived was carried on through it. It embodied and transmitted much of the

Roman heritage, modified and partly moulded by the Gospel.

The fact that the Patriarch of the West, whom we must now call the Pope, was the Bishop of Rome, furthered that achievement. As a city, Rome dwindled in population. Its inhabitants lived amid the physical remnants of former greatness, and the public buildings fell into ruin, despoiled by invaders and the remaining citizenry. However, as the barbarians became Christian and either through their conversion or by abandoning Arianism became members of the Catholic Church, they looked to Rome as the geographic centre of their faith, made pilgrimages to its shrines, and regarded the Popes as the successors of Peter and as possessing the authority which, they were taught, had been entrusted by Christ, as His representative, to Peter. The eventual capping of Trajan's Column with a statue of Peter was doubly significant. It was a symbol of the triumph of Christianity in the realm of the Caesars. It was also, unwittingly, witness to the penetration of the Catholic Church by *Romanitas,* the Roman tradition. In the West the Catholic Church was henceforth in actuality, even though not officially, the Roman Catholic Church.

Before the end of the seventh century the Roman Catholic Church had triumphed over Arianism. That achievement was part of the process of assimilating the Germanic invaders— Goths, Vandals, Lombards, and Burgundians—to *Romanitas.* During the early stages of their conquest the Germanic peoples held to their own laws, in contrast with their subjects, Roman citizens who were governed through Roman laws. Their adherance to Arianism was associated with their purpose to maintain their ethnic and cultural identity. As time passed they conformed to such Roman civilization, badly garbled, as survived, and conformation included incorporation in the Roman Catholic Church.

The steps by which in the West the barbarians were won to the Christian faith were evidence both of the close association of the Catholic Church with the State and of the embodiment in the Church of a spirit independent of the State. On the one

hand, the faith was adopted by a people as a whole at the instance of the secular ruler. The prince was baptized and his
subjects followed, either willingly or at his behest. On the other
hand, the large majority of the missionaries were monks, men
who had in theory made a full commitment to Christ.

In the brief summary to which we must condense the record,
we can call attention only to a few examples which are fairly
typical. As we have noted, in 496 Clovis, the King of the Franks,
was baptized. His warriors followed his example. His descendants, the Merovingians, were the first ruling house of the Frankish
realms. Some of the Romano-Gaulish clergy helped in the instruction of the converts, but much of the advance towards Christian standards of life was accomplished by Irish monks. During
the seventh, eighth, and ninth centuries, up to the beginning of
the Viking raids, Ireland was very little troubled by the invasion
of pagans. Its peoples adopted the Christian name. Monasticism
flourished. From the monasteries many went forth, some as individuals to live as hermits, and others in groups, often of twelve
with a leader in imitation of the Apostles and Christ. Many were
active as missionaries to non-Christians. Others sought to raise
the level of Christian living among those nominally of their
faith. Among other devices, they compiled elaborate penitentials
as a guide to hearing confessions and giving pastoral care.

Pagans on the island of Great Britain were won in part by
missionaries from Ireland and in part by monks dispatched from
Rome. The Anglo-Saxon invasions had reduced to paganism
much of the former Roman Britain. The descendants of the
Roman provincials retreated westward and there maintained the
faith inherited from the days when the Empire was ostensibly
Christian. In the North were peoples who had never been under
Roman rule, and had never been Christian. To them and to the
Anglo-Saxons came monks from Ireland, the most notable being
Columba (c. 521-597). He established himself on Iona, an island
off the west coast of Scotland, whence Christianity was carried
to peoples in Scotland and to Anglo-Saxons in the North-east of
England. In 596 Pope Gregory the Great sent a contingent of

monks from Rome. One of them, Augustine, became the first Archbishop of Canterbury. Through these pioneers and their successors sent from Rome many of the Anglo-Saxons were converted and a hierarchy was organized. Much of the organization of the Roman Catholic Church in England was accomplished by Theodore of Tarsus (602-690), a monk commissioned by the Pope (668) to be Archbishop of Canterbury. Although arriving in his mid-sixties and living well into his eighties, when most men find it necessary to slow down, Theodore travelled extensively through the island, creating dioceses, consecrating bishops, and improving the education of the clergy and the public worship.

The English had a large part in the conversion of the Low Countries and Germany. In 690 Willibrord went to the Frisians, a people in what is now the Netherlands. He had the support of the Pope and the Franks. In 695 or 696 the Pope created him the first Archbishop of Utrecht. Significantly, for it is evidence of the rapid success of the mission in England, that was almost exactly a hundred years after the first Roman mission to the Anglo-Saxons. The most famous English missionary to the Continent was Winfrith, better known as Boniface (c. 672 or 675 to 754). A monk, a scholar, having gifts of administration, Boniface could have risen to a high post in the Church in England. Instead, he chose to go as a missionary to the Continent. He worked first among the Frisians, then farther up the Rhine among the Germans. Supported by the Franks and the Pope, he won many pagans to the faith and did much to improve the quality of the existing Christianity. He summoned many from England, both men and women, to aid him. In his late seventies he returned to his first field, Frisia, and there suffered martyrdom. An indication of his character was his dying request that no vengeance be wreaked on his murderers.

Late in the eighth century the conversion of the Saxons who had remained on the Continent was accomplished by Charlemagne, the greatest of the Frankish rulers. Charlemagne equated baptism with submission to his rule. The independence-loving

Saxons resisted and again and again revolted. As often as they rebelled Charlemagne marched his armies into their country and forced submission. Charlemagne's programme included the sending of missionaries, through whom instruction and much of the creation of an ordered church life were accomplished.

Before the middle of the tenth century a beginning had been made in the conversion of the Scandinavians. The chief pioneer missionary was Anskar (801–865), who first went under appointment of Louis the Pious, the son and successor of Charlemagne. He was probably a Saxon, evidence of the rootage of the faith among that people. He made few converts. The adherence of the Scandinavians to the faith had to wait until the latter part of the tenth century and the eleventh and twelfth centuries.

The Development of Western Monasticism

A large proportion of the monks who shared in the conversion of the Germanic peoples in Western Europe followed the rule formulated by Benedict of Nursia (c. 480-c. 544). Born of a good family north-east of Rome, as a youth Benedict went to Rome to study. Distressed by the vices of the nominally Christian population, in his teens he left the city and adopted the life of a hermit. His austerities brought fame: many who were seeking to follow the perfect Christian life came to him. It is said that from them twelve monasteries arose, each with twelve monks and an abbot—as with the Irish *peregrini* in imitation of Christ and the twelve Apostles. When about fifty years of age Benedict moved to the summit of Monte Cassino, between Naples and Rome, destroyed a temple where the worship of Apollo was still maintained, and founded a monastery which became the mother house of the order bearing his name. He remained a layman, but some of his company were priests and maintained the observance of the sacraments. He had come to believe that the full Christian life should be lived in community rather than by solitary anchorites. For his rule he drew ideas from earlier regimens, including that of Basil of Caesarea. The rule discouraged extreme asceticism, but enjoined a poverty which forbade personal possessions, commanded chastity and obedience, and included labour (for idleness was held to be an "enemy of the soul"), communal worship, private meditation, and the reading aloud of religious books at meals. Obedience was to the abbot. Worship was called the *opus Dei* ("the work of God") and occupied four or five hours out of each twenty-four. Labour was largely in the fields, but later it came to include literary pursuits as well. The community was predominantly self-supporting. Clothing was simple but sufficient and sufficient hours of sleep were provided to maintain health. Physically the standard of living was no more austere than that of the average peasant of the day.

Benedict envisioned no comprehensive organization embracing many monasteries. Each community was independent and self-governing. Not for several centuries was a plan devised for coöperation among the several houses. However, Benedict's rule won wide endorsement and hundreds of monasteries which took it as a model sprang up in Western Europe. They did not slavishly conform, but devised modifications to meet their particular needs.

The other form of monasticism most widely adopted in the West during this period was that of the Irish. In Ireland the Church was organized around the monastery. The bishops as bishops did not have administrative functions and were without dioceses. Unless they were abbots, they were simply members of the community who administered ordinations. However, apart from an Irish nucleus, the Irish tradition was not widely followed; the Benedictine rule prevailed.

Cassiodorus (c. 490-585), a contemporary of Benedict, founded a quite different kind of monastery, but one which was not widely reproduced. Of Syrian ancestry, he long held civil offices in Italy. In these posts he sought to bring Goths and Roman citizens together, thereby fusing the two cultures. At about the age of fifty he retired, founded a monastery, and assigned to its inmates study, editing, and writing. Through them many

Greek classics were translated into Latin, and other works, religious and secular, were copied or compiled and were a means of transmitting to posterity much of the Greek and Roman knowledge that might otherwise have been lost.

THE DEVELOPING ROLE OF THE PAPACY

The Papacy had an important role in the perpetuation and ordering of the Roman Catholic Church, both in the West and in its later extensions. Its incumbents varied greatly, not only in ability but as examples of Christian standards of life. Before the sixth century several of the Popes had risen to prominence. As imperial power in Italy declined, some of them defended Rome against barbarian attacks. For the most part they took doctrinal positions which were adopted by the Catholic Church. Leo I, "the Great" (reigned 440–461), was outstanding. He protected Rome against barbarian invaders, notably the Huns and Vandals, asserted the authority of his see in the Catholic Church, with Roman clarity provided the formula adopted by Chalcedon as the orthodox statement of the relation of the divine and human in Christ, and suppressed much of heresy in the West.

A century and a half later another Roman, Gregory I (reigned 590–604), the only Pope to share with Leo I by general consent the title of "Great," and with Leo I one of several Popes officially regarded as a saint, did a great deal to shape the Roman Catholic Church and to make the Papal see the controlling centre of that Church in Western Europe. A scion of a prominent and wealthy Roman family, he lived at a time when imperial Rome was falling into ruins and when the city's importance was becoming exclusively ecclesiastical. His notable administrative gifts were representative of the best of the pre-Christian Roman tradition. The Emperor appointed him to head the civil administration of the city. He was strongly attracted to the ascetic life, was a warm admirer of Benedict of Nursia and wrote a life of that saint, devoted his inherited wealth to founding six monasteries in Sicily, and turned over the family mansion in Rome to a monastic community. He reluctantly consented to the popular election which elevated him to the Papal throne, but rose to the challenges of the office. In spite of chronic ill health he administered the vast estates of the Church, saw to it that the poor of Rome were fed, and renovated the church fabrics of the city. He raised armies, successfully withstood the attacks of the Lombards, the latest of the Germanic barbarians to invade Italy, made his authority respected in Italy, Sicily, Gaul, Spain, and North Africa, attempted to curb the abuses in the Church in the Frankish domains, inaugurated the Roman mission to Britain, preached frequently, endeavoured to enforce clerical celibacy, prompted monasticism and improved the quality of life in some of the houses which were lapsing from their professed ideals, and was the author of voluminous writings on theology that were long standard in the West. The kind of chant called by his name seems to have been indebted to him. A phrase on his epitaph, *consul Dei* ("God's consul"), is both terse and apt. In two words it epitomizes his perpetuation of the Roman administrative genius, now dedicated to God. He also employed a traditional description of the role of the Popes, *servus servorum Dei* ("servant of the servants of God"), as embodying his ideal for his high office.

A half-century after Gregory I, Nicholas I (reigned 858–867), also later canonized, insisted on the authority of his see in all the Catholic Church and over all governments. Among other achievements, he supported the appeal of a Frankish bishop against a powerful Frankish archbishop, compelled a great-grand-son of Charlemagne to take back his divorced wife, excommunicated two bishops for supporting the divorce, and enforced his power over another archbishop who defied it.

The Papal claims were backed by a collection of documents, some genuine and some spurious, which appeared about the middle of the ninth century: the *Decretals of Isidore.* They depicted the Bishops of Rome as claiming prerogatives over the Catholic Church from the beginning, permitted all bishops to appeal directly to the Pope, and regarded bishops and Popes as of right free from secular control. They included the *Donation of Constantine,* composed about the middle of the eighth century and purporting to have Constantine as its author. The *Donation of Constantine* professed to describe that Emperor's conversion, baptism, and healing from leprosy through Pope Sylvester I, and said that out of gratitude Constantine was handing over to the Pope and his successors the imperial palace in Rome and "the city of Rome and all the provinces, districts, and cities of the Western regions." In an uncritical age the Isidorian Decretals were accepted as genuine. During centuries of disorder the Papal power kept the Catholic Church in Western Europe from falling apart into a welter of tribal, royal, and feudal churches, dominated by secular princes.

TEMPORARY REVIVAL UNDER THE CAROLINGIANS

For a time in the eighth century and the early part of the ninth century recovery from the forces which had threatened to extinguish Christianity in the West appeared to be in progress. Although weakened, the Roman Empire still had a foothold and was presumably strengthened when, on Christmas Day, in the year 800, Charlemagne was crowned Emperor by the Pope in St. Peter's. The Pope's act was symbolic of the fashion in which the Roman Catholic Church was perpetuating the Empire—but an Empire which sought to embody Christianity. The outward conversion of the Germanic invaders had been all but completed. The raids of the Northmen, with the renewed inroads of paganism, had begun, but thus far only on the periphery. In the Battle of Tours (732) Charles Martel had checked the northern advance of the Arabs. In Western Europe the Moslem tide had come to its crest and had begun its slow ebb. That ebb was not completed until, in 1492, the Kingdom of Granada, the last political stronghold of Islam in the Iberian Peninsula, fell to Christian arms and in 1609 the Moriscos, the nominal converts from Islam, were expelled from Spain.

The recovery in Western Europe is associated with the Carolingians, the ruling house of the Franks. The Franks had the strongest realm in Western Europe. The Merovingians, the royal line which looked to Clovis as its founder, became progressively weaker. In the 750's Pepin the Short, the son of Charles Martel, was proclaimed king in their stead and had the support of the Pope. The latter crowned him in 754, thus confirming an earlier coronation in 751. Here was a precedent for the Papal claim to remove and appoint secular rulers. Pepin also rescued the Pope from the threat posed by the Lombards and turned over to the Pontiff lands which he had taken from that foe, an act usually regarded, not quite accurately, as having inaugurated the temporal power of the Pope and the Estates of the Church. On his death (768) Pepin the Short was succeeded by his two sons, Charles and Carloman. The latter died in 771 and Charles was left as sole monarch.

Charles, better known as Charles the Great, or Charlemagne, then reigned alone until his death (814). Under his nearly half-century of rule the Frankish power reached its height. Charlemagne was genuinely religious. He rejoiced in Augustine's *City of God* and set himself to make his realm the embodiment of its ideal. He continued a reformation of the Church which was already under way. He furthered the parish system, a form of territorial organization especially adapted to the spiritual care of a predominantly rural population. He perfected a system of tithes for the support of the clergy. He created bishoprics in the lands he conquered. He multiplied archbishops for the better administration of the diocesan bishops. He sought to improve the standards of Christian living of the clergy and through them of the laity: in theory all Christians were to know the Lord's Prayer and the Apostles' Creed. He improved education and to this end called to his court the Englishman Alcuin, a relative of Willibrord. He repaired and constructed church buildings and sought to improve public worship. He considered himself an expert in doctrine and under him synods were held to define it. During his reign considerable theological activity developed, some of it displaying marked originality.

Yet Charlemagne fell far short of Christian standards. He was a semi-literate barbarian who had only partly met the demands of Christ. In his marital relations he was notoriously lax and he encouraged a similar laxity in his daughters. As we have noted in his attempts to impose the faith and his rule on the Saxons, he was cruel in his wars. He insisted on dominating the Church. Although many years after his death he was canonized, that action was only a local one and was never officially confirmed by Rome. But even local canonization—with the implication that he was an ideal Christian—was evidence of how far the Frankish populace was from attaining to Christian standards.

Moreover, in the life of high and low, superstition flourished. It was seen, among other ways, in the reverence paid to the relics of saints and martyrs. As an example, one of Charlemagne's favorites, a scholar and Charlemagne's biographer, prided himself on having obtained by theft relics from the vicinity of Rome and erected a shrine for them.

We must also recall that in the total world scene Charlemagne was a minor figure. In population, wealth, area, and culture the Carolingian realms were far inferior to the contemporary T'ang Dynasty in China or the Arab empire.

THE TENTH-CENTURY NADIR

After the death of Charlemagne darkness again descended, and by the middle of the tenth century Christianity had sunk to a lower nadir than, to the date when these lines were written, it was ever to know. In Western Europe the Carolingian empire fell apart. The raids of the Scandinavians mounted. In their longboats the Vikings ravaged the coasts and ascended the rivers, sacking monasteries. They established themselves in England and in parts of the Continent. In the last quarter of the ninth century Alfred the Great made headway against them in England, but after his death fresh inroads in North England were made by Scandinavians from Ireland. In the last part of the ninth and the first half of the tenth century the Magyars, pagan invaders from Asia, overran much of Central Europe, defeating the Germans, now Christian. They pressed up to the walls of Constantinople and were bought off by the Byzantine Emperor. Monastic life ebbed. In the welter which followed the waning of Carolingian might in Italy, in the first half of the tenth century the Papacy sank to the lowest level of weakness it ever reached. During much of the time the Papal throne was filled by scions of a family which dominated what was little more than a village housed in the ruins of former imperial grandeur. Between 897 and 955 seventeen Popes followed one another in rapid succession. John XI, Pope from 931 to 935, was placed in the office at the age of twenty-one. John XII, who reigned from 955 to 964, is said to have been the worst of the lot. At the age of eighteen he was both Pope and the secular ruler of Rome. In Asia, Christianity died out in its easternmost frontier, China.

CHAPTER VI

Revival and Involvement in Medieval

Europe, A.D. 950-1350

Not long after A.D. 950 a recovery began from the low ebb of the preceding half-century. Within a few decades the Scandinavians, led by their rulers, became professedly Christian—those in the West conforming to Rome and those in the East to Constantinople. The same decades witnessed a similar movement of the Magyars, with adherence to Rome. In Western and in much of Central Europe formal paganism was theoretically on the way out. Not far from the same time efforts were begun to bring the nominal Christianity closer to the standards set forth in the New Testament. They were seen in reforms in monastic communities, in the emergence of new types of monasticism, and in the endeavour to make the Papacy an instrument for helping the European peoples and the entire structure of the Church more nearly to approximate these standards. Efforts proliferated to approach the goals held up in the New Testament. Some Christians remained within the Catholic Church. Numbers of others were denounced by that church. In every aspect of the collective life earnest souls strove to bring conformity to the ideals of the faith: in the State, in the realm of the intellect, in economics, in the family, and in the relations between the sexes. Heroic attempts were also seen to win European peoples not yet in Christendom and to plant the faith outside Europe.

These movements saw striking contrasts between ideals and results. The culture which developed had features unmistakably bearing the impress of the Gospel. On the other hand were repudiations of these ideals, either covertly or openly. Fully as striking were fruits of movements undertaken with what professed to be Christian motives but actually in stark contradiction to the fruits valued by the New Testament.

In the four centuries between 950 and 1350 Christianity was confined to Europe, chiefly Western Europe, to a few enclaves in Western Asia and North-east Africa, remnants of the pre-Moslem churches in these areas, and to minorities scattered across Asia. The area which might be called Christendom was only a small segment of the globe and was mostly the western peninsula of the land mass of Eurasia. It embraced but a slight percentage of even civilized mankind, a percentage smaller than in the fourth and fifth centuries.

PROGRESS IN THE "CONVERSION" OF WESTERN AND CENTRAL EUROPE

In the second half of the tenth century the Scandinavian hordes who as pagans had laid waste much of Europe began their outward conformation to Christianity. Hints of the transition appeared as early as the first half of the ninth century. As we have seen, Louis the Pious, son and successor of Charlemagne, promoted a mission to the Danes and Swedes. In 878 Alfred the Great required a Danish invader whom he had defeated to receive baptism as a price of peace, and eventually many of the Danes in England adopted the religion of the country. In 882 a Viking chief accepted baptism at the behest of one of the later Carolingians and was assigned territory on the lower Rhine. In 911 the first of the Vikings to rule as duke in Normandy was baptized in return for the confirmation of his title by the King of France. After ebbs and flows in the tide of conversion, in the first half of the eleventh century Canute, King of Denmark and

England, gave the weight of his office to the spread of the faith. He made a pilgrimage to Rome and is said to have commanded all his Danish subjects to learn the Lord's Prayer and to go to Communion three times a year.

Some Norwegian raiders were baptized while in England. One of them, Olaf Tryggvason, who in 995 became King of Norway, sought to extend his authority by giving the local chiefs the option of baptism or battle. In the first half of the eleventh century the formal conversion of the land was completed under another king, Olaf Heraldsson. Much of the instruction in the newly accepted religion was by priests and bishops whom Olaf invited from England. Also in the eleventh century the faith was carried to Norwegian settlers in Iceland and Greenland.

Roughly contemporaneously with the firm planting of Christianity in Norway, the mass acceptance of the faith made progress in Sweden, likewise under the leadership of the kings and through clergy from England. However, not until the twelfth century did Christianity become dominant in Sweden. There, at Uppsala, on the site of the chief pagan temple of the country, a cathedral was erected.

In the second half of the tenth century Christianity was firmly planted in Kiev, the chief town of the Scandinavian principality in what later became Russia. Christianity had been introduced slightly earlier, but Vladimir, a vigorous ruler, led his people in the adoption of the faith. In contrast with Denmark, Norway, and Sweden, where the new Christian communities looked to Rome, the Christianity of Kiev was derived from Constantinople. In view of the prestige of that city in the river valleys which had their outlet into the Black Sea and through the Bosporus to the Mediterranean, this was to be expected.

The movement of the Magyars into the Church took place in the closing decades of the tenth and the opening decades of the eleventh century. The chief agent was Stephen, who became king in 997 and reigned until his death in 1038. As in several other countries in Europe, the adoption of the new faith was associated with the strengthening of the power of the monarch.

Also as among some other peoples, the death of the masterful king was followed by a pagan reaction which was an attempt both to return to ancestral ways and to revive local autonomy.

The Slavic peoples in Central Europe were badly divided politically. As we have noted, in the second half of the ninth century Cyril (Constantine) and Methodius were sent from Constantinople to the Slavs in Central Europe. Partly through them Christianity gained a foothold in Moravia. The German clergy, affiliated with Rome, sought to dominate the nascent Christianity. Indeed, even as late as the twentieth century rivalries continued in Central Europe between the two wings of what had been the Catholic Church—the one owning allegiance to Rome and the other, Orthodox, affiliated, although more loosely, with Constantinople. Not until the thirteenth century did the majority of the Serbs call themselves Christians. Their ecclesiastical ties were chiefly with Constantinople and its Ecumenical Patriarch. In Poland the spread of the faith became marked in the second half of the tenth century. It occurred mainly through the Germans and was associated with the growing political power of that people. West of the Poles and along the lower courses of the Elbe and Oder and their tributaries were Slavs whom the Germans called Wends. They were divided into several tribes. About the middle of the tenth century Germans, who were now officially Christian and among whom the Saxons were politically dominant by armed force began the extension of their authority over the Wends. As had Charlemagne in the ninth century in his policy towards their ancestors, the Saxon rulers identified submission to their rule with the acceptance of baptism. Protracted and sanguinary fighting followed. Only in the twelfth century was the adherence of the Wends to Christianity completed, partly through the efforts of earnest missionaries, partly by German political supremacy, and partly by compulsory transfer of Wends into German and therefore officially Christian areas and the settlement of Germans in the former Wend territories.

Among non-Slavic, non-German peoples on the shores of the Baltic the faith was spread chiefly through conquest. The Prussians and those in the later Estonia and Latvia were "converted" mainly by Germans, partly through arms of two crusading orders, the Knights of the Sword and the Teutonic Knights and partly by settlers. The "conversion" was completed in the thirteenth century. North of the Gulf of Finland, Christianity prevailed through Swedish conquest and settlement. The Finns, an Asiatic people, were subdued. Swedes, now professedly Christian, moved in and constituted a controlling minority. Here, too, "conversion" was finally accomplished in the thirteenth century. In the preceding century, in the early days of the Swedish invasion, some missionaries came from England.

Christianity was challenged by the "conversion" of Western and Central Europe. To what extent, if at all, would these so-called Christians be shaped by the faith which they now professed? The "conversion" of the peoples of that small portion of the earth's land surface which lay north of the Mediterranean and west of the Dnieper Valley (for by 1350 only the fringes of Europe east of that valley had begun to be touched) had required nearly a thousand years. Even of that small portion of the globe much south of the Pyrenees had been conquered by the Moslem Arabs. The prospect was not promising. By long tradition these peoples were far from Christian in their customs. The Germanic folk (including the Scandinavians) glorified the warrior and had an aristocracy recruited from the warriors, a cultural feature that, indeed, continued into the eighteenth and in part into the twentieth century. They had gained the mastery by migrations which had been preceded and completed by armed conquest, usually utterly ruthless. "Conversion" had been obtained by the example and often at the behest of the rulers. Often it had been imposed by force. During the four centuries from 959 to 1350 force had been dominant also in the initial stages of the "conversion" of non-Germanic peoples.

Conquest had been followed by partial acceptance of the culture of the Mediterranean world as represented by the Roman Empire. Conquest by the "barbarians" had been limited to the northern shores of the Mediterranean and to regions which bordered on them in the north and immediately to the east. By the time most of the conquest and occupation had been accomplished, that portion of the Mediterranean world was officially Christian. But the culture of the area was a mixture of pre-Christian and Christian elements and had only partially—except for small minorities only slightly—conformed to Christian ideals. In the contact with the civilization of the Mediterranean the inherited customs and institutions of the invaders tended to disintegrate, with a decline in the traditional forms of social control and in morals. Under such unfavorable circumstances, how far could Christianity bring these rude barbarians to accept the ideals set forth by Christ and His Apostles as recorded in the New Testament?

Not all the conditions were unfavorable. The inherited mores of these peoples had partly disintegrated. Their culture was in marked transition and therefore malleable. Western and Central Europeans now regarded themselves as Christians. Here was both challenge and opportunity.

The "conversion" of the peoples of Western Europe was paralleled by the slow rolling back of the tide of Islam in that area. In the Iberian Peninsula it began in the eighth century. The professedly Christian kingdom carried on intermittent war with the Moslem states. By the middle of the thirteenth century Islam was driven back politically to the small state of Granada, in the extreme south-east. The conquest of Sicily in the eleventh century by the Normans, now Christian, brought the extinction of Islam on that island.

CHRISTIANITY AMONG MINORITIES IN EASTERN EUROPE AND IN ASIA

In the four centuries between 950 and 1350 Christianity won converts in Eastern Europe and Central Asia. But, in contrast with Western and Central Europe, the numerical gains were only among minorities.

In the first half of the thirteenth century the Mongols created the largest empire the world had yet seen. It stretched from the China Sea into Europe. In Europe it embraced much of the area north of the Caspian and Black seas. The Mongols who ruled that region became Moslems but tolerated the existing Christianity. To escape Mongol rule many Christians migrated northward, where numbers of monks established themselves and began to spread the faith.

In Central and Eastern Asia the eleventh, twelfth, thirteenth, and fourteenth centuries witnessed the renewal of the spread of Nestorian Christianity. Several peoples, led by their rulers, accepted that form of the faith. Under the initial stages of Mongol rule some advances were made. The Mongols conquered a people who were Nestorians and as a result some of the Mongol princes had Nestorian wives. Favored by the Mongols, Nestorians and some contingents of other Eastern Churches established themselves in China. A few courageous Roman Catholic missionaries made their way to Central Asia, India, and China. But in Central Asia the Mongols became Moslems and in China and their native haunts they adopted Buddhism. The existing Christian communities, minorities as they were, dwindled.

THE SHAPING OF WESTERN EUROPE

From 950 to 1350 striking progress was made in meeting the challenge and the opportunity presented by the formal acceptance of Christianity by the "barbarians" in Western and Central Europe. In all its aspects the resulting culture was more nearly shaped by Christianity than had been that of the Roman Empire in the five centuries when the peoples of that realm were adopting the Christian name.

As was to be expected, the effects were more profound in those who were brought into the Western wing of the Catholic Church than among those who looked to Constantinople. In Western Europe the disintegration of the Roman Empire and of the associated civilization had gone much further than in the portion of that realm which had its capital on the Bosporus. Thus in

Western Europe culture was more in a state of flux and more easily remoulded than was the civilization of the eastern heir of the Empire. This meant that the "barbarians" who conformed to the Eastern wing of the Catholic Church had to adjust themselves to a régime which, while profoundly alerted, kept much of the pattern inherited from pre-Christian days with its domination of religion by the State. Therefore the Christianity they adopted had different effects from those of the Christianity transmitted through the Western wing. And more aspects of the culture of the peoples who looked to Rome as their religious centre than of that of the former "barbarians" who had Constantinople as their religious capital bore the impress of Christianity.

Deepening of the Christianity of Europe by Monastic Movements

Fresh monastic movements were both an expression of and a channel for the deepening of the effects of Christianity on the peoples of Western and Central Europe. Even before the death of Charlemagne monastic reform had begun. Charlemagne's successor, Louis the Pious, supported it and ordered a stricter observance of the Benedictine rule in his domains.

In the first half of the tenth century a revival centred in the monastery of Cluny, north of Lyons. Cluny was founded in 910. It stressed the *Opus Dei*—the services of worship—lengthened and elaborated, and in the first half of the twelfth century erected what was said to be the largest church in Western Europe. Cluny enforced a strict discipline. To prevent corruption by lay proprietors, as had been the fate of many earlier foundations, it was placed directly under the Pope. Cluny had a notable succession of able abbots. Daughter houses were erected and others sought affiliation. The abbots travelled widely among the Cluniac houses to hold them to their professed standards. Significantly, the abbots and many of the monks were from the aristocracy. Since a conviction was widespread that full obedience to Christ was best achieved and entrance to eternal life attained through the monastic life, hundreds, many of them from the upper classes, were attracted by the rigorous discipline of Cluny with its emphasis on silence and dedication to worship. By the twelfth century the houses embraced in the movement numbered more than three hundred. Their growth and their endowment by pious benefactors were evidence of a widespread longing to meet the requirements of the Christian faith. In time the high devotion which inspired the movement was dulled and the Cluniac regimen became routine. But before that stage had been reached, men caught up in the initial enthusiasm were seeking to lift the level of the entire Church in the West.

Contemporaneous with Cluny but not organizationally connected with it were other attempts at raising the level of the professed Christianity. They also stressed monastic reform. Men inspired by them endeavoured to improve the quality of the parish clergy and through them of the rank and file of Christians. One such movement in England in the tenth century had as its outstanding representative Dunstan (c. 909–998). Of aristocratic stock, Dunstan was monk and abbot of Glastonbury, a monastery which claimed foundation by Joseph of Arimathea, to whom the New Testament ascribes the burial of Jesus and who unsupported late tradition says came to Glastonbury. Dunstan was eventually bishop of two sees and then Archbishop of Canterbury. He coöperated with others of like mind in strengthening monastic discipline, in lifting the moral and educational level of the parish clergy and through them curbing the drunkenness and sexual promiscuity of the upper classes and of the rank and file of the populace. He endeavoured to bring Danes and English together in a common Christian fellowship. In his archiepiscopal court he sought to reconcile enemies. The story of Dunstan could be paralleled again and again on the Continent. Thus a younger contemporary, Bernard of Menthon (923–1008), of a wealthy noble family, became a priest and archdeacon, was the means of converting a neighbouring savage mountain folk who robbed travellers crossing the Alps, and to serve those who passed by its doors founded the monastery in the pass which still bears his name. The monastery of Bec, in Normandy, founded in the first half of the eleventh century, was a centre of learning and of the training of monks who did much to raise the discipline of the Church in wide areas. For example, from it came Lanfranc and Anselm, successively Archbishops of Canterbury, who stood resolutely for the Church against forces which sought to use it for selfish ends. Anselm we shall meet again as one of the greatest intellectual forces of the period.

As it grew older many a monastery tended to decline from the fervour which had given it birth. Often lay lords attempted to divert the houses and their revenues from their avowed purpose. Efforts were made to preserve their original spirit. Increasingly common was the removal of a monastery from lay and even episcopal control in order to place it directly under the Pope. When the Papal see was filled by high-minded, able men, this made for an independence which could be wholesome. But corrupt, worldly, or weak Popes used their power to appoint as abbots men who had the emoluments of the office but seldom if ever were in residence.

Again and again movements arose which sought afresh to embody the monastic ideal of what constituted the full, uncompromising Christian life. The twelfth century witnessed as its most widespread new monastic endeavour the founding of the Cistercians, from Citeaux (Latin Cistercium), the mother house, in what is now North-eastern France. In general the Cistercians conformed to the Benedictine pattern, but they had a rule of much stricter poverty than did most Benedictine houses. They established their monasteries far from other human habitation, where the monks, aided by lay brothers, with their own hands cleared the land and erected their buildings. The churches were more austere than those of the Cluniacs. The Cistercians observed the rule of silence except in their common worship and for necessary communication. In contrast with the practice of many monasteries which recruited numbers of their members from boys dedicated to them in childhood and reared within their walls, the Cistercians would admit no novice below the age of sixteen and thus sought to assure an intelligent personal commitment.

Near their outset a marked impulse was given the Cistercians by Bernard of Clairvaux (1090–1153), the most influential figure in the religious life of Europe of his generation. Bernard was born not far from Citeaux to devout parents of the nobility. Deeply religious from childhood, in his early twenties he entered Citeaux, bringing with him five of his brothers and about a score of others who had been won by his enthusiasm. In 1115 at the age of twenty-five, Bernard became the first abbot of a new foundation, at Clairvaux, in a rugged mountain valley, about a hundred miles west of Citeaux. He retained the post until his death. Like many other Christian mystics he was a man of action. He was an eloquent preacher, travelled extensively, and interested himself in the Church at large. Partly because of him, hundreds sought membership in the Cistercians.

From a seventeenth-century reform of the Cistercian abbey of La Trappe, in Normandy, at that time decadent, came the Trappists, with an even more austere way of life than the original Cistercians. In the nineteenth and twentieth centuries Trappist houses multipled—evidence that their form of dedication still had an appeal.

Less numerous than the Cistercians were the Carthusians, begun late in the eleventh century at Chartreuse, in a valley of the Alps, slightly west of Grenoble. In the last decade of the century the founder, Bruno, began two other monasteries, in Calabria in Southern Italy. Like the Cistercians, the Carthusians followed an austere regimen. Unlike the Cistercians and somewhat after the manner of the early anchorites in Egypt, they adopted a semi-solitary rule. Each monk had a separate hermitage where he meditated, prayed, and worked. The hermitages were grouped together around a church and a refectory. Three times daily and on feast-days and Sundays the monks met in the church for common worship. Once a week and on Sundays they had a common meal in the refectory. Weekly they came together for recreation and a walk outside their grounds. In England, where they were introduced in the twelfth century, their communities were known as charterhouses.

We must not take the space even to mention other monastic orders which were founded in the eleventh and twelfth centuries. We should, however, call attention to a similar movement, that of the canons regular. They were clergy who were not monks, strictly speaking, but who lived together in community, serving churches or cathedrals, somewhat after the manner of Augustine and his friends, and followed a rule (regula, thus "regulars"). Many were known as Augustine Canons. Some communities differed from monasteries chiefly in leaving their members free to exercise their functions, mainly preaching, outside monastic walls. They multiplied in the twelfth century and eventually spread widely. One order of Augustine Canons was founded in 1120 at Premontre by a friend of Bernard of Clairvaux; its members were called Premonstratensians. In its austerity the Premonstratensian rule resembled that of the Cistercians.

The thirteenth century was marked by the appearance of another kind of monastic movement, that of the mendicant orders, the friars. The members took the standard monastic vows of poverty, chastity, and obedience. Like the older orders they lived in communities. But unlike the others, with the partial exception of the canons regular who, as we have said, might have parishes and preach, they sought to bring the Gospel by word and example to the nominally Christian masses and to non-Christians. To some degree their origin and growth coincided with the increase in the urban population, a feature of the thirteenth century, but that association was not necessarily responsible for their beginning and their popularity. The two largest of the mendicant orders were the Franciscans and the Dominicans. Several others came into existence, notably the Augustinians. The first two were the only ones which in the twentieth century continued to be prominent.

The Franciscans, officially the *Ordo Fratrum Minorum,* or the Order of Little Brothers or Brothers Minor, were begun by Francis of Assisi (1181 or 1182 to 1226). Like Benedict of Nursia,

Francis always remained a layman. Also like Benedict, he was an Italian. But in contrast to the other he was past his early youth before he entered the way of life for which he is remembered. A native of Assisi, a hill town in the upper valley of the Tiber and opposite Perugia, he was the son of a prosperous merchant. Ardent, charming, sensitive, he led some of the scions of the local aristocracy in their revelries. Late in adolescence illness and disappointment contributed to the inception of his religious pilgrimage. To the distress and anger of his father, he gave himself to the ministry of the lepers and the poor and to the repair of a decrepit chapel whose crucifix had contributed to the love of Christ which was to dominate his life. In 1209, then in his late twenties, Francis felt himself called to be an itinerant preacher, imitating Christ and obeying Him to the letter, proclaiming the Kingdom of God, subsisting on whatever food was given him, and radiating the love of Christ. Others were attracted and went about two by two preaching and helping peasants in their work. In 1210, the year after he began his preaching, Francis and eleven companions went to Rome, where they sought and obtained Papal permission to continue preaching. Francis was a radiant spirit, joyous, loving all living creatures. He urged love for God, neighbours, and enemies, the forgiveness of injuries, humility, and abstention from the vices of the flesh. He called his companions the Minor, or Humbler Brethren, enjoining on them complete poverty. Soon Clara, a girl of sixteen from a wealthy family in Assisi, joined him and began a second order, of women, the Poor Ladies or Poor Clares. Within a few years the third order developed, made up of those who remained in the world and owned property but followed a disciplined life of food and drink, receiving the sacraments and remaining loyal to the Catholic Church.

The Franciscans had a rapid growth. They provided a channel for following what many regarded as the full Christian way of life rather than the nominal Christianity professed by the majority of the population. Francis was no organizer. Before his death, to his great grief many of his followers were compromising the rule by which he attempted to restrain departure from what he deemed the poverty commanded by Christ. To his distress they established themselves in the universities which were beginning to emerge. One of the early companions of Francis, elected the second minister general, within less than a decade after the death of the founder gave the order a comprehensive structure, extended its mission, and raised large sums to erect in Assisi a huge memorial church to Francis.

The course of the Franciscans was stormy. The order mounted in membership and spread to many countries. A minority—Zealots or Spirituals—sought to keep to the pattern enjoined by Francis. Others demanded the complete relaxation of the rule of poverty. In between were moderates who, willing to maintain something of the primitive poverty, built houses in the universities and sought influence in the Church.

The Dominicans, or Order of Preachers, were founded by Dominic (c. 1170–1221), a Spaniard. Unlike Francis, Dominic was a priest and a student. As an Augustinian Canon he was attached to a cathedral. Ascetic, a man of prayer, remembered as always joyful, he might have remained one of the obscure but worthy clergy honoured in his lifetime by a small circle of intimates but quickly forgotten. Not until he was in his mid-thirties was he confronted with the challenge to which his response brought him unsought fame. The challenge was the religious situation in what is now the South of France. There the moral and intellectual quality of the Catholic Church was low and the Cathari, an heretical religious movement of which we are to speak more in a moment, were deeply rooted. With the endorsement of the Pope a crusading army was engaged in stamping them out. Traversing the country barefooted and in extreme poverty, preaching, Dominic sought to win the Cathari to the Catholic faith and to improve the quality of the Catholic Church. In 1214 or 1215 he was given a house in Toulouse where he and a small company sharing his purpose lived in community. In 1215 he gained Papal permission to constitute them a new order. At first they followed the regimen of the

Augustinian Canons, but soon Dominic adopted some of the features of the Franciscans, notably the rule of poverty which forbade not only personal but corporate possessions, except monastic buildings and churches, and prescribed begging as the means of obtaining food. By the time of Dominic's death the Order of Preachers was said to have more than five hundred members in sixty houses. Dominic was especially concerned to have houses in the universities.

From their inception the friars were missionaries. At times friction arose between them and the bishops and parish clergy, for the latter resented their preaching in towns and countryside which in theory had been assigned to these earlier representatives of the clergy. Before the middle of the fourteenth century both orders had missions among non-Christians in Eastern Europe, Africa, and Asia. Both had been in India and the Franciscans had penetrated to China.

The Rise of Movements Which the Catholic Church Branded as Heretical

The surge of religious devotion which gave birth to the monastic movements also found expression in other movements. These too sought to conform fully to the standards set by the New Testament but, unlike monasticism, were denounced as heretical by the Catholic Church. We can take the space to mention briefly only the more prominent. In contrast with the monastic movements, initiated, with the exception of the Franciscans, largely by members of the aristocracy, their original leadership was chiefly in the newly emerging urban population. They seem to indicate that the faith was penetrating to non-aristocratic elements of the populace and was stirring them to fresh expressions of the religion their forefathers had accepted under the direction of their princes. Significantly, almost all of both kinds of movements—monastic and heretical—had their origin and their major rootage in areas which had once been within the Roman Empire. Few made their first appearance among the "barbarians," now officially Christian, outside the former boundaries of that realm. Although many were begun and drew much of their strength from the descendants of the Germanic invaders, in the former Roman realms these "barbarians" had been partly assimilated to the culture into which pre-Christian Roman and Christian elements had entered.

We have already mentioned the Cathari ("Pure"), also known as Albigenses, (from Albi, one of their chief centres). The Cathari were a religious movement which flourished in the twelfth and the fore part of the thirteenth century in what are now Northern Spain, Northern Italy, and Southern France. They were a Western European wing of a dualistic religion resembling Manichaeism and having elements of Christian origin which also flourished among the Slavs east of the Adriatic and was represented in Constantinople. Their chief stronghold was in Southern France. There the Catholic clergy were largely corrupt and gave an impression of the faith represented by their Church which provoked criticism. The Cathari insisted that they were faithful to the New Testament, especially to the Gospel of John. They rejected parts of the Old Testament, saying that these were the work of the Devil. They declared that the Church of Rome was evil and that theirs was the true Church of Jesus Christ. Dualists, they taught that the material world is evil and the immaterial world good. Those of their numbers who fully followed their teachings were called the "perfect." They were to be celibate and were not to eat the products of reproduction such as eggs, milk, or meat. In their worship the Cathari followed simple ceremonies including preaching, readings from the Scriptures, and a common meal of bread. They had a vernacular literature, including translations from the Bible. They were ardently missionary and won followers not ony in the areas where they were strongest but also in Northern France and Flanders, chiefly among artisans in the cities. Beginning about 1179, at the command of Popes, including the most prominent Pontiff of the period, Innocent III, a crusade was launched against the Cathari. Political motives entered. Kings of France and nobles of Northern France were glad of an excuse to reduce the prosperous South and to profit by its wealth. Peaceful preaching, such as that of the Dominicans, was employed. The Inquisition, strengthened by the Popes and Church councils, was invoked. As a result, before the middle of the thirteenth century the Cathari ceased to be a major menace to the Catholic Church.

The other most widely spread movement branded by the Catholic Church as heretical was that of the Waldenses—also known as the Poor Men of Lyons and as the Poor in Spirit. Their founder was Peter Waldo, a rich merchant of Lyons who, seeking salvation, in 1176 took to heart the advice of Jesus to the rich young ruler, paid off his creditors, provided for his wife and children, gave the remainder to the poor, began begging his daily bread, and traversed the countryside and the cities preaching the Gospel as he found it in a vernacular translation of the New Testament. He attracted adherents, who followed his example. They sought authorization from the ecclesiastical authorities, including the Third Lateran Council (called by the Roman Catholics the Tenth Ecumenical Council), were refused, and, along with the Cathari, were condemned (1179). Yet they multiplied. Numbers went about two by two, preaching, subsisting on what was given them. They said that women and laymen could preach, that the Church of Rome, being corrupt, was not the head of the Catholic Church, that only priests and bishops who lived as did the Apostles were to be obeyed, that prayers for the dead were useless, that sacraments administered by unworthy clergy were of no effect, that taking life is against God's law, that every lie is a deadly sin, and that oaths, as in courts, are clearly contrary to Christ's command. Their only forms of prayer were the "Our Father" and grace at meals. Increasing rapidly in several parts of Western Europe, they divided into several sections and were not uniform in teaching or organization. The Waldenses were in the tradition of earlier twelfth-century leaders, such as Peter of Bruys and Arnold of Brescia, who led a life of poverty, denounced the clergy for unworthy luxury and grasping for political power, and condemned many of the current customs of the Church. All were persecuted by the ecclesiastical authorities and were eventually stamped out. A few of the Waldenses survived in remote Alpine valleys and in the sixteenth century conformed to the Reformed wing of Protestantism. Profiting by the protection of the secular, anti-clerical Kingdom of Italy, late in the nineteenth and in the twentieth century some moved into the cities. Others sought refuge in Latin America.

ATTEMPTS AT A THOROUGHGOING REFORM OF THE CATHOLIC CHURCH IN WESTERN EUROPE

Attempts to make the nominally Christian peoples of Western Europe fully to conform to the standards of their faith were not confined to monastic movements and to groups which the Catholic Church branded as heretical. The attempts were also by earnest men who remained within the Catholic Church and sought to purify its entire life and impact. Like the monastic movements they grew to large proportions in the tenth century and in the thirteenth century seemed, if not fully successful, to be achieving distinct progress. They sought especially to improve the character of the clergy, from bishops through parish priests, for if the level of the laity was to be raised their pastors must lead. The clerical evils which were most vigorously denounced were simony (the purchase and sale of ecclesiastical offices), nicolaitanism (laxity in sexual relations, including clerical marriage and concubinage) and the lay control of ecclesiastical appointments, with the requirement of loyalty to the secular lord.

The reform began locally and eventually captured the Papacy. We have noted it in England. Roughly contemporary with the awakening in that land of which Dunstan was the most prominent figure was one in the Rhine Valley. In the second half of the tenth century and in the first half of the eleventh it was augmented by the policies of monarchs who bore the designation of Holy Roman Emperor of the German Nation. The first to hold the title was Otto I (King of the Germans 936–973), on the female side descended from Charlemagne. He extended his authority into Italy and in 962 while in Rome was crowned Emperor by the Pope. He sought to use the Church to strengthen his power. To this end he created great ecclesiastical states in Germany, for, since their princes, being bishops and celibate, could not be hereditary, by controlling their election he could use them to support the royal authority. Otto III, grandson of Otto I, was brought to the throne at the age of three by his father's death (983). Reared under ecclesiastical influence, he not only dreamed of restoring the Roman Empire to its pristine glory but was as well deeply concerned for the purity and welfare of the Church. He brought about the election to the Papacy of his tutor who, as Sylvester II, struggled to eradicate simony and clerical marriage and concubinage. Otto III was followed by Henry II, who, ardently religious and later, with his wife, canonized, collaborated with Pope Benedict VIII, a friend of the Abbot of Cluny, in promoting reforms. After an interval of fifteen years filled by the able but secular-minded Conrad II, Henry III came to the throne in 1039 and in 1046 was crowned Emperor. Henry III succeeded in ridding the Papacy of three competitors, each of whom claimed to be the legitimate Pontiff, and obtained the election of Leo IX (reigned 1048–1054).

ATTEMPTS BY THE PAPACY, REFORMED, TO RAISE THE RELIGIOUS LEVEL OF CHRISTENDOM

Leo IX, related by blood to the Emperor, had been a soldier and had had an excellent record as an administrator. With him the full tide of reform swept into the Papacy. A friend of the Abbot of Cluny and of the ardent reforming hermit and Abbot Peter Damien, he travelled widely, fighting simony, enforcing clerical celibacy, and insisting that bishops be elected by their people and the clergy and not appointed by the lay lords. He himself, although chosen by an assembly in Germany at the instance of Henry III, refused to assume the functions and title of Pope until after he had entered Rome garbed as a humble pilgrim, his election was confirmed, according to long-established precedent, by the people and clergy of the city. He improved the cardinalate, the body of leading clergy in and near Rome, by appointing to it men of reforming zeal outside Rome and its environs, thus making it more representative of Western Europe as a whole.

The mastery of the Papacy by the reformers was not easily accomplished. Local factions sought to resume the control of the office to which the low ebb it had sunk to had been largely attributable. They set up men who claimed the title but were not able to win the support of more than a minority.

The leading role in keeping the Papacy on its reforming course was taken by Hildebrand (c. 1023–1085). Reared in Rome, in his early twenties he became a monk, probably in a branch Cluniac house in that city. It was he who was chiefly instrumental in obtaining the election of Nicholas II. In a pontificate which lasted only from 1059 to 1061, Nicholas took important actions. Outstanding was a decree declaring that the Papal election should be by the cardinals, that it need not be in Rome, that the Pope was not required to be a Roman, and that, in case of necessity, he might exercise his functions from another centre than Rome. These principles were never abrogated. The Roman nobles, combined with others who disliked reform and with German bishops who wished to reassert the power of the Holy Roman Emperor in the choice of a Pope, elected an Italian bishop. Throughout most of the pontificate of Nicholas II this rival constituted a problem. Factions fought in the streets of Rome and each expended large sums to win the support of the Roman populace.

As a successor to Nicholas II Hildebrand obtained the election of a reformer, a friend of Peter Damien, who as Alexander II reigned from 1061 to 1073. Supported by Hildebrand and Peter Damien, he actively and effectively made the weight of his office felt in several phases of the life of Europe. He gave his approval to the invasion of England by William the Conqueror (1066), and his legates intervened in ecclesiastical affairs in many countries. Appeals to Rome were encouraged, thus augmenting the authority of the Holy See.

Alexander II was followed by Hildebrand. As Gregory VII he reigned from 1073 to 1085, and under him the powers of the Papacy were further strengthened. He strove to keep all bishops under Papal authority and stood out against their investiture by lay princes. He compelled archbishops to come to Rome to receive the *pallium,* the symbol of the formal recognition of their office, and thus ensured their recognition of the prerogatives of the Pope. His greatest struggle was with the King of Germany, Henry IV. The issue was the right of investiture. Could the monarch appoint the bishops and compel them to swear fealty to him? The Pope held that this subordinated the Church to the State and tended to corrupt the faith. Gregory enlisted support in Germany which threatened Henry with the loss of his throne. To placate the Pope Henry came to Canossa, a castle in Italy where the Pope had ensconced himself on his way to Germany to enforce his deposition of the King. There Henry stood for three days barefoot, asking mercy. The dramatic spectacle of the mightiest prince in Western Europe abjectly suing for pardon from a monk appeared to ensure the victory of the principle for which the Pope contended. However, before the death of either, the outcome of the struggle seemed to be reversed. Henry placated his domestic enemies, induced a synod to declare Hildebrand deposed, had one of his creatures chosen as Pope, took Rome, and had his Pope crown him Emperor. Hildebrand was rescued by Normans from the South and died in exile among them.

The contest between the Catholic Church and lay rulers was not confined to the Popes and the Germans. It was prominent in most of the countries of Western Europe and took several forms. In England it was spectacular between the Kings and the Archbishops of Canterbury, especially between William II and Henry I and Anselm (roughly contemporary with that between Henry IV and Gregory VII) and between Henry II and Thomas Becket in the next century.

Paschal II (reigned 1099–1118), a monk of Cluny, the second after Gregory VII, sought to resolve the conflict between Church and State by ordering that all ecclesiastics surrender their temporal possessions to the Emperor and that the latter renounce his power of investiture. Paschal wished the clergy to live by tithes and voluntary offerings and thus approach the clerical poverty advocated by some of the reformers. Protests were so emphatic that under pressure from the Crown Paschal reversed his stand and conferred the right of investiture on the Emperor. To this, too, the bishops were opposed and the decree was annulled. A compromise was reached in the Concordat of Worms (1122), but it did not terminate the struggle. In Italy the continuing conflict, complicated by other issues, helped to prevent the political unification of that land.

Had the civil monarchs early scored a complete victory, in Western Christendom the Church would have been divided into many national churches and Christianity would have been fully subordinated to secular interests. Eventually this was the outcome. By the seventeenth century in the states predominantly Roman Catholic the Church was subordinate to the Crown. In Protestant lands it was even more under the control of the princes. As a result, Christianity entered the revolutionary age, which beginning late in the eighteenth century transformed Europe, handicapped by alliances with a political structure that was being rapidly undermined.

For a time after the death of Hildebrand, under the impulse of the reform movement, the power of the Papacy mounted. Urban II came to the See of Peter in 1088, three years after the death of Gregory VII, and occupied it until 1099. A Cluniac monk educated by the founder of the Carthusians, he vigorously pressed the reforms and enhanced the prestige of his office. Even Paschal II, who followed Urban, and whose involvement in the investiture controversy detracted from his memory, by extensive travels did much to improve the quality of the Church. Adrian IV (reigned 1154–1159), the only Englishman ever to hold the office, compelled the powerful Emperor Frederick I (Barbarossa) to hold his stirrup as a sign of vassalage. Alexander III (reigned 1159–1181), after having to face claimants to his office who had the support of Frederick I and having three times been compelled to leave Rome, in 1177 in a memorable scene in Venice had the satisfaction of seeing that monarch kneel and kiss his feet.

The outstanding Pope of the era was Innocent III (reigned (1198–1216). Under Innocent the Papacy reached a peak in the political life of Europe which it was never again to attain and made its authority felt in the Roman Catholic Church to a degree not to be surpassed until the nineteenth and twentieth centuries. Innocent believed that in all mankind under the guidance of the Roman Pontiffs the Christian ideal was to be attained. He wrote that Christ had "left to Peter the governance not of the Church only but of the whole world." The Popes, he maintained, as had others who held the office, were the divinely commissioned heirs of Peter. Innocent was the guardian of Frederick II, the infant grandson of Frederick I. He intervened in contests for the crown of Germany, insisted that the Pope had the right to pass on the validity of elections to the imperial office, crowned the King of Aragon in Rome as his vassal and induced the Kings of Castile and Navarre to bury their quarrels and to unite against the Moslems. He brought King John of England to heel, first excommunicating and deposing him and then restoring him to favour on the condition that that hapless monarch become a vassal of the Pope. Under Innocent the Kings of Portugal, Poland, Hungary, and Serbia also became Papal vassals. Innocent compelled Philip Augustus, the powerful King of France, to take back his divorced wife and to restore to the Church confiscated lands. In ecclesiastical affairs he brought more of the Eastern churches under the control of Rome than had been done before or has since been achieved. He insisted that in the Catholic Church as a whole only the Pope could transfer a bishop from one see to another, could create new dioceses, or could change the boundaries of existing dioceses. He attempted to enforce clerical celibacy, forbade pluralism (the holding of two or more church offices and drawing the income from them), endeavoured to exclude lay interference in ecclesiastical affairs, affirmed the right of Rome to review important cases under canon law and thus increased appeals to the Holy See, ordered that tithes for the support of the Church be given precedence over all other taxes, and took vigorous measures for the suppression of heresy.

Innocent III called and dominated the Fourth Lateran Council (1215), regarded by the Roman Catholic Church as the Twelfth Ecumenical Council. In its legislation it was the most important in the series between Chalcedon (451) and Trent (1545–1563). It brought together about fourteen hundred patriarchs, bishops, abbots, and priors and promptly endorsed measures previously prepared under Papal direction. Among other actions it sought to improve the education and morals of the clergy, endeavoured to raise the level of marriage and family life, provided for confession to the parish priest at a minimum of once a year, reaffirmed the obligation of all Christians to take Communion at least at Easter, forbade charging interest on loans, stressed the supremacy of the Papacy, condemned specific heresies, and tried to heal the schism between the Eastern and Western wings of the Catholic Church. The Fourth Lateran Council made doctrinal pronouncements, among them the affirmation of transubstantiation. The precise manner in which Christ is present in the mass had long been in debate. Now the issue was officially determined.

After the time of Innocent III the power of the Papacy declined. To be sure, Boniface VIII (reigned 1294–1303) in the bull *Unam Sanctum* (1299) declared "that it is altogether necessary to salvation for every human creature to be subject to the Roman Pontiff." But in practice the authority of the Holy See was more and more flouted.

THE PAPACY AT AVIGNON; "THE BABYLONIAN CAPTIVITY"

In the closing decades of the thirteenth century the Papacy became the victim of national and dynastic rivalries. French in-

fluence became strong. Germany was falling apart into semi-in-
dependent states, and the contests between the Popes and the
Holy Roman Emperors lapsed. A few able Popes sought to
restore the dignity of the office, but their reigns were too short
to permit effective action. Boniface VIII quarrelled with the
King of France and was about to excommunicate him when
the King's supporters made him prisoner. He did not long survive the humiliation but died a few days after his release. His
successor, the head of the Dominicans, reigned less than a year.

After an election which was deadlocked between French and
Italian factions, a French archbishop, a friend of the King of
France, was chosen (1305). Presumably because of the bitter
dissensions in Italy, he never set foot in Rome. After a few
years he fixed his residence in Avignon, a city on the left bank
of the Rhone, immediately across that river from the then
France. He appointed a number of Frenchmen to the cardinalate
and annulled recent decrees unfavourable to the King of France.
The next four Popes resided at Avignon. The fifth went to
Rome for a time but, disheartened by the disorder in that city,
returned to Avignon. His successor, who reigned from 1370 to
1378, eventually sought to make his headquarters in Rome but
to escape the riotous upheavals there he left and soon died in
a neighbouring city.

The Avignon period, lasting about seventy years, is usually
referred to as the Babylonian Captivity. French influence was
strong. Some of the Avignon Pontiffs were men of high character and desired much-needed reforms. The decades saw a continuation of the Franciscan and Dominican missions in what
is now Southern Russia and in India and China. However, on
the whole the Avignon years were marked by mounting corruption in the Papal court. A magnificent palace was erected for
the Pontiff. Cardinals and others associated with the curia lived
in luxury. To sustain the costly structure various devices were
employed to compensate for the decline of Italian revenues.
The burden was distributed where possible over all countries
which professed allegiance to the Holy See and was the source
of widespread complaints. In seeking to make their office a

means of elevating the character of the entire Church, the great reforming Popes had stimulated the growth of a bureaucracy at headquarters which under less able successors, some of them far from single-minded, attracted men who desired prestige, wealth, and power. The result, a decline in morals at the very centre of administration, was reflected in much of the rest of the Church. Earnest Christians were scandalized as the Bishops of Rome absented themselves from their historic see.

DEVELOPMENTS IN THEOLOGY

The centuries which witnessed the mounting vigour in the Catholic Church in Western Europe were also marked by striking efforts to think through afresh basic issues of the Christian faith. For the most part they were made by scions of the Germanic peoples who had been won to that faith during and following their settlement in the Roman realms. All the major creative figures were born and reared in what had formerly been the Roman Empire. Most of the men best remembered were from the early and most creative years of the monastic movements through which those who wished to commit themselves fully to the Christian faith sought to express that purpose. In general the leaders in this intellectual ferment and the majority of their followers were called schoolmen. Their theology and philosophy are known as scholasticism. Inevitably, heirs as they were of the Greco-Roman world in both its pre-Christian and its Christian stages, the schoolmen utilized the forms of thought developed by the Greeks, the creeds shaped in the early centuries, of the faith, the writings of the Church Fathers of those years, and always with reference to the Bible. Some were also influenced by the contemporary Moslem philosophers and theologians, chiefly as they came in contact with them through the Iberian Peninsula. Notable among the latter was the daring Averroes (or Averrhoes) of the twelfth century. The schoolmen were impressed too by current Jewish thought, particularly by

Maimonides (1135–1204), a warm admirer of Aristotle. Through them, as through the monastic and popular, often "heretical," movements, and through the Papacy and other ecclesiastical organizations, Christianity was being assimilated by the Germanic peoples, and these peoples were placing on it a distinctive stamp.

Outstanding was Anselm (c. 1033 or 1034 to 1109). Of mixed Lombard and Burgundian stock, Anselm was born in North Italy. A contemporary of Gregory VII and Urban II, as a youth he was deeply stirred by the religious awakening of which they were symbols and leaders. In his early manhood he crossed the Alps and soon became a member of the monastic community of Bec, then in the first flush of the devotion which gave it birth. Against his wish he was elected its abbot, succeeding the founder. Equipped with a first-class mind, he disciplined it to penetrating thought on fundamental problems of the Christian faith. Seeing no conflict between faith and reason, he had the conviction long familiar among Christian thinkers that he believed that he might understand—that prerequisite to valid theology is a commitment of the whole man to the Christian faith. He was convinced that when that commitment is made, the foundations on which Christian faith rests can be demonstrated to be in accord with reason. In compact, carefully formulated statements he gave what seemed to him conclusive proof that God exists and that He must be Father, Son, and Holy Spirit. He also explained why, as he saw it, God became man. Much of his writing was done in the monastery where he had adimnistrative duties and while in exile on the Continent because of his unwillingness to submit, as Archbishop of Canterbury, to the demands of the English Kings William II and Henry I.

A younger contemporary of Anselm was the brilliant Abélard (or Abailard, c. 1079–1142). A scion of Breton nobility, Abélard early had a thirst for study. Enjoying controversy, asking provocative questions, he proved immensely popular as a teacher. At the height of his career he was on the staff of the cathedral

school in Paris. A love affair with the beautiful and educated
Héloïse, niece of a canon of the cathedral, issued in lifelong
tragedy for them both. Abélard wrote extensively. One of his
more famous books was *Sic et Non (Yes and No)*. It was meant
to stimulate thinking, and it did so by propounding questions
on science, ethics, and theology, and giving quotations from the
Scriptures and the Fathers which could be used to support
contradictory answers. Abélard rejected the view of original sin
set forth by Augustine. He also formulated a theory of the
atonement which differed from that of Anselm. Anselm held
that the moral order of the universe could be preserved only
by making adequate compensation for sin and that this had
been accomplished by Christ, who is God and man. Abélard,
in contrast, maintained that God is love and in Christ, Who he
agreed with Anselm, is both God and man, had voluntarily
assumed the burden of man's suffering brought by sin and
thus had sought to awaken in man response to His love. Bernard
of Clairvaux, a mystic and not a theologian, the opposite of
Abélard in temperament, assailed the latter for views which he
held weakened the faith of good Christians. As a result, Abélard
was condemned by the ecclesiastical authorities and was excommunicated. Eventually he and Bernard were reconciled and he
spent his later years in prayer and reading.

We must pass over with only the barest mention Hugo (or
Hugh) of St. Victor (1096–1141), son of a Saxon count, and
a contemporary of Abélard, who wrote extensively on the Bible
and religious subjects. He held that philosophy and theology
are distinct but saw no necessary conflict between them. Nor can
we do much more than name Peter Lombard (c. 1110–1160), a
younger contemporary of Abélard and a protégé of Bernard
of Clairvaux who died as Bishop of Paris. We mention him
because his *Four Books of Sentences,* known briefly as *Sentences,*
for many generations constituted a major textbook in theology.
Not professing originality, the *Sentences* set forth in a systematic
and comprehensive fashion the theology held by the Roman
Catholic Church supported by appropriate selections from the
Church Fathers.

The high tide of the theological activity of the period and of the schoolmen coincided with the early years of the mendicant orders. Its outstanding figures were either Franciscans or Dominicans. The incentive came partly from the religious devotion which was stimulated by them and channeled through them and partly from the intellectual ferment associated with the study of Aristotle and the writings of such non-Christians as Averroes and Maimonides. In the universities which were emerging, many, stirred by these powerful minds, were questioning the Christian faith. The schoolmen made it their mission to restate the Christian faith in terms of this challenge.

The Franciscans had a leading part. Alexander of Hales (died 1245), English born and reared, was the first of the schoolmen to write a systematic theology which took account of Aristotle. He was one of the teachers of Bonaventura (John of Fidanza, 1221–1274). A native of Italy of whose parents and ancestry little is known, Bonaventura was a distinguished head of the Order of Brothers Minor but is best remembered as a theologian. He won a place for the Franciscans at the University of Paris and held a chair in that institution. In contrast with Alexander of Hales, he was more influenced by Plato as seen in Augustine and Dionysius the Areopagite than by Aristotle. A mystic, he maintained that our highest knowledge of God comes through union with God in meditation and prayer rather than through logic.

With their early emphasis on scholarship, the Dominicans made what proved to be the most influential continuing contributions to theological thought. Albertus Magnus (Albert the Great, c. 1193 or 1206 to 1280) was a German, possibly of the nobility, born in Swabia, an area which had been on the border of the Roman Empire. After studying in Italy, he taught in Paris and Cologne. As a bishop (an office taken reluctantly at the command of the Pope), he reformed the life in his diocese. He was a teacher of the younger and even more famous Thomas Aquinas (c. 1225–1274).

Thomas Aquinas was born in Italy, of the high nobility. His mother was of Norman and his father of Lombard stock, his father being a nephew of the Emperor Frederick Barbarossa. From childhood Aquinas was deeply religious and aspired to be a monk. His family, because of the prestige attached to the office, wished him to accept the headship of the famous Benedictine abbey of Monte Casino, where he had received part of his boyhood education and where his uncle had been abbot. Instead, to their distress, he insisted on joining the Dominicans, then without the acclaim which eventually came to them. He taught in various places. Deeply committed as a Christian, he was a man of prayer. He wrote prodigiously, and with a clarity as well as a depth which made his works of lasting significance. His *Summa Contra Gentiles* was designed to equip missionaries in their arguments with Moslems, the major body of non-Christians with whom the Catholics of the period were in contact. His *Summa Theologiae* (less correctly *Summa Theologica*) was left uncompleted by his early death. Aquinas believed that all truth is one and from God. Some truth, he held, including the existence of God, can be verified by man's reason. Much can be known only through God's revelation and can be apprehended only by faith. The goal of man, so Aquinas declared, is the vision of God. Although corrupted by sin, man of himself can cultivate four virtues—prudence, justice, courage, and self-control. The distinctly Christian virtues—faith, hope, and love—can come only through God's grace. Through grace a new birth is wrought in the Christian by the creative act of God. Grace, Aquinas maintained, both stirs man to repentance and enables him to repent. It is primarily through Jesus Christ, he said, that God's grace is mediated to man. God became incarnate through Christ, the God-man. Aquinas believed that Christ was born of the Virgin Mary and venerated her as the mother of Christ. But, in contrast with the Franciscans, he did not hold that Mary was conceived without the taint of original sin—the immaculate cenception. As we shall see, Roman Catholics continued to differ on that issue, and not until the mid-nineteenth century was the immaculate conception declared to be dogma, to be believed by all the faithful. Aquinas combined the views of Anselm and Abélard on the atonement. In his generation Aquinas, taking account of Aristotle, enabled many earnest intellectuals, troubled by the use made of that philosopher by sceptics, to see that without violating their integrity of mind they could remain Christian. In the nineteenth and twentieth centuries his writings performed the same function for many who were perplexed by the science of that day.

Concurrently with the decline in the vigour in the Christianity of Western Europe which began to be marked after the high tide of the late thirteenth and the early fourteenth century, schoolmen questioned the formulations arrived at in the creative years. The absence of the appearance of significant new monastic movements and of "heresies" as potent as those of the Cathari and the Waldenses, and the waning of the Papacy, culminating for the time in the Avignon Papacy, were paralleled by developments in scholastic theology which seemed to herald the breakdown of that approach as a bulwark of the Christian faith. The first important indications were in the theology of Duns Scotus (c. 1265–1308). We know little about the origin and family background of Duns Scotus. He was born somewhere in the British Isles, but whether in Ireland, Scotland, or the North of England was long debated. We know that he was a Franciscan and that he lived and taught in Oxford, Paris, and Cologne. He wrote in a cryptic style which has made understanding difficult. The fact that the word "dunce" is derived from his name is an indication of opinions of later critics—and the critics of the scholastic method—of what seemed to them to be futile hairsplitting. We have from the pen of Duns Scotus no systematic treatment of philosophy or theology. Much of our knowledge of him comes from his attack on positions with which he disagreed. He was particularly critical of Aquinas. Aquinas held that nothing God does is out of accord with reason. By the use of his reason, therefore, man can know much about God. Even though some of God's acts, such as the incarnation and the work of Christ, could not have been discovered through reason, they are not contradictory to reason. Duns Scotus maintained that God is completely free and is not bound by reason. He did not mean that God is capricious, but he believed that it was God's will and not His reason which brought the world into being. He held that although men are tainted by original sin they have not lost the power of free decision. He would not say, with Anselm, that if God wished to forgive men's sins He was bound to become incarnate and die on the cross, nor did he hold, with Aquinas, that the incarnation and the crucifixion were the wisest way to achieve man's salvation. Instead, he said that they were the way chosen by God. He declared that it is the Christian's duty to believe what the Church teaches and to conform to what it commands, even when that is not supported by reason and to men appears irrational.

Younger than any of the preceding was the Englishman William of Occam (c. 1280–c. 1349). William of Occam early became a Franciscan and is said to have studied in Oxford, possibly with Duns Scotus, and in Paris. He protested against what he believed were the subtleties of the schoolmen and attempted to simplify philosophy and theology. In contrast with the greatest of the schoolmen he maintained that through his reason man cannot prove the existence, unity, or infinity of God nor immortality. Right and wrong, he held, depend on the will of God. William of Occam recognized the authority of the Church in spiritual matters and said that, although they cannot be proved, such tenets of Christianity as the existence of God and the immortality of the soul must be believed because they are taught by the Church and the Bible. He gave up hope of reconciling the wisdom of man with the wisdom of God.

Not all theologians agreed with William of Occam and the debates went on. But the trend was towards the bankruptcy of reason when addressed to the basic Christian convictions.

CHRISTIANITY AND OTHER ASPECTS OF THE CULTURE OF MEDIEVAL EUROPE

As we have seen, long before the year 1350, except for the Moslems in the Iberian Peninsula and the Jews, Christianity

had become the professed religion of the overwhelming majority
in Western and Central Europe. We have noted the several
ways in which that religion had displayed marked vigour and
the distinctive forms it had taken in stimulating monastic movements and "heresies" and in furthering the growth of the
Papacy and the development of theology. It remains to sum-
marize the extent to which Christianity shaped other aspects
of the civilization of the region.

Here the results were ambiguous and often contradictory.
Every aspect of that civilization gave evidence of attempts at
conformity to the high and seemingly unattainable standards
set forth in the New Testament. Yet striking failures were seen,
and at times appeal was made in the name of the faith to under-
take enterprises which issued in actions and results utterly at
variance with the Gospel.

How far was religion shaped by Christianity? Systematic efforts
were put forth to bring the ostensibly Christian masses to an
understanding of the faith and conformity to it. Geographically
the region was divided into parishes grouped in dioceses supervised by bishops and their assistants. Each parish had one or
more priests, charged with the duty of teaching their parishioners
and, by catechizing, preaching, and the administration of the
sacraments bringing them to a knowledge of the faith and to
conformity with it. Through the sacraments the Church followed
the Christian from the cradle to the grave. Of the seven sacraments six were primarily for the laity: baptism, confirmation,
penance (with confession to the priest), Holy Communion, marriage, and extreme unction. The seventh, ordination, was, obviously, only for the clergy. The observance of the Christian
calendar, with its special days and seasons, furthered community
participation. To Sunday, Advent, Lent, Easter, and Pentecost
others were added, among them Trinity Sunday, Corpus Christi,
saints' days, and All Souls' Day (for prayers for the dead). As early
as the thirteenth century we hear of the Angelus, at first only
in the evening, with its ringing of a bell in recognition of the
incarnation and with a petition to the Virgin. The bishops confirmed the faithful, ordained the clergy, and through various

assistants, such as archdeacons, supervised clergy and laity. Pilgrimages to sacred shrines were popular. The coming of the friars brought more preaching. The Franciscans gave a marked impulse to the use of breviaries. As the name indicates, the breviaries were abridgements, a compilation of prayers, hymns, and passages of Scripture for the use of clergy, monks, and lay folk. They seem first to have appeared in Carolingian times, and Benedictines early developed them. Friction arose because the friars did not respect parish boundaries and competed with the resident priests. Prayers for the dead led to endowments, presumably perpetual, for the saying of masses for the repose of the souls of the departed. From this custom came the multiplication of chantries and of the priests assigned to them.

Yet there were contradictions. Numerous beliefs and customs inconsistent with the Gospel survived from pre-Christian religions, often thinly disguised under Christian names. A large proportion of the priests were poorly educated. Many were married or had concubines. Numbers engaged in business and in hunting. Bishops were often political administrators rather than pastors and spiritual leaders. Some bishops were warriors. With rare exceptions, as they grew older monasteries lost the initial dedication which had brought them into existence and in their common life became comfortable and routine or worse. Although some Popes attempted to protect them, the Jews were discriminated against and confined to ghettos, and at times anti-Jewish massacres broke out. The economic factor entered, but an excuse often given was that the Jews had killed Christ. Countless individuals who dissented from the Catholic Church were burned. The burning was done by the civil and not the ecclesiastical authorities, but it was in the name of Christ. A reason given was that "heretics," by teaching doctrines which imperilled the eternal welfare of souls, were even more dangerous than murderers who took physical life. But the fact could not be gainsaid that the Christian religion was given as a reason. A faith whose primary command is love and which professes to be based upon the self-giving love of God in Christ was then, as in later centuries, in a variety of ways used to justify barbarities starkly contradicting that love.

Something of the same contrast was seen in the political aspects of Western and Central Europe. The kings were professedly Christian and were crowned with Christian ceremonies of which participation in the Communion was a central feature. Aquinas echoed a widespread conviction when he declared that a ruler exercises his power as a divine trust and that a monarch who has betrayed that trust has lost his right to the obedience of his subjects. As we have suggested, the dream cherished by many of the choicest spirits was of a Christian society, the *Corpus Christianum,* of which the Popes and the Holy Roman Emperors were the heads, each with distinct but complementary functions. At least as some Popes conceived it, all mankind should be brought into the *Corpus Christianum.* The Christian conscience put forth valiant efforts to curb and redirect to its ends the traditions of the former "barbarians" by which the rulers emerged from the professional warriors and retained their power by prowess in battle and skill in directing their subjects in military objectives. Thus arose chivalry; when the young noble reached man's estate and formally assumed his arms, the Church blessed his sword with the prayer that he would devote it to the defense of widows, orphans, and the servants of God. The Christian knight was to keep his plighted word, be loyal to his lord, fight the infidel, and at his death make his confession and receive the Communion. The Church attempted to forbid jousts and tournaments, a favorite pastime of the aristocracy, for they entailed the shedding of blood. For example, the Second Lateran Council (1139, called the Tenth Ecumenical Council) forbade them. Toward the end of the tenth century agitation began for the Peace of God, which sought to exempt from attack all persons and places consecrated to the Church—churches, monasteries, clergy, monks, and virgins. Later were added those protected by the Church—peasants and their implements, the poor, pilgrims, and merchants on their journeys. Here seems to have originated the principle, in theory and to a degree in practice honoured until World War II in the twentieth century, that in war non-combatants are not to be attacked. Early in the eleventh century the Truce of God was added. It sought to prohibit the chronic fighting of the nobility over the week-end and during Advent and Lent as hallowed by events associated with the life, death, and resurrection of Christ. Many synods endorsed the Peace of God and the Truce of God, and several dioceses formed what were known as confederations of peace. In the twelfth century, as a phase of the reform movement, agitation arose for a Papal prohibition of all wars among Christians, for the adjudication by the Pope of all disputes between princes, and for the penalty of excommunication on those who did not abide by his decision. Again and again Popes and Church councils condemned such crude practices of administering justice as trial by fire and water and by battle.

Many bishops were appointed by their princes to help in administration. Some were worldly, but others sought to bring Christian principles to bear upon the discharge of their duties. Some bishops participated actively in national affairs in other capacities. Among them was Stephen Langton (died 1228), who in the University of Paris won recognition as a theologian. Appointed by Innocent III to the Archbishopric of Canterbury, he was notably free from self-seeking. He was a peacemaker between King John and the Pope, had an important share in the negotiations leading to the Magna Carta and to its reaffirmation, and was a mediator between the nationalism of the English and the demands of the Pope. In representative bodies which shared in government, such as the emerging English Parliament and the Estates General of France, the clergy had seats and at least in theory endeavoured to see that recognition was given to Christian standards.

A thought-provoking contrast in the effects of Christianity on the political life of Western Europe is seen in the Crusades, initiated (1095) by Urban II. Urban II, zealous reformer, successor of Gregory VII, and even more successful than the latter in carrying through reforms, presided at the Council of Clarmont, called by him to enact reform legislation. The Council gave formal approval to many of the measures taken by Urban and Gregory in their effort to raise the level of the Christianity of Western Europe. It also made the Truce of God obligatory in all Christendom. Apparently with no thought of inconsistency, in a powerful sermon Urban II urged the great company of warriors who were present to turn their swords from fighting their brethren to fighting the Moslems, at that time in possession of the places held sacred by Christians and oppressing the pilgrims who thronged them. He also wished the warriors to succour the Eastern wing of the Catholic Church. The cross was worn as a symbol of dedication, and plenary indulgence—that is, remission of the temporal penalties for sin —was promised to those who engaged in the enterprise with singleness of heart. Jerusalem, Bethlehem, and other sacred places were taken, with great slaughter of Moslems, and the crusading Kingdom of Jerusalem was set up.

The fall of Edessa, a stronghold of that kingdom (1144), was the occasion for the Second Crusade. Bernard of Clairvaux employed his eloquence in urging princes and warriors to join in it. His palpable sincerity and the reverence inspired by his reputation for sanctity contributed to the enrolment of thousands. However, many of the participants perished before reaching Syria, and the survivors were foiled in their attempt to take Damascus. The Third Crusade, in which Philip Augustus of France and Richard "the lion-hearted" of England participated and Frederick Barbarosso lost his life, was undertaken in the effort to retrieve the defeat (1187) and near annihilation of the warriors who were supporting the Kingdom of Jerusalem, followed by the loss of Jerusalem and many of the Christian strongholds. The recapture of Acre was the chief result. The fourth Crusade, called by Innocent III, stormed Constantinople (1204)—although that had not been the Pope's wish—placed one of its leaders on the imperial throne, and seemed to promise the reunion under the Pope of the Western and Eastern wings of the Catholic Church. A few years later (1229) by diplomacy and force the sceptical Holy Roman Emperor Frederick II obtained possession of Jerusalem, Bethlehem, and Nazareth and was crowned King of Jerusalem. However, in 1244 Jerusalem once more fell to the Moslems and was not again to be in "Christian" hands until the twentieth century.

Originally to protect the Christian pilgrims to the Holy Land great crusading orders arose—the Templars, Hospitallers, and Teutonic Knights. Their members took the customary monastic vows of poverty, chastity, and obedience.

The crusading spirit persisted. For several generations the Popes invoked it, partly against Moslems and partly, as in the case of the Cathari, against those whom they labelled as heretics or against others of their foes. The Teutonic Knights employed their might to "convert" non-Christians on the shores of the Baltic and ruled there for centuries.

The net effect of the Crusades was to weaken the Byzantine Empire, to deepen the gulf between the Eastern and Western wings of the Catholic Church, and permanently to embitter relations between Christians and Moslems. The Crusades are a striking example of that perversion of the devotion evoked by Christianity which has been seen again and again.

In the intellectual life of Western Europe in the four centuries covered by this chapter Christianity was potent. Not only did it stimulate thousands, including a number of first-class minds, to wrestle with basic problems of theology and the closely related philosophy. It was as well the major inspiration in education. Around cathedrals, notably in Paris, schools clustered. They were in part for the training of the clergy, but students with other purposes were also attracted. The twelfth century saw the emergence of the first universities, several of them developments from earlier schools. Some universities specialized in medicine and some in canon law, but several centred on the preparation of clergy. Most of the educated were clergy. Pioneers in science were found in the universities. Among the most distinguished were Roger Bacon and Albertus Magnus, who had been enlisted in the early enthusiasm of the mendicant orders.

To what extent the stimulus to their creative thinking stemmed from that commitment it would be impossible to determine. Nor is it possible to say whether the foundation of the science of later centuries, based as it has been on the conviction that the universe is orderly, is from the Christian belief in the creation and governance of the world by God and from the discipline given the European mind by the debates in theology and the associated philosophy.

We need also note the effect of Christianity on literature. The most famous of the European poets of the period, Dante (1265–1321), wove his greatest work, the *Commedia*, about the Christian faith.

In art and architecture Christian purposes and Christian themes were a major inspiration. The cathedrals and parish churches were for the worship of God. Much of the painting and the sculpture had Christian subjects.

Christianity had a marked although not a dominant effect on the economic life of Western Europe. Much of the clearing of the land and putting it into cultivation was by monastic communities. In principle charging interest on loans was forbidden to Christians, but ways of circumventing the prohibition were devised. Indeed, for more than a century the Templars were great international bankers. In industry and trade attempts were made, presumably from motives of Christian origin, to fix a just price for manufactured goods and for labour.

Many other aspects of society bore the impress of Christianity. By classifying matrimony with the sacraments the Church sought to give sanctity to the marriage tie. The validity of individual marriages and of divorce were among the functions of the church courts and were regulated by the law of the Church. The manumission of slaves was encouraged by the Christian faith. In 1179 the Third Lateran Council formally decreed what had long been a widespread conviction, that no Christian should be enslaved by another Christian. For such care of the poor, the sick, and the stranger as existed the Christian conscience was chiefly responsible.

Far from conforming fully to the ideals of the faith as Western Europe of these centuries was, in that small fraction of the earth's surface Christianity had more nearly free course over a longer period of time than in any other part of the world. That the faith entered into the formation of Western civilization and so into the global revolution produced by that civilization in the twentieth century is clear. But precisely to what degree it was responsible for that civilization and its distinctive characteristics cannot accurately be determined. For example, to what extent, if at all, is the activism which is so prominent in Western civilization ascribable to Christianity? Later we shall see that Christianity was a source of democracy in its various expressions and that it was potent in the idealism and the humanitarianism among peoples both of Europe and of the larger Europe which arose from migrations. But we shall also note that from these peoples came the largest-scale exploitation of other segments of mankind and the most widely destructive wars in history.

DEVELOPMENTS IN THE EASTERN CHURCHES

While Christianity was entering into the formation of Western European peoples, what was happening to the Christianity embodied in the Eastern Churches? Clearly, Western Europeans, malleable as they were because of the weakening of the Greco-Roman tradition and the disintegration of the inherited cultures of the invaders by contacts with such of that tradition as survived, were in large part shaped by that religion. But what developments were seen in the churches centred in Constantinople and in those segments of the pre-eighth-century Christendom in which a portion of the Roman Empire continued without interruption?

Here we need to remember four concomitant facts: (1) In the surviving portion of the Roman Empire the pre-Christian tradition of the control of religion by the State persisted. In the professedly Christian State the Church was not so fully dominated by the State as the pre-Christian religions had been, but it was not so nearly autonomous as in the West, and occasional struggles towards autonomy were less prominent and less successful than in the West. (2) The Greco-Roman culture had not been as badly shattered as it was in the West and hence was less readily moulded. (3) The non-Chalcedonian churches survived. (4) On all the churches the pressure of Islam mounted. As a result, the churches, especially those of the non-Chalcedonian tradition, became increasingly ghetto communities, on the defensive. To preserve their existence they sought to hold firmly to what had been transmitted from the past and were resistent to change.

The Eastern and Western wings of the Catholic Church continued to drift apart until the rupture became so unmistakable that attempts to heal it had only temporary and partial success. A major obstacle was the insistence of the Popes that, as successors of Peter, they were the rightful heads of the Catholic Church. In 1054 that claim led to a formal breach when legates of the reforming and vigorous Leo IX laid a sentence of excommunication on the altar of St. Sophia when it was ready for the Eucharist, and the Ecumenical Patriarch, in return, excommunicated the legates. The Crusades widened the gulf. The attempts to bridge it were made in part by Byzantine Emperors who sought support from the West in their perennial resistance to the Moslem advance. In the mid-thirteenth century and again in 1274 success appeared to be in sight, but in the East the popular resentment against Latins blocked it.

In the Eastern (or Orthodox) wing of the Catholic Church monasticism persisted, but it was far less activist than in the West. No great orders arose comparable to the Cluny movement, the Cistercians, the Carthusians, the Franciscans, and the Dominicans. Monks seldom if ever engaged in preaching or pastoral care of the laity but tended to withdraw from the world. Monasteries arose in mountain fastnesses, notably on Mount Athos, on a peninsula jutting south from Macedonia into the Aegean. From the eleventh into the fourteenth century a major theological controversy arose over a monastic mystical practice known as Hesychasm. Eventually Hesychasm won the endorsement of the Orthodox but it was frowned on by the Roman Catholics. That it loomed so large and continued to be characteristic of Orthodox monasticism was evidence of a retreat from the world and emphasis upon a special form of mysticism which was alien to the West and which widened the gulf between the Orthodox and the Roman Catholics.

The Byzantine form of Christianity continued to spread in non-Moslem territories north and west of Constantinople and looked to the Ecumenical Patriarch in that city as its ranking bishop. As we have said, the spread was most marked among the Bulgars, the Serbs, and the Russians.

Of the non-Chalcedonian churches, minorities from several were brought to an acknowledgement of Papal supremacy and either retained their liturgies and clerical forms or were fully assimilated to Roman customs. Relatively secure in their mountain fastnesses, the Ethiopians and most of the Armenians preserved their independence of Rome, Constantinople, and Islam. For a time the Nestorianism was widely represented in Central and East Asia, but only among minorities. The Coptic Church survived, but in spite of periodic persecution and less spectacular attrition.

Retrospect

In the mid-fourteenth century Christianity was in somewhat better condition than four centuries earlier. It had completed the winning of the professed allegiance of the large majority of the "barbarian" invaders in Western and Central Europe and had spread beyond the former confines of the Roman Empire there and in much of what we know as Western and Northern Russia. Small minorities in Central Asia and dwindling remnants in Northern Africa held to it. In Western Europe it had had a major share in the acculturation of the Germanic and Slavic peoples and had shared in the emergence of a civilization which was an heir of the Greco-Roman pre-Christian and "Christian" world. It had given rise to vigorous religious movements, especially in what had been the western portion of the Roman Empire.

But in the mid-fourteenth century Christianity appeared to have passed its zenith. In the West it was threatened, in part by unanticipated perversions of its inherent vitality. In the East, after a pause, the tide of Islam was again surging and was threatening the remnants of such churches as had survived its first onrush. From the standpoint of historical and global perspective, in A.D. 1350 Christianity counted for less in the total life of mankind than it had eight and a half centuries earlier.

CHAPTER VII

Geographic Losses and Spiritual Decay:

Partly Offset by Fresh Religious Movements,

A.D. 1350-1500

Shortly after the mid-fourteenth century several factors combined to pose a major threat to Christianity. Although the
prospect was not as bleak or the losses as extensive as during
the four and a half centuries which were ushered in by the
decay of the Roman Empire, the "barbarian" invasions, and
the conquests of the Moslem Arabs, the situation was sufficiently
serious to have warranted the prediction that in spite of its
resurgence in the preceding four centuries Christianity was
doomed. That appraisal would have been supported by the
fact that geographically Christianity was confined to a smaller
proportion of the earth's surface than it had been at the close
of the fifth century and that the cultures into which it had
entered were held by fewer of civilized mankind than had been
true at the close of the preceding height of the Christian tide.
As in the earlier recession of that tide, a chief cause of the new
ebb was the conquests by non-Christian peoples. Another factor,
akin to that at the close of the previous decline, was lassitude
and corruption within the ecclesiastical bodies which bore the
Christian name. Yet, also as earlier, indications of vigor could
be discerned, some in fresh and vigorous movements.

A Succession of Moslem Conquests

The invasions most seriously threatening Christianity were by Moslems. One was led by Timur (Tamerlane), whose life span was 1336–1405, the other by the Ottoman Turks.

Timur was of Mongol descent. Before his birth the slight mixture of Christian heritage among the Mongols of Central Asia had disappeared and the Mongols in that region had accepted Islam. By devastating wars, in the second half of the fourteenth century Timur erected an empire which had Samarqand as its capital and embraced much of Central Asia, Persia, Mesopotamia, and North-west India. His exploits contributed to the destruction of the Dominican and Franciscan missions in Central Asia and to the drastic shrinkage of the Nestorian, Jacobite, and Armenian minorities—a shrinkage that has never been fully repaired.

The Ottoman Turks were one of several peoples whose early home was in Central Asia and among whom Nestorian Christianity had formerly counted adherents. Before the middle of the fourteenth century they had become Moslem and had begun a spectacular advance in Western Asia. By that time they had wrested much of Asia Minor from the Byzantine rulers and had taken Nicaea. In the next fifty years they crossed into Europe, established temporary headquarters in Adrianople, and conquered Bulgaria. In 1453 Constantinople fell to their arms and was made their capital. In 1500 the Ottoman Turks were still advancing. They had mastered Greece and such of the Balkans as were not already under their sway and had taken much of Hungary. By 1550 they had more than once pressed to the gates of Vienna. In spite of frantic appeals by the Popes, the crusading spirit had so far become an anachronism that in Western Europe, divided into rival nation-states, no effective united effort was made to stem the Turkish tide. Under the Ottoman rule, many Christians were killed or forcibly made Moslem. Numbers of children were taken from Christian parents and reared as Moslems. St. Sophia and scores of other church buildings were transformed into mosques. Yet the majority of the Christians in territories in Europe subject to the Turks held to the faith. Only in mountainous Albania did the majority become Moslems. Minorities in Asia also were loyal to the religion of their fathers. The Turks permitted the office of Ecumenical Patriarch to continue, but the incumbents had, in effect, to buy their posts from the Turkish rulers. Increasingly, with Turkish support, Greeks from Constantinople were appointed to govern the Orthodox churches of non-Greeks in Europe. In time the Turks created a form of administration for the Christians in their domains. They treated adherents of the respective Eastern Churches—Orthodox, Armenian, Jacobite, and the like—as distinct communities or nations and recognized their ecclesiastical authorities as the heads through which to deal with them.

Russia was the one country in which large contingents of Orthodox who looked to the Ecumenical Patriarch as their ranking bishop escaped Turkish rule. There the centre of government was established at Moscow. As Mongol power waned, Moscow became the capital of a realm under Russian rulers. The metropolitans of Moscow helped to strengthen the Moscow grand dukes. In 1480 one of the latter, Ivan III, completed the emancipation of his realms from the Mongols. He married the only niece of the last Byzantine Emperor, and he and those who followed him at Moscow claimed to be the successors of the Byzantine Emperors and as a symbol appropriated the two-headed eagle.

In addition to its Orthodox connexions, Russian Christianity developed distinct forms. From its early days it had what was called the kenotic tradition—the emptying of self in humility as Christ did in His incarnation. Kenoticism had been embodied in Theodosius (died 1074), the first Russian to be canonized and the chief pioneer and inspirer of Russian monasticism. True to its Byzantine tradition, Russian Christianity gave prominence to monasticism, but, somewhat differently from the Byzantine monasticism with its aloofness from the world, due in part to the initiative of Theodosius many Russian monasteries served the sick and the poor, and the monks were guides and confessors to the rank and file of the laity. The kenotic humility, asceticism, mysticism of the Hesychast type, and service to the poor and the laity in general were exemplified in Sergius (died in 1392), later to be the patron saint of Russia. Sergius was first a hermit, but about him others gathered, and reluctantly, for he saw in the position a temptation to pride, he was ordained priest and was made abbot of the monastic community which grew up around him. That monastery, the Troitsa (Trinity), about forty miles from Moscow, became the mother of many other houses.

Especially in North-eastern Russia, monasteries were pioneers in colonization. Around them villages arose. The monasteries gave hospitality to travellers, cared for the sick, and conducted schools. Eventually they were partly transformed into refuges for the wealthy in old age. To them many of the wealthy retired, keeping their property but leaving it to the community on their death. Monasteries became centres of culture. Art and such intellectual life as existed was nourished in them, and the icons were painted which were means of strengthening the religious life and became prominent in Russian Christianity.

Towards the end of the fifteenth century two contrasting movements developed for the reform of the Russian monasteries. One, founded by Joseph Volotsky (born in 1440), insisted that the inmates of monasteries engage in long fasts, work hard, and study diligently. Encouraged by him, huge monastic buildings were erected; services were elaborated and lengthened and were equipped with gorgeous vestments, costly vessels, and ornate altars. In the monasteries following the Volotsky pattern were trained many of the aristocracy who became abbots and bishops and rose to prominence in public affairs. The other reform developed in the North. Those who conformed to it preferred to live alone and without property, giving themselves to meditation and prayer, either singly or in community, They were known as the Non-possessors. They did not mingle in the world, except to give spiritual counsel to laymen who sought them out. A leader of the Non-possessors, Nilus Sorsky (c. 1433–1508), combined the way of the hermit and life in community. But the communities were small, were remote from other habitations, and owned no property; their members worked with their hands for the bare necessities of existence. The Non-possessors regarded the goal of the religious life as the union with God of the soul which had given itself fully to the love of God. The two types of monasticism came into conflict. In 1503 a crisis was reached: the Non-possessors lost and the followers of Joseph won. Through their advocacy of the participation of monks in public life the Josephites furthered the close association of Church and State which characterized Byzantine and most of later pre-Communist Russian Christianity.

In the fourteenth century a movement headed by the Strigolniks ("barbers") arose—evidence that Christianity had sufficiently penetrated the Russian masses to stir them to differ from the tradition of the Orthodox Church. The Strigolniks believed that the fees charged by the Church for ordination and by the priests for the sacraments were contrary to the practice of the primitive Church. They held that the official church, with its wealth and formalism, was apostate. They formed congregations led by laymen who refused financial remuneration, taught the Bible to their flocks, and set an example of humble, earnest living. The Strigolniks were persecuted by the bishops and clergy and were either stamped out or driven underground.

The fifteenth century saw the entrance into the Russian Church of a kind of crypto-Judaism. It influenced some in high position in Church and State but within a few years was crushed by burnings and imprisonments.

Gradually, in spite of corruption in the official Church, something of Christianity filtered through to the Russian masses. In the services of the Church the public reading of the Scriptures in the Slavonic translation helped to acquaint the rank and file with the faith, even if imperfectly and accompanied by non-Christian beliefs inherited from the past.

Late in the fifteenth or early in the sixteenth century it began to be claimed that Moscow was the third Rome, the guardian of the apostolic faith. The first Rome, so ran the argument, had fallen victim to the heresy of the Latins and had lost the primacy that because of Peter it had formerly held. Constantinople, the second Rome, now subject to the infidels, had gone the way of its predecessor. Moscow, free from non-Christian domination, so it was held, had the responsibility of preserving and championing the unadulterated Gospel.

WESTERN EUROPE: THE CHANGING SETTING

While the Eastern Churches, especially the Eastern wing of the Catholic Church, were losing ground to resurgent Islam, and only in Russia were the Orthodox winning their independence of the Moslem and advancing into new territory, Western Europe was moving into a new era in which Christianity appeared an anachronism, a hold-over from a vanishing age. While admittedly still strong, the Church was honeycombed with corruption and seemed to be perpetuating an outmoded structure and intellectual climate.

The new age in Western Europe had several features. Cities were growing. Nation-states under monarchs with mounting power were bringing together areas formerly loosely bound together by feudal ties. Although still powerful, feudalism was waning, and the ecclesiastical structure adapted to feudalism and to an almost purely rural economy seemed anachronistic. Printing by movable type was invented. The use of gunpowder was beginning to make the chronic wars more destructive. The Holy Roman Empire persisted, and to the Emperors remained something of the prestige attached to their office, but it did not command as much as formerly the imagination of the dreamers and of the practical men of affairs. The conception of a *Corpus Christianum* with the Emperor and the Pope as the two foci was being relegated to the past. The Renaissance was in full tide.

The Renaissance was multiform and was more a state of

mind and a climate of opinion than a single, concrete movement. It was in part an outgrowth of the Christianity of the
preceding period and in part an expression of new social, economic, aesthetic, and intellectual trends. The Renaissance had
begun before the mid-fourteenth century, but it was to reach
its apex in the fifteenth and sixteenth centuries. Its exponents
took joy in the literature and art of pre-Christian Rome and
Greece. One of the expressions was a humanism which found
its goal not in life beyond the grave but in an exuberant appre-
ciation of life in the present world. The men of the Renaissance
were self-confident, believing in themselves and in man. They
took pleasure in nature and in the beauty of the human form.
They rejoiced in verbal expression. Few openly rejected the
Christian religion—some were deeply religious—but many were
content to pay lip service to the faith and regarded man as the
competent architect of his own future. They looked with dis-
dain upon the schoolmen and scholasticism.

THE CATHOLIC CHURCH HANDICAPPED
BY DIVISION AND CORRUPTION

The Catholic Church, the dominant representative of Christianity in Western Europe, entered the new age badly hampered by division and corruption. The division took the form
of the Great Schism, an outgrowth of the Avignon Papacy. Many
earnest Christians were unhappy over the absence of the Bishops
of Rome from Rome and the subservience of the Papacy to
France. Early in 1377, Gregory XI moved his residence to Rome,
thus ending the "Babylonian Captivity." When, in the following year, he died, the Roman populace insisted that a Roman,
or at least an Italian, be chosen to succeed him. Yielding to
pressure, the cardinals complied and elected a Neopolitan. But
the new Pope, Urban VI, antagonized many of the cardinals by
commanding them to live in the posts whose titles they bore
and to give up the profitable pluralism—enjoying the revenues
of two or more offices without fulfilling their functions or doing

so only through poorly paid substitutes—which made possible their luxurious existence in Avignon. Within a few months the cardinals left Rome, declaring that they had the right to depose the Pope as well as to choose him. They said that Urban had been elected under duress from the Roman mob and called on him to resign. The French majority proceeded to name another Pope, one of their own number, who took the title of Clement VII. They and he soon settled in Avignon. Urban VI denounced their action and appointed a new group of cardinals. Europe was now divided: some countries supported Urban VI and others Clement VII. The corruption which had mounted in the Avignon period became, if anything, more notorious.

HEALING OF THE BREACH BY AN ECUMENICAL COUNCIL; EFFORT TO SUBORDINATE THE POPES TO THE COUNCILS

Earnest and able men were scandalized by both the schism and the corruption. They demanded that a general council of the Church be called to deal with both. They did not at first succeed, but in 1409 cardinals from Rome and Avignon yielded and called a council. In the meantime both Avignon and Roman Pontiffs had died, a successor to each had been chosen, and the schism was continued. The Council, meeting in Pisa, called on both Popes to resign, and the cardinals appointed a new Pontiff. But both the Avignon Pope and the Roman Pope refused to surrender their posts and Europe was confronted by the spectacle of three Popes.

To end a situation which was becoming intolerable, Sigismund, King of the Germans, later (1433) to be crowned Holy Roman Emperor, called a council. It met in Constance from 1414 to 1418 and is regarded by Roman Catholics as the sixteenth in the ecumenical series. The Council deposed one Pope and persuaded another to resign, and since the third declined to do so, it deposed him. He persisted in his claim to the office but retained only a dwindling following. Thus the Great Schism was ended, not by Papal initiative but by a general council of the Church. The Constance gathering was too badly divided to take many effective measures against the widespread corruption. Drastic action would have curtailed the privileges enjoyed by many of the members. One act was negative: it condemned John Hus, of Bohemia, who had advocated what seemed to the majority radical measures to cleanse the Augean ecclesiastical stables. In spite of the pledge of safe conduct from Sigismund under which he had been induced to come to Constance, the Council turned Hus over to the civil authorities for burning. On the positive side, decrees were enacted in an effort to curb several of the most obvious evils, including some of the financial exactions of the Papacy.

The Council of Constance endeavoured to further the remaining needed reforms by ordering that general councils be convened at specified intervals. The Council said expressly that it and other general councils drew their authority directly from Christ and that all, including the Pope, were "bound to obey" them "in all those things which pertain to the faith, to the healing of schism, and to the general reformation of the Church."

For a time what was called the conciliar movement seemed to give promise of accomplishing the needed reforms and of confirming the authority of councils over the Popes. In 1431 the council provided for at Constance assembled in Basel. Although the Pope recognized it and sent legates to it, and although Papal prestige was weakened by the proof (1433 and 1440) by humanist scholars that the Donation of Constantine which had so long been used to bolster Papal claims was a forgery, Basel failed to accomplish the drastic reforms which the situation demanded and permanently to confirm the authority of the councils over the Popes. For a time it appeared to succeed, but numbers of its members withdrew, leaving the control in the hands of the radicals. By the middle of the fifteenth century the Basel gathering was clearly moribund. With its demise the conciliar movement was patently a failure. The effort to employ a general council to effect the clamant reforms had been frustrated.

CORRUPTION IN THE PAPACY

The failure of the conciliar movement to bring reform was followed by a similar defeat in the use of the Papacy for that purpose. A few of the Popes of the latter part of the fourteenth century were pure in their private lives and sought to do what the best consciences of Western Europe desired, but they either were lacking in resolution and force of character or compromised. They faced formidable obstacles which might have baffled abler and more determined men. Italy was torn by domestic quarrels between the many states into which it was divided, and in the attempt to avoid domination by one or another faction the Papacy became a partisan. The Popes sought to confirm their authority in the Papal States and in doing so became further embroiled in Italian affairs. The monarchs of the growing nation-states were seeking, with success, to dominate the Church within their borders. From time to time the French attempted to resume the dominance over the Papacy which they had exerted in the Avignon period. Leading Italian families struggled with one another for a similar control. More than once the cardinals endeavoured to reduce the Pope to a puppet status.

Some Popes were notorious for nepotism in their appointments. Several of them attempted to solve the finances of themselves and the Papal curia by the sale of ecclesiastical offices. In Papal elections lavish bribery was common. Now and again a Pope expended much effort in futile attempts to rouse Western Europe to a crusade against the Ottoman Turks. The Popes became patrons of the Renaissance and the humanists. Nicholas V is credited with founding the Vatican Library; he made Rome a centre of the new humanism and art and adopted the plans for the new St. Peter's, which in the twentieth century is still the largest cathedral in Christendom. Paul II represented an anti-humanist reaction. He sought to curb simony, insisted on strict discipline in the curia, and appointed worthy men to office. Under him the cardinalate became predominantly

Italian. In 1471 the General of the Franciscans was elected Pope as Sixtus IV (reigned 1471-1486), but, although a scholar and of blameless personal life, he strove to make the Papacy the centre of a strong Italian state. He engaged in wars, built the Sistine Chapel, named for him, spent vast sums on new buildings and streets in Rome, reorganized the Vatican Library, and attracted scholars and artists to Rome. Among his aides were men who were essentially pagan. Some of his appointees to the cardinalate debased the already low moral quality of their office.

In the closing decades of the fifteenth century the Papacy sank to a nadir from which it did not recover until the next century. Sixtus IV was followed by Innocent VIII, who reigned from 1484 to 1492. Before his ordination he had been married and had a son by his wife and two illegitimate children. While in his private life he seems to have reformed after being ordained priest, his election was obtained by heavy bribes. During his pontificate most of the cardinals were worldly and several were openly dissolute. They lived like secular princes, hunted, gambled, and had mistresses. Innocent's appointees lowered rather than raised the level. One was the thirteen-year-old son of the influential and wealthy Florentine Lorenzo de Medici, who even before that early age had been given an abbacy and before he was twelve had been made abbot of Monte Cassino, the mother house of the Benedictines. Later, as Leo X (1513-1521), he was addicted to hunting, had a cardinal executed and others severely punished for plotting against his life, and utterly failed to sense the importance of his contemporary, Luther.

Innocent VIII was succeeded by Rodrigo Borgia, who, as Alexander VI, was in the chair of Peter from 1492 to his death in 1503. From his early youth he had been given ecclesiastical posts with large incomes and entailing an intimate knowledge of the Papal administration. He was able and hard-working and from long experience knew the etiquette and machinery of the Vatican. Handsome, imposing, he presided with dignity at pontifical functions. He did much to improve the architecture and streets of Rome. He encouraged art. He gave his support to the Angelus and stood for the immaculate conception of the Virgin Mary. Yet when all that can be said in his favour is recorded, the fact remains that no one in the long succession of Popes combined marked ability with personal conduct and political actions to bring so much discredit to his office. Others had been as vicious but they did not compare with him in ability. He was notorious for his mistresses and his illegitimate children. He strove to promote the ambitions of his offspring. He sought and sometimes obtained among the high nobility matrimonial alliances for his daughters. He gave his sons lucrative ecclesiastical preferments and promoted their political ambitions. One son, Caesar Borgia, was made a cardinal in his teens, but when he developed political ambitions he was released from his ecclesiastical status. Utterly selfish, daring, courageous, noted for his perfidy and cold-blooded cruelty to all who stood in his way, he sought to make himself the leading prince in Italy. His father's death, presumably from the endemic Roman disease, malaria, deprived him of the powerful Papal support and his enemies quickly accomplished his ruin. Within four years of Alexander VI's passing his adventurous career was ended by death in battle.

Corruption Outside Rome

With such corruption in Rome, similar conditions could be expected throughout the Catholic Church. Pluralism and absenteeism were prevalent. Concubinage was common among clergy, high and low. Kings and other political grandees provided for their illegitimate sons by having them appointed bishops, and bishops obtained offices, either clerical or secular, for their illegitimate male progeny. Many bishops behaved more like secular lords than pastors of their flocks. Masses were hurriedly said, and in the chantries established for prayers for the dead, masses were often neglected or grouped together. New monastic movements, evidence of deep religious conviction and dedication, were few, and in existing monastic houses luxury, lethargy, laxity, and even stark immorality were usual. Nunneries were favourite places for providing homes for daughters of the aristocracy. Many women so domiciled had private incomes which made possible physical comforts and often went outside the enclosing walls.

Evidence was accumulating that Western Europe was in danger of de-Christianization. The gains painfully won in earlier centuries were apparently being lost. In practice Christian ideals were repudiated and a secularism was emerging which in morals would have shocked high-minded pagans of pre-Christian days. Western Europeans seemed to be resolving the tension between Christian and un-Christian customs so prominent in the Middle Ages by abandoning any attempt to live up to the standards of the New Testament.

Fresh Indications of Continuing Vitality

The facts just summarized, undoubtedly grim, were only one side of the picture. By that contrast which from the beginning has characterized the course of Christianity, the century and a half covered in this chapter witnessed not only a seeming retreat but also indications of continuing vigour. As in Russia, so even more in Western Europe, that vigour expressed itself partly through old channels and partly in fresh ways. Among the old channels were monasteries which held to their original ideals and bishops and parish clergy who laboured conscientiously to fulfil what was rightly expected of men in their posts.

In Italy, where much of the scepticism and worldliness of the Renaissance centred and where the corruption radiating from Rome was most conspicuous, individuals and groups who stood for loyalty to the faith were not wanting. Among them was Catherine of Siena (1347-1380), who in her brief life had a wide influence in reconciling enemies and warring factions and in contributing to the return of the Popes to Rome. She also sought to prevent the Great Schism and attempted to restore peace between the Popes and Florence. In the fifteenth century Florence, a centre of Renaissance art and humanism, had a circle of brilliant intellectuals who were earnestly Christian. At the close of the century Florence was the scene of the labours of Girolamo Savonarola (1452-1498). A Dominican, by his sincerity and his eloquence Savonarola endeavoured to bring moral and religious reform to that city. For a time in the 1490's he seemed to succeed. But he ran afoul of Alexander VI, for he denounced that Pontiff as neither a true Pope nor a Christian and appealed to the sovereigns of four leading countries to call a general council of the Church. Public opinion in Florence turned against him, and he and two of his disciples were condemned and hanged, and their bodies were burned. From Florence, too, came Michelangelo, a warm admirer of Savonarola. As a Christian Michelangelo dedicated his skill to some of the greatest sculpture and painting of the age.

North of Italy humanism had less of paganism than in that land. Outstanding, for example, was Jacques Lefèvre d'Étaples (c. 1455-1536), a priest who taught in the University of Paris. He pled for a return to primitive Christianity, held the Bible to be the primary authority for Christians, and gave much time to the study of the Scriptures and their translation into French. More famous was Desiderius Erasmus (c. 1466-1536), a native of Rotterdam. A master of the Latin style admired by humanists, Erasmus was widely read in their circles. An intense individualist and having no use for monks or scholasticism, reluctantly a priest, he was sincerely Christian and wished to see the Church purged of superstition and to return to the ethical teachings of Christ. In a politically divided Europe, racked by war, he pled for peace.

A few new monastic movements emerged. One of the more notable was the Brethren of the Common Life. They sprang up in the Low Countries in the fourteenth century and combined some of the features of monasticism with non-monastic life. They spread chiefly in the Low Countries and in Germany and were closely related to other movements which stimulated monastic reform in Germany. By the close of the fifteenth century the Observants among the Franciscans, holding to a complete adherence to the ideal of Francis of Assisi, multiplied rapidly. One of their number, Ximénes de Cisneros (1436-1517), in his later years Archbishop of Toledo, endeavoured to bring all of the Brothers Minor of Castile to the Observant discipline and to purify the entire church in that Spanish realm. A Dominican, Vincent Ferrer (1350-1419), severely ascetic, of an aristocratic family, travelled widely, preaching repentance and impending judgement.

Varied expressions of the rising tide of devotion appeared through mysticism. One channel was what were known as the Friends of God. They began early in the fourteenth century and were found chiefly in Germany and the Low Countries. Among their pioneers were two Dominicans, John ("Meister") Eckhart (c. 1260-1327) and John Tauler (died 1361). Related to the movement but not of it was the Fleming John Ruysbroeck (1293-1381), who with a few companions followed the rule of the Augustinian Canons. His writings had a profound influence on the Friends of God and the Brethren of the Common Life. From the awakening represented by the Brethren of the Common Life came the New Devotion. Its chief literary legacy was—and is—*The Imitation of Christ*, composed early in the fifteenth century. To the latter half of the fourteenth century belong influential English mystics. One of them, Walter Hilton, an experienced spiritual director who died in 1396, wrote *The Scale of Perfection*, to guide the soul in its progress towards God. It is said to have been the book of devotion most widely used in England in the fifteenth and sixteenth centuries.

MOVEMENTS CONDEMNED BY THE CATHOLIC CHURCH

The latter part of the fourteenth and the fifteenth century witnessed two movements which were closely related, which sought to bring the Church to a closer approximation to the New Testament, but which were branded by the Catholic Church as heretical.

One was that begun by John Wyclif (c. 1320-1384). Wyclif

spent much of his life in Oxford and was an outstanding teacher in that university. When he was already in middle life, possibly because he was scandalized by the Avignon Papacy and the Great Schism, he began giving pen to views which antagonized the conservatives. He declared that Popes might err and were not necessary for the administration of the Church. He said that a worldly Pope was a heretic and should be removed from office. Later he insisted that the true Church is made up only of those elected by God and that no visible church or its officers could control entrance to it or could exclude its members. He maintained that every one of God's elect is a priest. He attacked transsubstantiation but held to the real presence of Christ in the bread and wine of the mass. He condemned the cult of the saints, relics, and pilgrimages. Wyclif was responsible for the translation of the Bible from the Vulgate into English. To give wide currency to the Bible he sent out itinerant preachers who won a following known as the Lollards. Wyclif was protected by some of the nobility who were powerful at court; he died peacefully in the parish at Lutterworth to which the Crown had appointed him. But his followers were persecuted. Among other charges, they were accused of stirring up the Peasants' Revolt of 1381. In 1415 the Council of Constance condemned Wyclif and ordered his writings burned. In 1428, at Papal command, Wyclif's remains were dug up and burned, and the ashes were thrown into a nearby stream.

Wyclif's writings came into the hands of a Bohemian priest, John Hus (c. 1373-1415), and reinforced him in the course on which he had already entered and for which he has been remembered. Hus was of humble birth but eventually became Rector of the University of Prague. In his preaching in Prague he advocated reform and stirred both high and low. He held that God had founded the Church on Christ and not on Peter, and that Popes might be heretics. His emphasis was more ethical than theological. He was condemned by the Pope and, as we have seen, was tried by the Council of Constance and, stripped of the priesthood, was turned over to the civil authorities for burning.

In his death Hus became a national hero of the Bohemians. His followers fell into two groups. One, largely from the aristocracy, wished the free preaching of the Gospel, gave the Communion to the laity in both the bread and the wine, not simply in the bread as had become the custom, and opposed only those practices of the Catholic Church which seemed to them to be forbidden by the Bible. The other wing was from the humbler ranks of society and rejected all in the Catholic Church for which they could not find express warrant in the Scriptures. The radical wing was defeated in battle by the moderates. In spite of Papal condemnation, the Bohemian Parliament gave the latter full equality with the Catholics. Another movement, the Bohemian Brethren (the *Unitas Fratrum*), combined elements from both wings and from the Waldenses. They were one of the sources of the Moravians, whom we are to meet later.

The many and varied movements, both within the Catholic Church and condemned by it, in which the inherent vigour of Christianity was finding expression contributed to vast tides that, beginning in the sixteenth century, were largely to reinvigorate and transform the Christianity of Western Europe. They started it on a course of geographic expansion which in the nineteenth and twentieth centuries attained global dimensions.

CHAPTER VIII

Revival, Reform, and Expansion,

A.D. 1500-1750

Not far from the year 1500 a new stage began in the course of
Christianity. It was concurrent with the beginning of a new era
in the history of Western European peoples. Because of the developments among these peoples, the sixteenth century also ushered
in a new stage in the history of mankind as a whole. For the
first time one segment of mankind began to impinge on all the
rest of mankind, and the foreshadowings were seen of the global
revolution which resulted from that impact. The revolution was
to mount until in the twentieth century every people, tribe, and
nation was profoundly altered and the whole human race was
ushered into a world which in time dimensions was rapidly
shrinking and which was displaying common cultural features.
The source of the revolution was Western Europe and those large
portions of the globe peopled by migrations from that area.
Since Western Europe was the segment of the globe in which
Christianity longest had the nearest approach to an opportunity
to mould culture, the question inevitably arises as to what share
Christianity had in the impact and the revolution.

In general, the four and a half centuries which followed the
dawn of this new age fall into four periods of unequal length.
One lasted roughly from about the closing decades of the fif-

teenth century to the middle of the eighteenth century. The second, much briefer, was from the mid-eighteenth century into the second decade of the nineteenth century. The third was from 1815 to 1914. The fourth was introduced by dramatic events in 1914 and had not ended when these lines were written. The present chapter is an attempt to cover the first period—from the closing decades of the fifteenth century to the mid-eighteenth century. As in the previous stages of our story, the boundary dates are only approximate. Some phases of the movements characterizing the period began before and some continued after the years which head this chapter. But those years are sufficiently near to marked transitions to be an aid in understanding what lies between them.

General Developments Between a.d. 1500 and a.d. 1750

In many ways, as was to be expected, movements which marked the fourteenth and fifteenth centuries continued into the sixteenth, seventeenth, and eighteenth centuries. The Renaissance did not end immediately: much of its legacy persisted and in the twentieth century is still potent. Such, for example, is the emphasis upon man, upon the this-worldly stage of human life, and upon man's confidence in his ability to explore the universe and to solve the problems which confront the human race. The use of the vernaculars in literature, begun before the sixteenth century, increased. Latin was still the vehicle of much of scholarship and thus helped to further unity in Western culture, but it was beginning to be supplanted by the several national languages. Printing by movable type made the written word available to thousands who had previously been illiterate. Cities multiplied and grew in population. With them the urban middle class, the *bourgeoisie,* became more important politically and culturally. The emergence of nation-states continued.

The Ottoman Turks were a chronic menace. For many decades their empire continued to expand and eventually embraced not only the Balkans, Greece, much of Hungary, the shores of the

Black Sea, Asia Minor, and Mesopotamia but also all the north coast of Africa from the Red Sea to the Straits of Gibraltar. For a time their ships made the Mediterranean a Turkish lake. The Ottoman Empire roughly approximated the Eastern Roman Empire at its height, but in contrast with the latter it was Moslem rather than Christian. The Ottoman menace to Western Europe reached its peak in the first seven decades of the sixteenth century. It was checked by the decisive Turkish defeat in the Battle of Lepanto (1571) by the fleet inspired by Pope Pius V. Never after that event were the Turks to dominate the Mediterranean.

In connexion with some of these movements were other developments which made the centuries introduced by the closing years of the 1400's distinct from what went before. The cities of Western Europe, including Antwerp, Bruges, Brussels, Seville, and Lisbon, outstripped the Italian cities—Venice, Genoa, Florence, and Pisa—as the chief centres of commerce and banking. That was because the Turks had taken some of the Eastern Mediterranean strongholds of the Italian cities and because of the expanding empires of Spain and Portugal in the Americas, Africa, and Asia. From human daring came a new astronomy of which Copernicus (1473-1543), Galileo (1564-1642, and Kepler (1571-1630) were pioneers. The telescope was invented. The earth was demoted from its central place in the heavens, and the sun was recognized as the centre of a system of planets. Symbols were devised or appropriated for the developing mathematics—for arithmetic, algebra, and geometry—and calculus was devised. By stressing the observation of facts Francis Bacon (1561-1626) did much for the development of natural science. Early in the seventeenth century Harvey discovered the circulation of the blood, thus opening a new door in the practice of medicine. Isaac Newton, born in 1642, the year of Galileo's death, observed "laws" which ever since have been basic in physics and astronomy. Descartes (1596-1650) contributed to mathematics and especially to philosophy—to the latter with his basic questioning and his principle of *cogito, ergo sum* ("I think, therefore I am"). Robert Boyle (1627-1691) is credited with being the father of modern chemistry. The microscope was improved, the air pump was invented, and the system of reckoning temperature was formulated which is still in use in English-speaking countries. Developments in botany and zoölogy laid the foundations for later achievements in biology. John Locke (1632-1704) made contributions to philosophy which profoundly influenced theoretical study in that field and as well had lasting repercussions on political thought and institutions. Pascal (1623-1662) and Leibnitz (1646-1716) elaborated calculus.

In the area of government, the development of nation-states which had begun earlier was accelerated. From the age of the "barbarian" invasions Western Europe had been a congeries of hundreds of units, large and small, some of tribal origin, bearing the pattern of feudalism, loosely held together in regional kingdoms, and for the most part recognizing a theoretical association through the Holy Roman Empire. Now these feudal units were coagulating in kingdoms under dynastic royal houses which claimed to rule by divine right and possessed absolute power. The Holy Roman Empire persisted in name, but for the most part its Emperors were chosen from the Hapsburg family by seven electors, all except one German. The Hapsburgs based their power on hereditary possessions, chief of which was Austria with its capital in Vienna. An imperial Diet, composed of the electors, lesser princes, higher clergy, and representatives of the free cities, acted for that incongruous combination whose cohesion was mainly geography, the Holy Roman imperial tradition, and language. In the seventeenth century the leading nation-states were France, ruled by descendants of Hugh Capet, who in 987 had been elected King; England, under the House of Tudor, whose first King was Henry VII and whose diplomatic marriage of a daughter paved the way for the union of Scotland and England which was realized late in the seventeenth century; Spain, its kingdom unified late in the fifteenth and the fore part of the sixteenth century; Portugal; Sweden; and Denmark-Norway. The rival royal families fought with one another for the aggrandizement of their power and the enlargement of their domains.

They waged their wars with professional armies equipped with the firearms made possible by gunpowder. The professional armies supplanted the former feudal levies and rendered the kings independent of these levies. The feudal nobility were either decimated by domestic struggles, markedly by the prolonged Wars of the Roses in England, or made subordinate to the kings. In their efforts to curb the feudal magnates the kings were often aided by the *bourgeoisie*.

Associated with the growth of the absolute monarchies were geographic discoveries and empire-building by the peoples of Western Europe. Spain and Portugal led the way, followed tardily by the English, the French, and the Dutch. Blocked by the Turks from enlarging the incipient expansion in the Eastern Mediterranean accomplished through the Crusades and the Italian cities, Western Europeans outflanked these formidable rivals by rounding Africa and, more than outflanking them, moved westward across the Atlantic. The initial explorations were directed by Prince Henry (1394-1460) the Navigator, of the royal house of Portugal. Henry was Grand Master of the Order of Christ, a military monastic body which in Portugal succeeded to the property of the Templars. Using that property to finance his enterprises, he founded an institution to study geography and navigation, to devise better ships, and to train men to sail them. How far his motives were of Christian origin even he might have found it difficult to say. One of his purposes was certainly to spread the Christian faith, presumably by circumnavigating Africa and so reaching South and East Asia without having to venture on the impossible feat of forcing a way through the Ottoman Empire. Africa proved to be much larger than Prince Henry had anticipated. By the time of his death his captains had made their way only along part of the west coast. But less than a generation later (1488) the Cape of Good Hope was reached, and in 1497 Vasco da Gama sailed round it to India. In the first half of the sixteenth century the Portuguese established trading posts along the coast of Africa and in India, Ceylon, Malacca, Japan, and the East Indies. Before the close of the century they were in possession of Macao, not far from Canton. In several places these posts were enlarged to embrace adjoining territory, but except in Ceylon and some of the East Indies that territory was of very limited extent.

From almost the beginning of the Portuguese voyages Africans were enslaved and sent to Europe. Here was the inception of the largest exploitation in all history of one race by another—with the heartless barbarity of the tribal wars whose victims were sold to the European slavers, the incredible suffering of the trans-Atlantic passage, and the cruelties inflicted in the plantations of the New World. If a Christian motive entered into the initial voyages, results followed which were a tragic contradiction of that motive.

Similar exploitation followed the discovery and settlement of the Americas by the Spaniards and the Portuguese. One of Christopher Columbus' objectives was the conversion of the Indians, but unspeakable cruelties and enslavement attended the initial impact of the Europeans upon the native races.

The English, French, and Dutch were later than the Spaniards and Portuguese in trade, conquest, and colonization. In the mid-eighteenth century their overseas domains, while extensive, were not as large or as populous as those of the two pioneering powers.

Similarly the Russians, with their political capital at Moscow, moved eastward across the vast northern plains of Eurasia and before the end of the seventeenth century had reached the Pacific, but their new territories had few inhabitants.

By the mid-eighteenth century European peoples had mastered a larger proportion of the earth's surface than had any earlier group of mankind. Even the Roman, Chinese, Arab, and Mongol empires had not approached the geographic magnitude of the European-dominated realms. In population totals the latter had not yet equalled these earlier domains. The Europeans had moved into relatively sparsely settled portions of the globe. Except in the Americas the cultural revolution produced by the impact of Western civilization had scarcely begun. Not until the twentieth century was it to attain global traumatic dimensions.

THE STATUS OF CHRISTIANITY IN THE NEW AGE: GENERAL FEATURES

In the new age which dawned at the close of the fifteenth century Christianity faced a major challenge. Could it mould the changing civilization of Europe and transform wholesomely or at least ameliorate the impact of Europeans upon the peoples coming under European influence? Would non-Europeans accept Christianity? Never had any religion been confronted by so nearly global a challenge.

The prospect was far from promising. As we saw in the last chapter, Christianity was not only seriously threatened, it was as well losing ground geographically and apparently was waning in inner vitality. It had either lost most of its outposts in Asia and North Africa or seen them greatly constricted. In Asia Minor and South-eastern Europe the churches were subject to the Ottoman Turks, Moslems. The Ottoman rulers were both the spiritual and the political head of the rapidly expanding Islam—for Islam was steadily winning peoples in Central Asia, China, and South-eastern Asia and the adjacent islands. In Europe the Papacy and much of the hierarchy of the Roman Catholic Church were largely staffed by men who regarded their posts as an opportunity for luxury or power or both. The attempts of the great reformers of the twelfth and thirteenth centuries to make the Papacy an instrument for lifting the entire body of professed Christians to a nearer approximation to the standards of the New Testament had brought that office functions which required an enlarged staff with increased powers and incomes commensurate with their importance. From quite other than Christian motives men sought positions on the Papal curia for themselves or members of their families, and the emoluments of the posts were augmented. On the eve of the movements which ushered in the new day the Papacy and the Papal court had become a stench in the nostrils of honest men. Such corruption at the administrative centre could not but prove contagious in the structure which radiated from it. The evils were further aggravated by the secularization attending the heightened control of the Church by the absolute monarchs. The struggle of earlier centuries to free the Church from domination by lay princes was increasingly resolved by the power of each King to appoint the bishops in his realm and to forbid any Papal decree from being published within his borders without his consent. As the decades passed the powers of the monarchs over the Church mounted.

Yet, by what seemed a strange anomaly, the sixteenth and seventeenth centuries witnessed a fresh surge of life in the Christianity of Western Europe. Through it Christianity permeated the life of that region more effectively and brought it nearer to the ideals set forth in the New Testament than in any earlier time. From that surge issued a missionary movement of unprecedented dimensions. The faith was planted among more peoples than had ever known it. By the middle of the eighteenth century no other religion had had as wide a geographic expansion as Christianity. Moreover, earnest Christians fought the evils attendant upon the chronic wars between the rival dynasties and sought to check the exploitation of peoples by European conquerors, explorers, merchants, and settlers and make the contacts with Europeans accrue to the benefit of non-Europeans.

To what extent, if at all, did a causal connexion exist between the fresh surge of life in Christianity in Europe and the vigour displayed in other phases of the life of that region? Was Christianity at least one of the causes and perhaps the major cause of the abounding creativity—political, intellectual, and economic —among Western Europeans of these centuries? Or was that creativity a cause of the new vigour in Christianity? That each influenced the other is clear. But whether the relation was causal and, if so, in which direction or in both directions seems impossible to ascertain.

The surge of life in Christianity was seen chiefly in Western Europe. There it had two main expressions—in the emergence of Protestantism and in a renewed animation in the Roman Catholic Church which purged it of much of the glaring corruption of the fourteenth and fifteenth centuries, gave birth to new monastic movements, and inspired the most extensive missionary activity that Christianity or any other religion had thus far produced.

A striking feature of the awakenings in Christianity was their regional division. In general Protestantism had its origin and flourished in areas which had not been within the Roman Empire, and the Catholic Reformation had its mainsprings and its most cogent expressions in what might be called Latin Europe—the countries in Western Europe which had been most extensively incorporated in the Roman Empire. To be more precise, Protestantism became the prevailing religion among the Germanic peoples who, with one exception, had not settled within the former confines of the Roman Empire. The exception—Great Britain—was more apparent than real, for here the Anglo-Saxon and then the Scandinavian invaders had never been under Roman rule and they had wiped out all cultural traces of the Roman occupation. The generalization has been made that Protestantism is the reaction of the Teutonic mind to Christianity. To put it another way, the Roman Catholic Church retained its hold on the descendants of those "barbarian" invaders who had settled within the former provinces of the Roman Empire and had conformed in part to the Roman culture when it was becoming officially Christian. That conformation—or acculturation—had proceeded further in Italy and the Iberian Peninsula than it had north of the Pyrenees and the Alps. There, significantly, or through individuals born in those regions, most of the great monastic movements had arisen and a large proportion of the outstanding theological systems had been formulated. Although a few individuals espoused it, Protestantism never won a substantial continuing foothold in Italy, Spain, or Portugal. In France, where, presumably, the acculturation had not proceeded as far as in Italy and the Iberian Peninsula, Protestants constituted a substantial minority. A leading Protestant, Calvin, was from a northern border of Latin Europe and was educated in France. Switzerland, also on the northern border of what had been the Roman Empire, divided about evenly between Protestantism and the Roman Catholic Church. In the Low Countries Protestantism prevailed in the portion which had not been within the Roman limes, and Roman Catholicism was dominant in the southern sections where Roman rule had been established. In Germany the Roman Catholic Church retained the allegiance of most of the Rhine Valley and Austria, formerly parts of the Roman domains, and Protestantism was strongest in the sections the Romans had never fully subdued.

Seeming exceptions can be cited. Although Ireland had never been conquered by the Romans, the majority of the population retained its Roman Catholic allegiance, but partly, at least, because the English, who eventually separated from Rome, ruled the island and the Roman Catholic form of the faith became associated with Irish nationalism and resistance to English rule. Except in Bohemia, Protestantism never gained a large continuing following among Slavic peoples. For a time Protestantism seemed to have some prospect of winning the Poles, but it was soon eliminated.

In the main the pioneers and creators of Protestantism were from the lower or middle social strata and most of the leaders of the Catholic Reformation were from the aristocracy.

In our survey of the course of Christianity in the sixteenth and seventeenth centuries and in the fore part of the eighteenth century we will address ourselves first to Protestantism and then to the Roman Catholic Church. Although the Catholic Reformation began a generation prior to Martin Luther, its later course was so consciously in opposition to Protestantism that it has often been called the Counter-Reformation. For that reason it should follow our account of Protestantism. Later we must say something of developments in the Russian Orthodox Church.

Protestantism took four main forms—Lutheran, Reformed, Radical, and Anglican. In addition anti-Trinitarian humanism won minorities.

THE RISE AND DEVELOPMENT OF LUTHERANISM

October 31, 1517, is usually regarded as marking the beginning of Protestantism. It was then that Martin Luther affixed to the chapel door of the University of Wittenberg ninety-five theses which he offered to defend in debate. The procedure was normal in university circles. What made it notable was the author, the occasion, the subject, and the sequel.

Martin Luther (1483-1546) was the eldest child in a prosperous peasant family. Sturdy physically, loving music, intelligent, and hard-working, he was reared in the Catholic faith as understood and practised by members of the peasant class. He was subject to periods of depression (*Anfectungen*)—a psychological characteristic with important fruitage. He acquired as good an education as Germany afforded. During part of his student days he had as a teacher one of the Brethren of the Common Life. He had embarked on the study of law with the purpose of going into the legal profession when, moved by the threat of death from a stroke of lightning, he suddenly vowed to become a monk. He entered a house of the Observant Augustinians, a reform movement which had begun in the preceding century, and studied theology, applying himself chiefly to masters of the Occamist tradition. He was assigned to teach theology in the University of Wittenberg, newly founded by the Elector Frederick III, "the Wise," of Saxony. The monastic life brought mental and spiritual agony, not peace. By the means enjoined by the Church of his day Luther sought to earn the assurance of the favour of God. But fasting, self-inflicted scourging of the body, and repeated confession and eventual ordination to the priesthood only intensified his distress. To distract his attention from his torturing introspection his superiors loaded him with administrative duties as well as teaching. Gradually the light dawned. A phrase in Paul's Letter to the Romans—"the just shall live by faith"—contained for him the answer. The Christian, he came to believe, is justified not by his deeds—by "work righteousness" including religious observances—but by trusting in the mercy and love of God, which can never be earned but is offered freely in Christ. Luther enlarged the word *fide* ("faith") by *sola* ("alone"), so that the verse read "the just shall live by faith alone."

Luther was moved to propose his theses by the hawking of

indulgences through parts of Germany by Tetzel, a Dominican. The proceeds were to be used, so the public was informed, towards the erection of the new St. Peter's in Rome. The public was not told, nor did Luther know, that half was to go to pay a debt which Albert of Brandenburg, of the aristocratic Hohenzollern family, had acquired in purchasing the Archbishopric of Mainz, the top ecclesiastical post in Germany. In promoting his sales Tetzel had declared that as soon as the money fell into the coffer a soul was released from purgatory. Luther's sense of justice was outraged. Luther declared that the Pope had no jurisdiction over purgatory and could remit only those penalties which he himself had imposed; that the indulgences bred a false sense of security and were positively harmful; that few Germans could worship in St. Peter's; that the Pope had enough money to build St. Peter's without impoverishing the Germans; and that the Pope would do better to appoint one good pastor to a church than to grant a multitude of indulgences.

To Luther's surprise the theses created an immense sensation. The relatively new device of the printing press was used to scatter them widely across Germany. The controversy so raged that the Pope, the pleasure-loving scion of the Florentine Medicis, Leo X, whom we have already met, was forced to take cognizance of it. He ordered the head of the Augustinians to silence Luther, but in a chapter of the Augustinians the offending monk won followers. Leo X then ordered Luther to Rome to stand trial for heresy and contumacy. The Elector Frederick obtained the transfer of the hearing to Germany. Public debates followed in which Luther was maneuvered into saying that not only Popes but Ecumenical Councils might err, and that Hus's views were "Christian and evangelical."

The issue between Luther and the Pope was now squarely joined. In 1520 Luther published five widely-circulated German tracts stating that good works were not limited to praying in church, fasting, and giving alms but also included "labouring at one's trade, coming and going, eating, drinking, and sleeping, and all other acts that help nourish the body and are generally useful." He declared that the "noblest of all good works is to believe in Christ" and that a Christian should seek "to please God and serve Him without hope of reward." He insisted that every true believer is a priest, without the aid of Pope or clergy, and is competent to interpret the Scriptures and to discern what is right, and that many Popes had been unbelievers and so were incapable of understanding the Scriptures. He attacked the pomp and luxury of the Popes and cardinals and said that the Papacy was the Babylon which had carried the Church into captivity. He would permit priests to marry. He denied transubstantiation and would give the cup to the laity. Of the seven sacraments he held that only baptism and the Lord's Supper are supported by Scripture. But he maintained that through baptism supported by the prayers of the Church the infant is cleansed and renewed and that in the Lord's Supper the bread and the wine contain the real flesh and the real blood of Christ. He advised youths not to take monastic vows, for he was convinced that the works of members of religious orders are not more praiseworthy in the sight of God than are those of the farmer in his field and of the woman in her household duties. Luther affirmed that "A Christian man is the most free lord of all, and subject to none; a Christian man is the most dutiful servant of all, and subject to everyone."

In these tracts Luther enunciated the distinctive convictions of Protestantism—justification by faith alone, the priesthood of all believers, the authority of the word of God as contained in the Scriptures, and the right and the duty of each Christian to interpret the Scriptures. If for no other reason, because of the right and the duty of each Christian to interpret the Scriptures Protestantism was multiform. Nor were all Protestants—not even Luther himself—willing to carry to their logical conclusion the basic principles peculiar to Protestantism, notably that of the right and the duty of the interpretation of the Scriptures by the individual. But with all its variety and its frequent hesitation fully to implement the convictions whch set it apart from other forms of Christianity, in its numerous expressions Protestantism bore the stamp of what Luther forthrightly formulated.

The inevitable followed. Early in 1521, less than four years after the appearance of the ninety-five theses, a Papal bull excommunicated the daring monk and the Papal nuncio pressed the authorities of the Holy Roman Empire to liquidate what Leo X called a "wild boar" in the Lord's vineyard. Luther was haled before the Diet of that realm. There, at Worms, in the presence of the newly elected Emperor, Charles V, the mightiest monarch in Europe, and of the dignitaries of Church and State, Luther, the son of peasant parents, declared that he could not accept the authority of Popes and councils, since they had often contradicted one another, and that unless he was convinced by Scripture and plain reason he could not in good conscience recant anything he had written. In May, 1521, the Emperor adjudged Luther to be "cut off from the Church of God" and commanded his subjects to refuse the "obstinate schismatic and manifest heretic" hospitality, food, or drink, to take him prisoner and turn him over to the Emperor, and to deal similarly with all Luther's friends and adherents. To protect Luther, the Elector Frederick had him taken to the nearly untenanted Wartburg castle. There, with the exception of a brief visit to Wittenberg in December, 1521, Luther remained until March, 1522, disguised as a knight and under an assumed name. In his nine months in the Wartburg, in spite of ill health and *Anfectungen,* Luther wrote nearly a dozen books and translated the New Testament from Greek into German. His translation of the entire Bible, completed later and polished by him again and again, continued to be standard and through its dignity and felicity of expression was epoch-making in the literary history of Germany.

In March, 1522, defying the imperial ban and contrary to the advice of the Elector Frederick, Luther resumed his residence in Wittenberg. There he took active leadership in the Reformation, a position which he held throughout his life. He taught in the university, preached, and continued his writing. Students came from other parts of Germany and from several countries to drink of the new spring at its source. Returning home, they profoundly influenced the Reformation in state after state and country after country.

Revolt against the Roman Catholic Church spread rapidly. As it proliferated it took many forms. The more radical rejected infant baptism, repudiated clerical and monastic vows, destroyed images and altars, and regarded the Lord's Supper simply as a memorial. The general unrest of which the religious element was a phase contributed to a peasants' revolt against both lay and ecclesiastical authorities. The revolt broke out in 1524-1525. It demanded emancipation from oppressive measures and customs. But it was suppressed in a blood bath. Luther took vigorous action. His was a middle course. While at first he urged the authorities to be moderate, he later came out against the more radical features of the extreme reformers and urged the use of force against what he called the "murderous and thieving hordes of peasants."

In other ways Luther shaped the form of Protestantism which has been known by his name. In a colloquy in Marburg in October, 1529, he took a position on the real presence of Christ in the Lord's Supper which made intercommunion impossible between those who held to him and those who did not agree with him on the nature of the presence of Christ in the bread and the wine. He permitted priests, monks, and nuns to marry. He himself married a former nun. He wrote a German mass utilizing much from the traditional liturgies, and said that, unless they were expressly forbidden by the Bible, what customs had come through the Roman Catholic Church were not necessarily to be repudiated. He stressed music, congregational singing, the family, and education. He encouraged the civil authorities to regulate worship and ecclesiastical structures and procedures within their respective domains and thus contributed to the emergence of *Landeskirchen* (territorial churches) in Germany and to state churches elsewhere. By his emphasis upon sin and man's inability without God's grace to attain forgiveness, he alienated some of the humanists, notably Erasmus. Erasmus openly differed from Luther and never broke with the Roman Catholic Church.

In Germany, politically divided into many states and cities, large and small, religious controversy contributed to wars, at times as the major factor. Fortunately for Luther and his fellow Protestants, Charles V was too much engrossed in wars with France and in Italy and with the Turkish menace promptly to follow up with vigour the ban directed against Luther and his friends decreed at the Diet of Worms. But in 1530, in an attempt to restore religious unity, returning from his coronation at Rome as Emperor, Charles called a meeting of the Diet at Augsburg and asked the Protestants to state where they differed from the Roman Catholic Church. Their statement, known as the Augsburg Confession, has continued to be regarded by Lutherans as the authoritative formulation of their convictions. The chief author of the Augsburg Confession was Philip Melanchthon (1497-1560). Melanchthon sought to make the documents as irenic as possible, endeavouring to show that the Protestant convictions were in accord with those of the Universal Church, but did not hesitate to point out what abuses had crept into the Roman Church. Roman Catholic theologians replied. The Emperor sought through conferences to bring agreement but failed. The Diet had a Roman Catholic majority and held that the Protestants had been refuted. Charles gave the latter until April, 1531, to submit. After some delay war followed between the imperial forces and the Protestant princes, now divided by Charles's skilful diplomacy. It was waged intermittently. In 1552 the Emperor was defeated and almost captured. The Peace of Augsburg followed (1555). A compromise, it followed the principle of *cujus regio, ejus religio*, permitting each lay prince, Lutheran or Roman Catholic, to determine which of the two forms was to prevail in his territory, but required Roman Catholic prelates who turned Lutheran to surrender their properties and incomes belonging to their offices.

The principle of *cujus regio, ejus religio* continued to govern the religious map of Germany. From 1618 to 1648 what was known as the Thirty Years' War was waged. Rivalries between Protestants and Catholics were a major and continuing factor. Eventually most of Western Europe was embroiled and in the later stages France entered in an attempt to enlarge its territories. Much of Germany was laid waste. The Peace of West-phalia (1648) ended the long agony and, among other features, checked the Roman Catholic anti-Protestant counter advance, gave recognition to the Reformed as well as the Lutheran form of the faith, and fixed the boundaries between Protestants and Roman Catholics roughly where they remained into the twentieth century. Each wing of Christianity had made gains. Some former Roman Catholic bishoprics, monasteries, and churches were left in Protestant hands, but Bohemia, formerly Protestant, became prevailingly Roman Catholic. In general North Germany emerged Protestant and much of the Rhine Valley remained Roman Catholic. Toleration was granted for private worship in a branch of the faith which differed from that of the prince.

The adherents of Lutheranism did not fully agree among themselves. Some wished accommodation to Roman Catholic practices. Others held good works to be an obstacle to the Christian life. Still others declared that man is completely without freedom of will. The Formula of Concord, framed in 1580, was an attempt to devise a statement to which all could agree. It represented the convictions of the large majority of German Lutherans, but a minority dissented. Then as later, Lutheranism did not present a solid front to the world. In time increasing emphasis was placed on dogma—a kind of Lutheran scholasticism.

Lutheranism spread beyond Germany. Before the Thirty Years' War began Scandinavia, Iceland, and Finland (ruled by Sweden) were solidly Lutheran. The transition from Roman Catholic allegiance to Protestantism was achieved partly by earnest individuals who had had contact with Wittenberg but chiefly on the initiative of the monarchs. The latter were moved partly by religious conviction and partly by the desire to control the Church in their domains and to profit from the ecclesiastical property confiscated in the transition. The transition began in the second decade of the sixteenth century and was completed soon after the middle of the century. The King of Denmark used Protestantism to consummate his control of Norway. Lutheranism also prevailed in the Baltic countries south of Finland and won substantial minorities in Hungary and Transylvania, at the outset largely among German settlers. Luther's writings were widely read outside Lutheran circles and contributed markedly to other forms of Protestantism.

THE "REFORMED" PHASE OF PROTESTANTISM

The "Reformed" phase of Protestantism, with an ecclesiastical structure which, although having many variations, was Presbyterian, arose almost simultaneously with Lutheranism. In the sixteenth and seventeenth centuries it was the major form of Protestantism in a geographic belt between the solidly Lutheran and the Roman Catholic portions of Europe. That belt stretched from Transylvania and Hungary through Switzerland, down the Rhine Valley into Holland, and across the North Sea into Scotland and North Ireland. Most of the French Protestants were Reformed and Reformed influence was potent in England. In general, the Reformed belt ran between the Latin South, once fully incorporated in the Roman Empire, and the portion of Europe which had never been in the Empire. In later centuries, largely by migrations, the Reformed became as widely spread and about as numerous as the Lutherans.

Why Reformed Protestantism arose and was originally strongest in the border between the areas thoroughly Latinized and those never in the Roman Empire must be conjectural. Reformed Protestantism was not a compromise between Roman Catholicism and Lutheranism. The Reformed much more nearly repudiated the Roman Catholic heritage than did the Lutherans. Luther, as we have seen, rejected only those aspects of the Roman Catholic Church which he felt contradicted the Bible. The Reformed retained from Roman Catholicism only what they believed was expressly warranted in the Bible. The contrast may have arisen from two quite different factors. Unlike Luther, whose education had been apart from humanism, the two outstanding creators of Reformed Protestantism, Zwingli and Calvin, had been under strong humanist influence. The humanistic tradition stressed the

study of the sources, and Zwingli and Calvin insisted on sub-
mitting the Roman Catholic faith to the test of its conformity
with the Scriptures. Luther was pessimistic about the possibility
of bringing human society to conformity with the will of God.
The Reformed Churches, while recognizing as keenly as Lutherans the depravity of man and the wonder of God's grace, were
more hopeful that through those who accepted the salvation
offered by His grace God would effect an approximation to His
Kingdom.

Huldreich Zwingli (1484-1531), the earliest outstanding leader
in the Reformed wing of Protestantism, was born in Switzerland
only a few weeks before Luther, and, like the latter, in a prosperous peasant home. He was a bright lad and his family
determined to give him an education and prepare him for the
priesthood. During his student years he was much impressed by
the writings of the Christian humanists. Unlike Luther, he seems
to have had no soul-shaking religious experience. He was ordained, eventually was on the staff of the Great Minster in
Zürich, and in his preaching advocated reform. He stressed the
authority of the Scriptures and rejected whatever in the Roman
Catholic Church did not, in his judgement, agree with them.
He preached salvation by faith and denounced monastic vows,
clerical celibacy, the invocation of the saints, belief in purgatory,
the sacrificial character of the mass, and the teaching that salvation can be won by good works. He was supported by the civil
authorities. By Easter, 1525, images, relics, and organs had been
removed from Zürich churches, the properties of monasteries
had been confiscated and the proceeds devoted to schools, the
mass had been discontinued, and a simple church service had
been developed in German with the sermon central. Zwingli
broke with Luther largely over the Lord's Supper, holding that
the Communion Service was simply a memorial of Christ's self-
sacrificial death. He perished in an inter-cantonal war which
arose from the attempt of the Zürich authorities to force Protestant preaching on neighbouring Roman Catholic cantons.

Even before Zwingli's death the kind of reform which he advocated was spreading in Switzerland and Strassburg. In 1536 what was called the First Helvetic Confession was drawn up, followed by the Second Helvetic Confession (1562–1564), which long remained standard for many of the Reformed. The Reformed Churches and the Lutherans were parting company.

The Reformed wing of Protestantism was so deeply indebted to Calvin that some of its branches have borne his name. Calvin was not as dominant an influence in the Reformed Churches as was Luther in Lutheranism, but he was the most prominent figure in shaping them and, as was true of Luther, his writings had a profound and continuing effect both within and outside the ecclesiastical circles which looked to him as their leader. John Calvin (1509–1564) was of humble ancestry but was reared in aristocratic society and had the manners of that class. He was born at Noyon in Picardy, about sixty miles north-east of Paris. Intended by his father for the priesthood, in his early teens he went to the University of Paris, still a major centre of theological study. He was there when those great figures in the Catholic Reformation, Ignatius Loyola and Francis Xavier, matriculated, but we have no evidence that he met them. At nineteen he left Paris to study law. His interests were those of the current humanism. He had developed a lucid Latin style and had acquired a knowledge of Greek and Hebrew. In Paris he was under the influence of a group out of which came several Protestants. Somewhere in his youth Calvin had a profound religious experience, but he was so reticent about it that we do not know the details. In his mid-twenties he was imprisoned for his Protestant convictions, was freed, and (1534) sought refuge in Basel, by that time a Protestant city.

In Basel, at the age of twenty-six, Calvin published his *Institutio Christianae Religionis* (usually translated into English as *The Institutes of the Christian Religion*). Repeatedly revised and enlarged by the author, the *Institutio* went into its fourth and final edition in 1559. Because of its clarity, orderliness of thought, and comprehensiveness, it became the single most influential book of the Protestant Reformation. In it Calvin attempted to set forth what he believed to have been the Christian faith before it had been obscured and corrupted by the Roman Catholic Church. Conforming to the outline of the Apostles' Creed, he explicated his idea of that early and generally accepted summary of Christian teaching. He stressed especially the Scriptures and Augustine. He set forth God as the Creator, Preserver, and Governor of the universe. With Luther and Zwingli, he stressed the sovereignty of God, declaring that God is omnipotent and that, "governing heaven and earth by His providence, He so overrules all things that nothing happens in it without His counsel." God, so Calvin held, is concerned for every individual. Calvin did not attempt to resolve the seeming paradox between God's sovereign justice and love and the evil in the universe, but enjoined a meek acceptance of what he found in the Bible. Calvin maintained that God created man in His own image, that the image is in the soul, and that the soul is immortal and has the power to distinguish between good and evil and between justice and injustice. He said that the first man, Adam, sinned, and that the essence of his sin was revolt against God, in which pride, ambition, and ingratitude were prominent. Through the sin of Adam, so Calvin held, all men at birth are tainted with sin. Because of "original sin," every man is totally depraved and can do no good work unless he is assisted by God's grace. Although God hated sin in man, He loved man and, following a plan which dated from the beginning of creation, gave man the law to keep alive the hope of salvation until Christ should come. God sent His Son, Who was fully God and fully man, to give Himself in sacrifice. Thus Christ satisfied the righteous judgement of God, removed the curse on man for his sin, and by His resurrection conquered death. At the last day, Calvin declared, Christ will appear as judge of all and redeemer of the elect.

According to Calvin, the faith by which the sinner accepts God's work in Christ comes through the Holy Spirit. Faith and repentance of sin are correlative. They issue in love towards God and man and in sanctity and purity. We are never perfect in this life but are to press on towards that goal. Because of the taint of "original sin," without the initiative of the Holy Spirit a man cannot have saving faith. With Augustine, Calvin held that God had chosen—"elected"—some to have that faith and had determined—"elected"—others not to have it. Why He chose one individual to receive it and another not to receive it man cannot know. God's justice is not thereby compromised, for no one deserves anything from Him. Also with Augustine, Calvin held that no one can be sure in this life whether he is among the elect. However, Calvin said, if a man meets the tests of a profession of faith, an upright life, and participation in the sacraments, the probabilities are that he is among the elect and he should not worry. Because of his belief in God's concern for every individual, Calvin maintained that each individual has a distinct calling of God to a particular work.

Calvin taught that the Catholic Church, embracing all the elect, has Christ as its head but is invisible and its membership is known only to God. But, although it contains many hypocrites, a visible church exists and is found "wherever we find the word of God purely preached and heard and the sacraments administered according to the institution of Christ." Calvin's outline for a structure for that church as he believed it to be found in the New Testament is followed in the main by Reformed and Presbyterian bodies.

As did the medieval Roman Catholic thinkers, Calvin said that the holy community contained both Church and State, each with its functions assigned by God. But his description of Church and State differed from that set forth in the Middle Ages.

Much of Calvin's work was accomplished in Geneva. That city traced its history back to Roman times. It was a commercial centre with a population of varied composition which had been pleasure-loving and had had low moral standards. Several of its bishops had been the offspring of the ruling Counts of Savoy and were of unworthy character. The clergy and monks and nuns were little better. Early in the 1530's the Reformation had been brought to Geneva by a fiery Swiss preacher, Guillaume

Farel (1489–1565). The bishop, a weak man, had been driven out of the city (1527). In 1536 Protestantism could be said to be fully adopted, with Farel as the dominant religious force. That year Farel persuaded Calvin to help him. The two sought to make Geneva a model community with Church and State working in harmony. But in 1538 a hostile element obtained control of the city government and Farel and Calvin were banished. Calvin took refuge in Strassburg, by that time a Protestant city, with a former Augustinian, the irenic Martin Bucer (1491–1551), an influential figure. There he was pastor of a French congregation, married, wrote, and taught. A shift in Genevan politics brought the element friendly to Calvin back to power. On its urgent invitation, in 1541 Calvin returned to Geneva and remained until his death. Although sometimes his authority was threatened, he succeeded to a marked degree in bringing the little city towards his ideal. He preached, taught, wrote, and advised in legislation, administration, and law enforcement. He did much to foster commerce and industry. Attracted by him, oppressed Protestants from many lands found refuge in Geneva, and returning to their native countries, they furthered the Reformation.

Calvin's mantle fell on Theodore Beza (1519–1605). Born about 150 miles south-east of Paris, Beza was of aristocratic stock and was given a humanist education. In his twenties, sobered by an illness, he cast in his lot with the Reformers. Elected as Calvin's successor, he continued to make Geneva a refugee centre for Protestants. He wrote prodigiously, took a leading part in shaping the constitution for the Reformed Church in France, and encouraged the development of church music, with metrical versions of the Psalms and tunes composed for them. In 1562 the definitive edition of the widely used *Geneva Psalter* was issued.

As we have suggested, the Reformed phase of Protestantism spread widely. It was not unifrom. But the extensive use of the Heidelberg Catechism, issued in 1563, the writings of Calvin and Beza, and the many individuals who had spent longer or shorter periods in Geneva contributed to a family likeness. The persecuted remnants of the Waldenses conformed and experienced a revival. In Hungary and Transylvania large groups of Magyars developed Reformed Churches. Reformed Churches flourished among Germans, notably in the Rhine Valley. Through many vicissitudes the majority in Scotland adhered to the Reformed faith, and the Church of Scotland became Presbyterian.

The Reformed Churches were persecuted, notably in the Netherlands and France. The Netherlands were peopled chiefly by the Dutch in the north, Flemings in the centre, and French-speaking Walloons in the south. Luther's writings early won a wide following, but in the latter half of the sixteenth century Calvinism largely supplanted Lutheranism. In the north Protestants were in the majority whereas the South was predominantly Roman Catholic. In 1571 the Dutch Reformed Church held its first synod. Charles V, who had been reared in the Netherlands, endeavoured to stamp out Protestantism and to construct a more centralized, autocratic administration. His son and heir, Philip II of Spain, sought to carry on what his father had begun. Revolt broke out, soon led by William of Orange, also known as William the Silent. After prolonged warfare the Protestant North formed itself into the United Provinces and in 1581 declared itself independent of Philip. By 1609 the Spaniards acquiesced to the inevitable, hostilities ceased, and the United Netherlands (as the United Provinces were called) had won their freedom. Not until the Peace of Westphalia (1648) did Spain formally recognize that status.

Political independence was followed by bitter doctrinal struggles in the Dutch Reformed Church. A minority, largely among the wealthy intelligentsia who favoured states' rights, protested against the doctrines of election held by the church. They were known as Remonstrants. Their leading theologian was Jacob Arminius, a former student of Beza who had become convinced that predestination as taught by Calvin was untenable. To meet the challenge a synod was held in Dort (or Dordrecht) in 1618–1619 to which delegates came not only from Reformed Churches in the Netherlands but also from Switzerland, Germany, and

England. It condemned Arminianism and reaffirmed the Heidelberg Confession and the Belgic Confession, strong Calvinistic documents.

In France Protestantism sprang from several sources but never enrolled more than a minority. Partly because of Calvin's writings circulated in French and by zealous missionaries trained in Geneva, Lausanne, and Strassburg, that minority held to the Reformed wing. In 1559 a national synod convened in Paris. It adopted a confession of faith based on one drawn up by Calvin and a form of organization which was to have a marked effect upon churches of the Reformed family in the Netherlands, Scotland, and America. The Protestants, from about 1560 also known as Huguenots, were strongest in the cities and had their following chiefly among artisans, tradesmen, and farmers. But some converts were among the nobility. Persecution soon broke out and civil strife followed. Although at their height constituting about a tenth of the population, the Protestants had determined and much of the time able leadership. The religious issue was complicated by personal rivalries and by the efforts of some of the kings and their counsellors fully to unify the country under an absolute monarch. The wars of religion are usually dated from the massacre of Huguenots assembled for worship (1562). They continued at intervals until, in 1628, La Rochelle, the last of the Protestant strongholds, surrendered to the royal forces. The wars were punctuated by such events as the Massacre of St. Bartholomew (August 24, 1572), which, beginning in Paris, spread to much of the rest of the country; by the accession to the throne of France as Henry IV of the Protestant Henry (Bourbon) of Navarre (1594), who to unify the country became a Roman Catholic; and by the promulgation through Henry IV of the Edict of Nantes (April 15, 1598), which guaranteed the Protestants religious freedom, but under certain restrictions.

The end of the wars and the confirmation (1643) of the Edict of Nantes did not mean the end of persecution. When in 1661 Louis XIV assumed the reins of government, it was renewed and was pressed with rigour and cruelty. In 1685 Louis XIV, intent on being absolute monarch and determined to be rid of a religious minority who constituted an enclave not yet fully integrated under his rule, revoked the Edict of Nantes. Within a few years several thousand Huguenots left France and found homes in Prussia, Holland, Ireland, the British colonies in America, and South Africa. By the end of the eighteenth century persecution gradually ceased, but the Protestants had been reduced to a small minority.

PROTESTANTISM: THE RADICAL MOVEMENTS

We now come to phases of Protestantism which differed strikingly from the Lutheran and Reformed Churches. They may be called radical Protestantism. Radical Protestants departed more sharply than these others from what had been inherited from the Catholic Church. For the most part the Lutheran and Reformed Churches retained the post-Constantinian tradition of being territorial or folk churches. They were allied with the State and embodied the conviction that all within a political unit should conform to them. Where, in some countries, as in Hungary and France, they were minorities, they tended to be political entities, *imperia in imperio*. In contrast with the Lutheran and Reformed, few of the many movements embraced in radical Protestantism aspired to include in their membership all the inhabitants of a political unit. Several were missionary, seeking to win others, and some dreamed of carrying the Gospel to the entire world. Most of them insisted on going back to the New Testament for their patterns and said that entrance into the membership of the Church must be by a new birth wrought by the Holy Spirit, registered by the acceptance of God's grace by the individual, and attested by baptism.

Anabaptists constituted a majority of the radical Protestants. They were called Anabaptists because they insisted that the baptism of infants was not true baptism, that only believers should be baptized, and that if an individual had been baptized in infancy, after he had the experience of being justified by faith he should be re-baptized. Numbers of Anabaptists rejected war. All stood for strict ethical standards and, in general, excluded from their fellowship any who departed from these standards. Some of their leaders were men of education and included several former Roman Catholic priests. For the most part they attracted men and women from the lower economic and social strata. They were multiform, divided into many groups and movements, had no one geographical centre, and agreed on no one formulation of the faith. A few endeavoured to construct idealistic communities with the common ownership of property. They were most numerous in Germany, Switzerland, and the Low Countries, mainly within and immediately outside the former borders of the Roman Empire. The majority emerged in the sixteenth century and the fore part of the seventeenth, but some arose in the eighteenth century. Severe persecution by Roman Catholics, Lutherans, or Reformed eliminated most of them. They were regarded as destructive of orderly society. That fear was accentuated by an episode in Münster, a prominent city in Westphalia not far from the Dutch border. There in 1533 the Anabaptists gained control and attempted to set up a Christian commonwealth framed on their principles. Lutherans and Roman Catholics joined in a siege of the city, took it, and wiped out the defenders. Anabaptists suffered severely in the Thirty Years' War. Similar movements arose in England and eventually constituted fully half the Protestants in the United States.

The Mennonites constituted the majority of the Anabaptists who survived on the Continent of Europe. They took their name from Menno Simons (1496–1561), a native of the Low Countries who was a Roman Catholic priest and only slowly came to Anabaptist convictions. In his fortieth year he publicly renounced his Roman Catholic connexion and became an Anabaptist minister and itinerant missionary. A fugitive and an outlaw, eventually he was given haven by a nobleman in Holstein, in Denmark. His followers were strongest in North Germany and the Netherlands. They were tolerated in the United Netherlands, but on condition that they be inconspicuous in their assemblies.

Mystics were another wing of the Protestantism. The majority were individualistic and at the most gathered about themselves only small groups. The writings of some, such as the two Germans Sebastian Franck (1499–c. 1542) and Jacob Boehme (1575–1624), had a wide circulation far outside these groups.

Radical Protestantism included many humanists, whose approach was largely but by no means purely intellectual. The outstanding figures were from Latin Europe, chiefly from Spain and Italy. They either continued outwardly to conform to the Roman Catholic Church there or, when that was no longer possible, found refuge in countries on the northern borders of or completely outside Latin Europe. Much but not all of the humanistic radical Protestantism was anti-Trinitarian. It honoured Jesus. Some of its representatives made Him unique, but they would not subscribe to the Apostles' or Nicene Creed or to the Chalcedonian formula. A continuing movement was Socinianism, taking its name from two highly placed Italians from a humanist background, Laelius Socinus (1525–1562) and his nephew, Faustus Socinus (1539–1604). The latter became a leader of an anti-Trinitarian minority in Poland. For a time in the sixteenth century Protestantism seemed to be sweeping Poland. But its internal divisions, a Roman Catholic monarch, and Jesuit missionary activity nearly eliminated it. Socinians found refuge in Transylvania, and there the anti-Trinitarians, soon called "Unitarians," obtained state recognition and, with the Roman Catholics, Lutherans, and Reformed, were granted official status. In Holland Socinianism influenced the Remonstrants and the Mennonites.

THE RISE OF PIETISM

Akin to radical Protestantism but seldom issuing in distinct ecclesiastical bodies was Pietism. It arose late in the seventeenth century and was potent in the Lutheran and Reformed churches. It sprang chiefly from a revival after the deadening effects of the Thirty Years' War and the arid dogmation of that century, but had rootage in earlier Roman Catholic and Protestant mysticism. It made much of conscious conversion, high ethical standards, and the deepening of the spiritual life. It issued in missions, among both nominal Christians and non-Christians. For the most part those committed to it did not leave the state churches but gathered in small groups for the cultivation and propagation of the Christian life. Early leaders were two German Lutherans, Philip Jakob Spener (1635–1705) and August Hermann Francke (1663–1727). Late in the seventeenth and early in the eighteenth century for more than a generation Pietism had a major centre in Halle and in the theological faculty of the newly founded university in that city. Largely under Francke's leadership an orphanage, schools for boys and girls, a printing house, and a centre for missions to Jews were inaugurated and maintained at Halle. From Germany, and especially from Halle, Pietism took root in Denmark, Norway, Sweden, and Finland. It was also potent in Holland.

Nikolaus Ludwig, Graf (Count) von Zinzendorf (1700–1760), a godchild of Spener, was the major figure in the emergence of the Moravians as a missionary force. Refugees of the *Unitas Fratrum,* Bohemian and Moravian Protestants who traced their origin to John Hus and who had fled from the Roman Catholic persecution in their native land which accompanied and followed the Thirty Years' War, found haven on the estates of Zinzendorf. There, at Herrnhut, Zinzendorf gathered them in a village, became a bishop of their church, and through them inaugurated missions among non-Christians in several parts of the world.

PROTESTANTISM IN ENGLAND

In England the Reformation combined indigenous elements with a number of influences from the Continent. The indigenous elements were the waning aftermath of Lollardy, earnestly religious humanists, resentment against interference in Church life by the Popes, the decisive action of monarchs, and native leadership. Foreign contributions were the writings of Continental reformers, notably Luther and Calvin, and contacts with Reformed Protestantism and Anabaptist movements.

The English Reformation is of peculiar importance because of its eventual global impact. In the vast area embraced in the British Empire at one time or another it had effects which were world-wide, partly through emigration, as in the United States, Canada, Australia, New Zealand, and South Africa, partly through missions to non-Christian peoples in Asia, Africa, and the islands of the Pacific, and partly through repercussions in ostensibly Christian lands, including some of the Eastern Churches. Of the global impact we are to hear more in later chapters.

The Reformation began slightly later in England than on the Continent. The ground was made fallow by the remnants of Lollardy, chiefly among the poor and with outward conformity to the Roman Catholic Church, and partly by other movements of the late Middle Ages. Visitors from the Continent remarked that the rank and file of the populace were devout. The writings of Luther attracted attention in Oxford and Cambridge, but only among limited circles. A few leading humanists wished a deeper religious life but had no thought of breaking with the Roman Catholic Church. William Tyndale (c. 1494–1536), a priest who had been in both Oxford and Cambridge, using Greek, Hebrew, the Vulgate, the Septuagint, the Latin translation by Erasmus, and Luther's German Bible, made an English translation of the New Testament and of much of the Old Testament which were of substantial assistance to later translators. He moved in the direction of Protestantism and in the Low Countries was tried for heresy, condemned, and killed (1536).

The separation from Rome was primarily at the instance of Henry VIII, who reigned from 1509 to 1547. Henry was a younger son of Henry VII and, like many younger sons of the aristocracy, had been slated for a high ecclesiastical post. The death of his elder brother Arthur in 1502, when Henry was about eleven, made the latter the heir to the throne. At the age of fourteen Arthur had been married to Catherine, daughter of the powerful Ferdinand and Isabella of Spain. The match was purely for purposes of state. On Arthur's death Henry VII, still for political reasons, had the future Henry VIII betrothed to Catherine. Since canon law forbade a man to marry his deceased brother's wife, an accommodating Pope granted the requisite dispensation and in due time marriage followed. Catherine bore Henry several children but all except one, Mary, died in infancy. Henry desired a male heir. He fell in love with Anne Boleyn and she would have none of his favours unless she was made Queen. Henry wished to have his marriage with Catherine annulled, but to this the Pope would not consent. Catherine was the niece of the Emperor Charles V. The Pope would scarcely have dared risk the enmity of the most powerful monarch in Europe for what was from the standpoint of canon law a dubious act. Long negotiations failed to obtain Papal approval. By successive steps Henry reduced the clergy of his realm to submission, and in 1534 a subservient Parliament declared that the King "is and ought to be the supreme head of the Church." In 1535 Henry announced himself the "supreme head on earth of the English Church." In the meantime the Pope had excommunicated him. The breach with Rome was complete. A few of Henry's subjects refused to acknowledge the royal supremacy over the Church and paid for their temerity with their lives. Among them were several Carthusians, the upright John Fisher, Bishop of Rochester and cardinal, and Thomas Moore, a former chancellor of the realm and friend of Henry. Henry was now master of both Church and State. He was one of the autocratic monarchs who were emerging in Europe.

In his ecclesiastical policies Henry had the support of Thomas Cranmer (1489–1556). Cranmer was a younger son of a farmer, a graduate of Cambridge, and a deeply religious priest. Without seeking it, Cranmer had come to the favourable attention of Henry by a suggestion for effecting the King's desired separation from Catherine. He seems to have been sincerely convinced of a monarch's divine right to absolute authority over the Church as well as the State. In 1532 Henry appointed him Archbishop of Canterbury. Papal approval was obtained and Cranmer was duly consecrated. One of his early acts was to nullify Henry's marriage to Catherine, but with the stipulation that Mary was legitimate.

Under Henry VIII the separation of the Church of England from Rome did not entail significant doctrinal changes. Henry was proud of his orthodoxy and earlier had affixed his name to a book which professed to refute Luther and had won for him from the Pope the designation of Defender of the Faith. In 1539 under authority of Henry Parliament passed a statement endorsing transubstantiation, the celibacy of the clergy, private masses, the observance of the vows of chastity taken by men and women, and auricular confession, and declaring that Communion in both kinds was not necessary. Although far from exemplary in his private and public life, Henry was regular in private confession and in hearing mass.

However, highly important innovations were made. All the monasteries were dissolved and their properties were confiscated. The chief shrines of the saints were dismantled and despoiled of their treasures. Some of the proceeds of the expropriations were assigned to national defence, to the creation of new dioceses, to the universities, and to various philanthropic purposes, but the larger proportion went to Henry and his favourites. Priests were commanded to set up a large English Bible in such manner that it might be read by all who wished.

At Henry's death his only surviving son came to the throne as Edward VI. He was then in his eleventh year and died in 1553, before he was sixteen, but not before he had given indications of having a mind of his own. Both he and his advisers moved in the direction of Protestantism. Images were removed from the churches, chantries were abolished, the marriage of priests was legalized, and several outstanding Continental reformers were welcomed and given important posts. In 1549 and 1552 Acts of Uniformity were passed which required the clergy to use the Book of Common Prayer. That book was the work of a commission headed by Cranmer. It utilized much of the liturgy and many of the prayers which had come down from the past. A second edition moved further in the direction of Protestantism.

Edward VI was followed by Mary, the daughter of Catherine. Deeply religious and loyal to the old church, she undertook to bring England back into communion with the Church of Rome. In the five years of her reign (1553-1558) she succeeded in restoring the connexion with the See of Peter and in renewing some of the practices which had been abolished in the preceding two reigns. About three hundred whom she and her advisers regarded as obnoxious heretics were sent to the stake, including three bishops, Latimer, Ridley, and Cranmer, burned at Oxford.

Mary in turn was succeeded by Elizabeth, daughter of Henry VIII and Anne Boleyn. During Elizabeth's long and eventful reign (1558-1603) the Church of England was given the form which, in its main features, it was to preserve into the twentieth century. How much personal religious conviction Elizabeth possessed is uncertain. Like her father, she was masterful. She was intent on holding her realm together and in order to succeed needed the loyalty of the majority of her subjects. In 1559 an obedient Parliament passed the Act of Supremacy. The Act again severed the tie with Rome. It made the Queen "the supreme governor" of her realm in ecclesiastical as well as secular matters, but it did not renew the title of the "supreme head" of the Church of England. In what is usually called the Elizabethan settlement, the effort was made to steer a middle course between the Catholic heritage and Protestantism. The apostolic succession was perpetuated through bishops who had served under Henry VIII and Edward VI and so directly or indirectly had received it from the undivided Catholic Church. An Act of Uniformity was passed which, among other features, restored with modifications the second edition of the Book of Common Prayer of Edward VI. Thirty-nine Articles of Religion were issued defining the faith as held by the Church of England. They modified the Forty-two Articles framed under Edward VI. Scholars defended the Church of England as thus constituted. Especially notable was Richard Hooker's massive *Laws of Ecclesiastical Polity,* left uncompleted by the death of the author (1600). It became a bulwark of the Church of England against Roman Catholics and the more extreme Protestants.

Dissatisfaction with the Elizabethan settlement was marked. On the one hand, the Roman Catholics, from headquarters on the Continent and representing the revival of the Catholic Reformation, sought the restoration of the tie with Rome. More numerous were the Puritans, who wished to "purify" the Church of England of what they regarded as the corrupting survivals of the Roman connexion. The Puritans did not fully agree among themselves. The more extreme wished the Church of England to be reorganized on the pattern of the Reformed Churches, with a Presbyterian government. Even more radical were the Separatists or Independents. They were akin to the Anabaptists and believed in "gathered" churches, not made up of all the inhabitants of a given area, but only of those who were consciously Christian.

Elizabeth's death brought to the throne James Stuart—James VI of Scotland and James I of England. He was a great-grandson of Margaret, daughter of Henry VII, whom that farseeing monarch had married to a king of Scotland. He had been reared a Presbyterian, but favoured episcopacy on the principle of "no bishop, no king." He continued the Elizabethan settlement, including the banishment of Roman Catholic priests. Puritans increased. Radical Protestants of varied views grew, although still small minorities. Chief among them were still the Independents. The Baptists appeared, distinguished from the Independents by their rejection of infant baptism and their insistence that baptism was only for conscious believers. The major religious achievement of the reign was what has been known as the Authorized Version of the Bible. It was prepared by a company of scholars appointed by James who went to the original languages and the best texts then available and took advantage of previous translations. The result was a translation which long remained standard and which had much influence on the English language and English literature.

James I was followed by his son, Charles I (reigned 1625–1649). Handsome, pure in his private life, and deeply religious, Charles was convinced that he ruled by divine right and that, although seeking the welfare of his subjects, he must not be controlled by them and need not keep his word, even when solemnly plighted, if it conflicted with his prerogatives. He staunchly supported the Church of England, but was firmly against the Puritans. In his ecclesiastical policies he was ably supported by William Laud (1573–1645), Bishop of London (1628–1633) and then Archbishop of Canterbury (1633–1645). Laud endeavoured to root out corruption in the Church. He also took vigorous measures against both Roman Catholics and Puritans and reintroduced some features in public worship which the Puritans abhorred as savouring of Rome.

In 1640 conflict arose between Charles and Parliament which came to a climax in civil war. On the one side were the King, most of the nobility, and those who held to the established order and the Catholic tradition in the Church of England. On the other side were Parliament, the growing urban middle classes, many of the lesser gentry, the Puritans, and the extreme Protestants. The religious factor was important, but the basic issue was political—whether there was a body of law which the King must obey. During the struggle Laud was imprisoned and after a long delay executed. To advise it on religious questions Parliament called the Westminster Assembly of clergy and laity, the majority of them Puritans; the most enduring accomplishments were what are usually called the Westminster Confession of Faith and the shorter and longer catechisms. Setting forth the Reformed system of theology and church government, they were widely adopted by Presbyterian churches in Great Britain and America and into the twentieth century continued to be standard in these bodies. The civil war ended in victory for Parliament and the trial and execution of Charles.

Now followed the Commonwealth, headed by Oliver Cromwell (1599–1658), who had emerged as the leading general of the Parliamentary forces. As Lord Protector he governed England from 1649 to his death. Cromwell sought to make England a truly Christian country. He was confronted with many movements on the extreme wing of Protestantism—among them Levellers, Diggers, Fifth Monarchy Men, and Quakers. Quakers, or as they preferred to be called, the Society of Friends, were founded by George Fox (1624–1691), a younger contemporary of Cromwell. Fox believed that men should be guided by the Inner Light, protested against formalism in religion, advocated an extreme democracy which would put men and women on a basis of equality, stressed simplicity in dress, food, and speech, opposed all participation in war, and insisted on truth-speaking. Even more than the other radical groups, the Quakers were popularly deemed enemies of society and were persecuted. Cromwell wished a national Church, supported by the State and tithes, but without bishops or the Book of Common Prayer. Yet he desired toleration of all Protestants except Quakers and permitted Episcopalians to worship, but only quietly. Even Roman Catholics were not molested if they did not disturb the public peace.

The Commonwealth had the support of only a minority. Within two years after the death of Oliver Cromwell a son of Charles I returned (1660) from exile as Charles II. In the reaction from the Commonwealth, episcopacy was restored, the Book of Common Prayer was ordered read in all the churches, and discriminatory legislation was passed against dissenters. Charles died in 1685 and was followed by his brother, James II. In his last hours Charles had been received into the Roman Catholic Church. James was an avowed adherent of that form of the faith.

During the Stuart restoration and in spite of adverse legislation, extreme Protestantism survived. One of its most famous representatives was a Baptist, John Bunyan (1628–1688), whose

The Pilgrim's Progress, begun while he was imprisoned for preaching in violation of the law, became one of the classics of the Christian life as held by thousands of Protestants. John Milton (1608–1674) had been a secretary to Cromwell but escaped the scaffold at the Restoration and completed *Paradise Lost,* presenting the human drama as conceived by Christians.

Widespread fear that James II would return England to the Roman Catholic fold led to his expulsion from the country (1688). He was followed on the throne by his Protestant daughter, Anne, and her consort, William of Orange. England was now clearly committed to Protestantism. The Church of England had both Catholic and Protestant elements, each represented in its clergy and constituency. Legislation against Protestant dissenters was lightened but not fully removed.

After the religious dissensions of the fore part of the seventeenth century, a period followed of partial lassitude and of impatience with theological and ecclesiastical controversy. Christianity was far from dead. John Locke (1653–1704), reared in a staunchly Protestant home and continuing to believe in God and revelation and having a deep reverence for the Bible, espoused religious toleration but not to atheists or Roman Catholics. His writings, rooted largely in his Puritan background, were major contributions to democracy as it developed in Britain and America. In spite of their minority status and restrictions placed on them, Protestant dissenters continued vigorous, as is seen, among other ways, in hymns which have since been cherished by the English-speaking world. Isaac Watts (1674–1748), for example, could write "Jesus shall reign where'er the sun doth his successive journeys run" in a day when it seemed improbable that the Gospel as he understood it would prevail even in England.

THE CATHOLIC REFORMATION

As we have suggested, the Catholic Reformation first arose in Spain. Unified at the close of the fifteenth century, at the outset by the marriage of Ferdinand and Isabella, in the sixteenth century Spain was the most powerful of the absolute monarchies of Western Europe. It reached the apex of its might under Philip II (reigned 1556–1598), great-grandson of Ferdinand and Isabella and son of the Holy Roman Emperor Charles V. The period during and after that reign saw the religious movement of which the Catholic Reformation was an expression reach its height. The same era witnessed the peak of Spanish creative genius in literature, art, and colonial expansion. Whether any causal connexion can be proved or whether all proceeded from other factors than appear on the surface is highly doubtful.

The most prominent figure in the Catholic Reformation and with prolonged and continuing influence was Ignatius Loyola (c. 1491–1556). A contemporary of Martin Luther, like Luther Loyola came to spiritual insight and devotion through deep agony which left its mark on the movement he founded. To both, Christ was the centre of their faith and devotion. Unlike Luther, sprung from peasant stock, a priest and monk who eventually denounced monasticism, Loyola was a scion of the nobility, at the outset a layman and a soldier, and was creator of the most widely influential monastic movement which emerged in the Roman Catholic Church after the Middle Ages. During a prolonged and painful convalescence from a wound received in war, Loyola began his momentous spiritual pilgrimage. That pilgrimage led him to dedication as a soldier of Christ. Out of the searing inner struggle which followed came the beginnings of the *Spiritual Exercises* through which he disciplined and nourished his life. Intent on helping those about him to full commitment to Christ, Loyola began giving the *Exercises* to others. Fearful of heresy from a theologically uneducated layman, the ecclesiastical authorities forbade him to continue teaching until he had gone through a course of study. As an obedient son of the Church, Loyola went to the University of Salamanca and then to the University of Paris, the most renowned centre of theological learning of his day. He was in Paris for seven years and received an M.A. There he gathered about him in intimate friendship a circle of students and younger teachers, won them to complete dedication to Christ, and put them through the *Spiritual Exercises*. In 1534 a little band of seven took the three-fold vows of chastity, poverty, and obedience. Eventually they made their way to Rome. Before reaching the Eternal City Ignatius and several of the others were ordained priests. In Rome, after some delay, they obtained Papal permission (1539) to constitute themselves an order, the Society (originally the Company) of Jesus. Ignatius was elected the first General. The Society of Jesus attracted many who were moved by the religious awakening of the day. Before his death Loyola saw it grow to a membership of about a thousand. The Jesuits were in several countries in Western Europe, established themselves in universities, and sought to convert Protestants and to deepen the spiritual and moral life of nominal Catholics. Typical of the revival of which they were the spear-head, the third General of the Society was Francis Borgia, a great-grandson of the notorious Pope Alexander VI. Under the direction of Loyola he had been an itinerant preacher in Spain. Possessed of marked administrative gifts, he has often been regarded as the second founder of the Society. The Jesuits improved education, brought many Protestants to the Catholic faith, and initiated extensive missions among non-Christians.

Contemporary with the origin and growth of the Society of Jesus were Spanish mystics whose example and writings did much to deepen the life of Roman Catholics. Outstanding were Teresa (or Theresa) of Avila (1515–1582) and her younger contemporary, John of the Cross (1542–1605).

Out of the Spanish Reformation issued, as we shall see, a vast missionary movement which carried the faith to the Americas, Asia, and many of the islands of the sea. We must also note that it strengthened the Inquisition and sought to eradicate dissent in Spain, as embodied in Protestants, Jews, and Moslems. Through a conviction which was compounded of religious zeal and economic, cultural, and political motives, incipient Protestantism was stamped out, the Marranos, nominally Christian converts from Judaism, either were driven into exile or secretly preserved their ancestral rites, and the Moriscos, proselytes from the widely prevalent Islam, were expelled from the country (1609).

The other chief radiating centre of the Catholic Reformation was in Italy, where the corruption against which the reform was directed was as marked as in any other country. As we have noted, the corruption had not been complete. In Italy were Christian humanists; Savonarola had borne his witness; the titanic Michelangelo, who had been deeply impressed by Savonarola, maintained a committed life and dedicated his talent to the faith. As in earlier centuries, the tide of reform gave birth to new monastic movements and to the elevation of the character of some of the older orders. Also as in previous centuries when fresh vigour was emerging in the Roman Catholic Church, some of these new movements made original approaches. The Oratory of Divine Love, a confraternity rather than an order, had its beginnings about the year 1497, when Alexander VI was on the Papal throne. Its members were highly placed, worked for the moral reform of the Church, and visited hospitals and prisons. The Theatines, consecrated to the cross of Christ and taking their name from the episcopal see in which their first head was bishop, had one of its sources in the Oratory of Divine Love. The Theatines sought the reform of the priests who ministered to the rank and file of the laity. Papal approval was given in 1524, and the Theatines rapidly grew in numbers and spread to other countries. The Regular Clerics of St. Paul, better known as the Barnabites, were founded in 1530 by three Italians of noble birth. They sought a revival of the care of souls by the clergy and set the example through catechizing, hearing confessions, and conducting missions. The Congregation of the Oratory, begun by Philip Neri- (1515–1595), a Florentine who received his early instruction in the Dominican house with which Savonarola had been connected, had its inception in Rome in 1556 but did not obtain official sanction until 1575. It worked to raise the level of the moral and religious life of the people

of Rome, widely know for their laxity. To this end it devised
novel methods. Among them were evening meetings for prayer,
reading the Bible and the Fathers, and lectures and sermons
of an informal kind. Hymns and music were prominent. Pales-
trina (1526–1594) contributed to them and in this and other
ways set a new standard for the music of the Church. The Congregation of the Oratory contributed to the development of the
oratorio, a drama, usually on a Scriptural theme, set to music,
and spread in Italy, Spain, and France. The Ursulines, a new
type of congregation of women, began in the last decade of the
fifteenth century and had teaching as their primary function.

The chief reform of Italian origin in the older orders issued
in the Capuchins. The Capuchins desired to conform strictly to
the rule which Francis of Assisi gave to the Order of Brothers
Minor and in time were made a distinct family within the
Franciscans. They attracted many who were eager to live the
full Christian life in unselfish service and by the end of the
sixteenth century had spread through much of the Roman
Catholic portions of Europe. By their poverty and austerity,
convincing evidence of their sincerity and devotion to Christ,
they made a wide appeal. They devoted themselves to the poor,
preaching, catechizing, hearing confessions, serving the sick, and
giving themselves to the sufferers from the many epidemics which
swept across Europe. Among other achievements they made
many converts from Protestantism.

The reform movement was given leadership by several Italian
bishops. Prominent among them were. men who renounced the
prevalent custom of drawing revenues from ecclesiastical posts
whose duties they did not perform. One was Giberti who,
drawn into the circle of the Oratory of Divine Love, took up
residence in the see of Verona of which he had been absentee
bishop. There he began a strictly ascetic life; he went from village
to village examining the priests, reconciling enemies, and caring
for the poor. He improved the services in the parish churches,
reformed both the secular and the regular clergy, and encouraged
confraternities for the care of the poor. Even more notable was

Charles Borromeo (1538–1584). Nephew of Pope Pius IV, at the age of twenty-two he had been made a cardinal, was entrusted with important administrative duties, and became the leading official in the Papal court. He was appointed Archbishop of Milan but employed the revenues of the see and of other benefices to maintain a life of splendour in Rome. Yet he won admiration for his humility and temperate life. After aiding the election of the great reforming Pope Pius V, he went to Milan and gave himself to promoting reform. He travelled through his diocese, improving decorum and dignity in public worship and cleansing the monasteries and religious confraternities. He administered relief of the poor, worked for conciliation in labour disputes, emphasized frequent Communion, established homes for beggars, and did much for the education of the clergy. During an epidemic of the plague, in complete disregard of his own safety, he gave directions for the care of the sick and the burial of the dead, sold his plate to aid the sufferers, and had his tapestries made into clothing for the destitute. Never sparing himself, he died in his mid-forties.

In the fore part of the eighteenth century new congregations of religious continued to emerge. In 1732 the Redemptorists (officially the Congregation of the Most Holy Redeemer) were founded for the purpose of preaching "the word of God to the poor." In 1741 Papal approval was given to the Passionists, begun in 1720 and combining the contemplative life of the Carthusians with the active missionary life of the Jesuits.

The Catholic Reformation was not confined to the deep Latin Europe—Spain, Portugal, and Italy. It was felt in Switzerland, Germany, Poland, and Hungary. France was late in experiencing its full impact, but in time what was sometimes called "the eldest daughter of the Church" was swept into the current. The Jesuits, the Capuchins, and the Oratory were influential. New movements were born. Especially notable was the Congregation of the Priests of the Mission, also called the Lazarists or the Vincentians. Its founder was Vincent de Paul (1576 or 1580 to 1660). An association of seculars, not regulars, it sought the nurture of the Catholic masses and the conversion of Protestants, conducted seminaries to train priests, and sent missionaries to other countries. In 1643 John Eudes (1601–1680) inaugurated what were known as the Eudists, more formally the Society of Jesus and Mary. They maintained seminaries for the training of priests and conducted missions. Out of the Catholic Reformation in France came great mystics, among them Pierre de Bérulle (1575–1629), who sought to subject himself fully to the Word made flesh and to the Virgin Mary, and his disciple Charles de Condren (1588–1641). Both contributed to a growing popular devotion to the Child Jesus and the Sacred Heart of Jesus. A great master of the life of the spirit, Francis de Sales (1567–1622) had marked influence on Vincent de Paul.

As had been true in the tenth-century nadir, the reform movement was late in placing its representatives on the Papal throne. For a brief time, in 1522–1523, the downward trend in the Papacy seemed about to be arrested. To break a deadlock in the college of cardinals over the election, a native of Utrecht, a former tutor of Charles V, was chosen and took the title of Adrian VI. Scholarly, ascetic, an experienced administrator, by his vigorous attempts at reform he might in time have overcome the stubborn opposition, but he died after less than two years in office. Incidentally, he was the latest non-Italian Pope.

In the four reigns which followed, halting progress was made. By the election of Paul IV, who held the chair of Peter from 1555 to 1559, the reform party appeared to have triumphed. Paul IV had been a member of the Oratory of Divine Love and the first head of the Theatines. He dreamed of restoring the Papacy to the commanding position attained under Hildebrand and Innocent III, but that was impossible in the Europe of his day. He achieved some needed reforms, but he appointed unworthy relatives to high posts and his high-handed rigour and lack of prudence aroused much needless antagonism. In his initial years in office the next Pope, Pius IV (reigned 1559–1565) maintained high standards, but later he scandalized some of the reformers by succumbing to the ease and the pleasures which had brought obloquy to his office. Pius V, whose pontificate was approximately the same length (1566–1572), a Dominican who continued in the Vatican his ascetic way of life and made the Papal court a model in morals, marked the apex of reform in the Papacy. He firmly avoided all nepotism, gave no special favours to his order, and discouraged animal-baiting, profanity, and prostitution. In his efforts to curb heresy he stiffened the Inquisition. He was responsible for a new catechism and a revised breviary and collaborated with Borromeo. He had a major share in assembling the naval forces which inflicted the decisive check on the Turks in the Battle of Lepanto. His stature in the Roman Catholic Church is seen in the fact that he was eventually canonized (1712). The last earlier Pope to be so recognized was Gregory X, of the thirteenth century, and the only one of his successors to be granted the title of saint was Pius X, of the fore part of the twentieth century.

Of the men who later wore the tiara in the sixteenth, seventeenth, and eighteenth centuries none reached the stature of Pius V, but none disgraced the Church as had the Pontiffs of the tenth, fifteenth, and fore part of the sixteenth centuries. Several aided their relatives in acquiring wealth, but the majority were virtuous in their private lives, several laboured to improve the moral quality of the clergy, and some encouraged the extensive missionary activity of which we are to speak in a moment. Nevertheless all were caught in the toils of European dynastic rivalries and the tangled skein of Italian politics. In country after country, their administrative power was curtailed by the control of the Church by the ruling dynasties. In France, Spain, Portugal, and the Hapsburg lands appointments to the episcopate and other ecclesiastical dignities were made by the monarchs, and no Papal decree could be recognized except with the consent of the State.

An outstanding feature of the Catholic Reformation was the Council of Trent. Meeting intermittently from 1545 to 1563 and not always at Trent, it has been regarded by Roman Catholics as the nineteenth of the series which began at Nicaea in 325. Some Protestant reformers had wished such a council.

Several of the German princes, troubled by conflicts between Protestants and Roman Catholics, hoped that an Ecumenical Council would heal the breach. From time to time the Emperor Charles V urged the Pope to call one, but at other times his friction with a Pope made him less eager. The ambitious rival of the Emperor, Francis I of France, blew hot and cold as what he deemed his political interests dictated. The degree to which the Pope should control the Council was important. The Spanish, French, and northern bishops resented Papal claims and advocated restricting the authority of the Pontiffs.

The Catholic reformers and the Pope had their way. Definitions on dogma ruled out specific Protestant positions, such as justification by faith alone and the priesthood of all believers. The Council slammed the door on those Protestants who had hoped that by stating a position which would be as irenic as was consistent with their convictions accomodation could be achieved with the old Church. Extensive legislation was enacted to remove the evils that had compromised the Church's mission. Earlier decrees were renewed requiring bishops to reside in their sees. Pluralism and absenteeism were either forbidden or closely restricted. Much attention was given to education in preparation for the priesthood. Ordination to the diaconate was forbidden until the candidate had reached his twenty-third year and to the priesthood before the age of twenty-five. The effective power of the bishops in their respective dioceses was augmented. Better supervision of the monasteries was prescribed, either by placing them under a bishop or by organizing them into provinces or general chapters and requiring the heads of the orders to visit their houses. Bishops were ordered to visit all the charges in their dioceses at least once in two years, either in person or through representatives delegated by them. Parish priests were commanded to preach and explain the sacraments in the vernacular. The authority of the Roman Pontiff was confirmed by the provision that the decrees of the Council were not to be binding until the Pope had officially approved them. The Pope was expressly declared to be the vicar of God and Jesus Christ, and all patriarchs, primates, archbishops, and bishops were to promise obedience to him. Thus the Roman Catholic Church put its house in order, excluded the dissidents, and sought to be more effective in the care of souls. The Council of Trent ushered in a new age in the Roman Catholic Church. Not until the mid-twentieth century did voices within the church speak hopefully of a post-Trentine era.

The Catholic Reformation was also the Counter-Reformation, for much of its energy was directed to curbing the advance of Protestantism and to winning back individuals and regions which had been lost to that wing of the faith. Much was accomplished by zealous missionaries, notably the Jesuits and the Capuchins. The Counter-Reformation was important in several bitter armed conflicts, notably the Thirty Years' War (1618–1648). By the end of that exhausting struggle the Counter-Reformation had spent its force. The Peace of Westphalia not only fixed the geographic border in Germany between Protestantism and the Roman Catholic Church where, with relatively slight modifications, it remained beyond the middle of the twentieth century. It was also an unintentional recognition that in Europe in their efforts to supplant each other the two wings of Western Christianity had reached a stalemate.

Retreat and Advance of The Eastern Churches

While the great surge of life was re-invigorating Christianity in Western Europe, in Eastern Europe and Western Asia the record was a contrast of stagnation and advance.

In the widely flung Ottoman Empire, committed as it was to Islam, nothing but defensive action could be expected of the Churches. That empire did not reach its height until the second half of the sixteenth century. As we have noted, the Turks administered the Christian minorities as separate entities. The Churches had a kind of ghetto existence, attempting to preserve themselves by resisting change in liturgy, theology, or customs. For a few years in the early part of the sixteenth century Cyril

Lucar (1572–1637), who became Patriarch of Constantinople in 1621, worked for the moral and spiritual improvement of the Orthodox Church. He entered into correspondence with church leaders in non-Roman Catholic Western Europe and sent young men to study in Protestant schools. A confession of faith which he either wrote or endorsed contained Protestant elements. The Jesuits, intent upon bringing the Orthodox Church into communion with the Roman Catholic Church, offered implacable resistance. Eventually the Sultan had Lucar strangled, and his views were condemned by a synod of his church. The Uniate Churches, gathered from the Eastern Churches into communion with Rome, continued, and some grew. Roman Catholic missionaries ranged through the East, seeking to augment the Uniate bodies. But for the most part the latter remained minorities, also with a kind of ghetto life.

The Gregorian (Armenian) Church displayed marked vitality. In the seventeenth century a striking awakening was seen. It began in the monasteries, and from them monks went to the rank and file, preaching, founding schools, seeking to reconcile enemies, to improve morals, and to eradicate superstition. One of the reformers eventually (1629) became Catholicos or Patriarch of the entire church. Armenian merchants ranged far in Western and Central Asia. In at least one city in Persia they constituted a centre noted for its religious devotion and its learning.

The sixteenth and seventeenth centuries witnessed important developments in the Russian Orthodox Church. As we have seen, in 1547 Ivan IV (1530–1584), known not unfittingly as "the Terrible," had himself crowned Tsar (Caesar) and thus professed to be the successor of the Christian Emperors who had ruled in Constantinople but had now been displaced by the Ottoman Turks. Ivan greatly extended the territory over which he ruled. Since some of the Russian Orthodox were claiming that Moscow, Ivan's capital, was the third Rome, they insisted that, to parallel Ivan's assumption of the imperial title, the head of the Russian Church should have the designation of

Patriarch. After long negotiations, in 1589 the Patriarch of Constantinople gave his consent, and the next year a council of the other Orthodox Patriarchs held in Constantinople confirmed the approval. After the see of Moscow was raised to the Patriarchate, the ecclesiastical structure of the Russian Orthodox Church was enlarged. Four sees became metropolitanates, several bishoprics became archbishoprics, and a number of new dioceses were created.

Soon after its recognition by the occupants of the other Orthodox Patriarchates, the Moscow Patriarchate became a rallying centre against foreign invasion. In what was known as "the Time of Trouble" which followed the extinction of the ruling dynasty for lack of a male heir (1598), the realm was torn by civil strife, and Poles and Swedes threatened Russian independence. The Russian Orthodox Church, led by the Patriarch, headed the nationalist resistance. The Patriarch was incarcerated by the Poles and died in prison. When, in 1613, the first Tsar of a new dynasty (the Romanov) was brought to the throne, his father, as Patriarch, closely coöperated with him; together they restored order and gave stability to the new ruling line.

A generation after the Time of Trouble Nikon, who became Patriarch of Moscow in 1652, sought to cleanse the Russian Orthodox Church of what he regarded as corruptions and weaknesses. In the effort to free the Church from local control which he believed made it subservient to secular influences he augmented the power of the bishops over the parish priests. He endeavoured to restore clerical discipline, which had suffered in the Time of Trouble. He encouraged preaching. He stood against the Tsar's control of synods, ordinations, and ecclesiastical courts. For some time a revision had been in progress of the books employed in the services to bring them into conformity with the Greek originals. Nikon insisted on the use of the revised versions. For about six years Nikon appeared to be attaining his goal, but as was to be expected, he met vigorous opposition from many of the nobility, clergy, and monks. About

1658 he lost the support of the Tsar. In protest he retired to a monastery, but without resigning. In 1666, after many complications and delays, a synod formally deposed him and sent him into exile. He died fifteen years later (1681).

As a sequel to the controversy a substantial minority withdrew from the Russian Orthodox Church. The ostensible reason was protest against the use of the revised service books. The synod that deposed Nikon avoided what to him had been the central issue, the control of the Church by the State, but it endorsed some of the innovations he had made, including the revised books. The opponents held to the old ways. They maintained that to depart from the familiar texts was to adopt the "errors" of the later Greeks who, wandering from the true faith, had become apostate. They were known as the Old Believers, Old Ritualists, or *Raskolniks*. *Raskolnik*, derived from a word meaning division or schism, could be applied to all who withdrew from the Russian Orthodox Church. The Old Believers were mainly from among the underprivileged, rebels against the upper ranks of society. They were largely monks, parish priests, and common people. No bishops joined them. They were visited with severe persecution but persisted into the twentieth century. Eventually they split into various groups. As the priests who had sided with them died, they could fill the gaps only with priests who joined them from the official church. Some refused to accept such priests and were known as the *Bezpopovsty*, or Priestless. They, too, divided into many sects. The *Popovsty*, or Priested, accepted clergy from the Orthodox on condition that only service books would be used which did not contain the changes endorsed by Nikon.

In addition to the Old Believers other dissenting religious movements arose. Some outwardly conformed to the Orthodox Church but had secret meetings. Persecuted, they were driven underground.

A few decades after the final deposition of Nikon, the Russian Orthodox Church was reduced to the status which that

Patriarch had persistently opposed, subordination to the State. The change was the work of Peter the Great. Masterful, after the manner of contemporary absolute monarchs of the Western Europe which he had opportunity to observe in his sojourn in that region, Peter was determined to bring the Church under his control. When, in 1700, the Patriarch died, the Tsar saw to it that no successor was appointed. In 1721 he created as a substitute a Spiritual College, later called the Holy Synod, completely subordinate to him. Although he commanded the laity to attend church every Sunday and feast day and to make at least an annual confession, he restricted the number of the clergy, tended to make the parish priests an hereditary class, regulated the interior life of the monasteries, and insisted that the Church keep out of civil affairs. He thus paralleled developments in Roman Catholic and Protestant countries in Western Europe.

In the sixteenth and seventeenth centuries and the beginning of the eighteenth century the Russian Orthodox Church both gained and lost territory. Partly at the instance of the Tsars and partly through the labours of zealous monks the borders of that church were pushed northward to the White Sea and the coasts of the Arctic, southward to the Caspian Sea, and eastward across the Urals. The losses were in the west. In the sixteenth century the Catholic Reformation gave support to attempts to win Orthodox to the Roman Catholic Church. Jesuits maintained efforts at penetration and conversion and were backed by Polish monarchs. The Poles were moving away from early Protestant tendencies and, in part because of Jesuit missions, were becoming loyal Roman Catholics. Their Kings used the Roman Catholic Church to extend their rule on their eastern borders. The Lithuanians, also Roman Catholics, aided. In 1570 the Jesuits opened a college in Vilna, on the Lithuanian and Polish border, which attracted sons of the Orthodox nobility. Near the end of the sixteenth century, under pressure from the Poles and Lithuanians, large numbers of Orthodox affiliated with Rome as Uniates, keeping their distinctive rites and customs.

World-wide Extension of Christianity

Accompanying the amazing voyages, commerce, and conquests of Europeans which began at the close of the sixteenth century and continued until the beginning of the twentieth was a territorial expansion of Christianity not only unequalled in its earlier history but more extensive than any other religion had achieved. Until the nineteenth century that expansion was chiefly made by the Roman Catholic Church and in connexion with the empire-building of the Spaniards and the Portuguese and the extended commerce of the Portuguese. The French shared, but to a smaller degree. Protestant expansion began more tardily and by the mid-eighteenth century had barely begun.

Acting on the conviction that the Popes as vicars of Christ had authority over all mankind and could assign the civil rule over all peoples to whom they would, in 1480 the Pope granted to Portugal a monopoly of trade, colonization, and political dominion in non-Christian lands from West Africa to the East Indies. In 1493 Alexander VI drew a line one hundred leagues west of the Azores from the north pole to the south pole, and handed over to Spain North America and most of South America and to Portugal Africa, Asia, and the eastern coast of South America.

The expansion of the Roman Catholic wing of the faith was augmented and its character was largely determined by the Catholic Reformation. As we have seen, the Catholic Reformation had its inception in Spain a few years before the voyages of Columbus inaugurated the vast Spanish empire in the Americas. That empire eventually included much of the West Indies, the more thickly peopled regions of South America, almost all Central America, all of Florida, Mexico, California, and Texas, and what are now Arizona, New Mexico, and a part of Colorado. It also spanned the Pacific and embraced the Philippines. The initial impact of the Spaniards in the West Indies and parts of the mainland was marked by incredible cruelty and ruthless exploitation. Most of the original settlers had come in search of wealth. To obtain it, either from mines or plantations, labour was essential. The *conquistadores* scorned soiling their hands or compromising their dignity with the use of tools. They therefore enslaved the Indians or relied upon Negro slaves.

However, from the outset an avowed purpose of Spanish exploration and conquests was the salvation of souls and the temporal and eternal welfare of the Indians. Isabella, Charles V, and Philip II, influenced by the Catholic Reformation, endeavoured to safeguard the Indians and to provide them with religious instruction and clerical care. *The Laws of the Indies* were extraordinarily humane and sought to protect the interests of the aborigines. But America was far away, and in spite of their theoretical absolutism the Spanish monarchs had difficulty in making their will effective. The prior of the first contingent of Dominicans to reach the New World led in denouncing the cruelties inflicted on the Indians, was imprisoned by the irate settlers, repeatedly wrote to Rome, and eventually went in person to Europe to protest the exploitation of the aborigines. He was at least partly responsible for the bulls of the worldly-minded and luxurious Paul III on behalf of the Indians.

The most famous champion of the Indians was Bartolomé de Las Casas (1474–1566). Symbolic of the role of the Christian conscience in the impact of one race upon another is the fact that Las Casas seems to have been the first Christian clergyman ordained in the Americas. Slow in protesting the evils which he saw about him, when his conscience awoke he became the outstanding leader in the struggle. Again and again he journeyed to Spain to prod the monarchs to action. He found fellowship with the Dominicans and joined them. When the laws demanded by the situation were enacted, he was fearless in having them promulgated in America. To demonstrate that the unarmed way of love was practicable, he headed a mission to an Indian tribe famous for killing Europeans and, without supporting troops, won them to the Christian faith. He refused appointment to an archbishopric which carried as much prestige

as any other in the Americas and at the age of seventy accepted
instead a see which was said to be the poorest in the New
World. There in the attempt to make the protective laws effective he met determined opposition from laity and clergy, for
with other Europeans they believed the laws would obstruct
their livelihood. Returning to Spain, until an advanced age,
supported by the Dominicans, he continued to espouse the cause
of the Indians and resisted theologians who declared that the
Pope and the Kings of Spain had the right to subdue by war
the peoples of the New World.

Similarly the Christian conscience sought to ameliorate the
lot of the Negroes. For example, a Jesuit, Pedro Claver (1581–
1654), for four decades ministered physically and spiritually to
the Negro slaves when they arrived in Cartagena, and made
long journeys into the interior to visit the blacks in the mines
and on the plantations. He braved the enmity of slave-dealers
and slave-owners and is said to have baptized more than three
hundred thousand.

In the meantime the conversion of the majority of the Indians was accomplished. In centres of pre-Columbian civilizations with large populations, notably Mexico and Peru, thousands moved into the faith *en masse*. Many of the early missionaries were from orders, among them the Observant Franciscans and the Jesuits, which embodied the devotion of the
Catholic Reformation. Missionaries were used to push forward
the borders of Spanish rule and civilization. The characteristic
frontier institution of the Spaniards was the mission, seen especially in the Jesuit enterprises in Paraguay and on the tributaries
of the Orinoco, in the work of the Capuchins and Observant
Franciscans in Venezuela, and in the Franciscan undertakings
in Texas and California.

The Spanish occupation of the Philippines had as its primary
objective the conversion of the peoples of those islands. Except
for the Moros (Moslems) in the southern portions of the Philippines and animistic tribes in mountain fastnesses, the Filipinos
were won to the Christian faith.

Five generalizations will serve to give some indication of the spread of Christianity under Spanish auspices. (1) The majority in Spanish America and the Philippines remained or became professedly Christian. This majority included all of European descent and the larger proportion of the indigenous stock. In Spanish America only in tropical jungles and thinly peopled plains did non-Christians remain. Here were the largest gains in territory and in numbers that Christianity had made since the winning of the Roman Empire. (2) These gains had been made by a combination of State initiative and support and the heroic devotion of hundreds of missionaries. State support also meant State control from Spain. All top and many minor officials of the civil government were appointed by the Crown. Most of them were Spanish-born and Spanish-educated and not of the American-born European stock. All bishops were appointed by the Crown and until the eighteenth century for the most part were from Europe. Theoretically they were subject to confirmation by the Pope, but often Rome was not even notified of their appointment. The Crown created new dioceses and altered the boundaries of existing dioceses. No Papal bull could be published without the permission of the Crown, no missionary could come to the New World without the approval of the Crown, and almost all the financial support of the missions was from the Crown. (3) Much of the Christianity was superficial. Especially in the mass conversions of hundreds of thousands no careful instruction could be given. Many of the pagan customs and beliefs survived, often under Christian guise. (4) Efforts were put forth to give the faith better rootage. Universities on European models were founded, notably in Lima and Mexico City. Indigenous clergy were trained. At the outset the conviction was held that Indians, mestizos (the results of unions of whites and Indians, in the beginning and to some degree later the fruit of irregular unions), and even American-born whites would not make worthy priests. Increasingly clergy were recruited from these classes, especially from the American-born whites. By the end of the eighteenth century the majority

of the bishops were American-born. Yet far fewer clergy were
obtained, either from Europe or in the New World, than were
necessary to give adequate care to those who bore the Christian
name. (5) By the end of the sixteenth century the impulse given
by the Catholic Reformation was waning. With the decline
went a lowering of the quality of the clergy. Indeed, from the
early years some priests of unworthy life were permitted—even
encouraged—to go to America to free their superiors of the
embarrassment of their presence. With notable exceptions the
quality and numbers of the indigenous clergy left much to be
desired. At the middle of the eighteenth century the Roman
Catholic Church in Spanish America and in the Philippines
was in poor condition to face the revolutionary changes of the
nineteenth century.

The share of Portugal in the geographic expansion of Christianity differed substantially from that of Spain. The Portuguese colonial empire was distributed over a much larger part
of the globe but in square miles and population did not equal
the Spanish possessions. It included Brazil, but the Portuguese
settlements were only on or near the coast and no such centres
of pre-Columbian civilization and population existed as in
Mexico and Peru. The Portuguese had trading posts in several
places on the west and east coasts of Africa, but they were
predominantly a source of slaves and did not embrace many
square miles. On the coasts of India were other small enclaves,
the chief of which was Goa. The Portuguese subdued much of
Ceylon but in the sixteenth century were expelled by the Dutch.
They had a trading post at Malacca, won a tenuous foothold at
Macao, in China, and in the East Indies had a few trading centres. In these widely flung domains, under grants from Rome
Portugal claimed the right to control the Roman Catholic missionary activity, including the appointment of bishops, and
attempted to embrace in that claim much of Africa and extensive portions of South and East Asia. In part of East Asia the
Portuguese came in conflict with the Spaniards. In none of their
empire were the Portuguese able to take advantage of the right

of patronage as effectively as did the Spaniards in the vast portion of the earth's surface over which their flag flew. One reason was the scattered extent of the Portuguese footholds; another was the fact that Portugal was much smaller than Spain; and, further, the Catholic Reformation did not stir Portugal as profoundly as it did Spain.

Although the Portuguese Crown attempted to prevent any missionaries from going to areas over which it claimed ecclesiastical control unless they went with its permission and through Lisbon, the majority of the more notable missionaries to South and East Asia were not Portuguese. The most famous was Francis Xavier (1506–1552). Of Basque stock, as was Loyola, while a student in the University of Paris Xavier was drawn into the original band from which came the Society of Jesus. Loyola received a request from the King of Portugal for four missionaries for the latter's possessions in the Indies. Having a far-ranging vision which was broader geographically than even that vast area, Loyola felt he could not spare so many from his then small company. He sent two, one of whom was retained in Portugal to quicken the life in the Church in that country. The other, Xavier, sailed for the East in 1541. He was first in Goa, but he traversed the vast area from India to Malacca, the East Indies, Japan, and China. A devoted friend, intensely interested in individuals, seeking by love, gaiety, and a timely word to win them to a Christian faith or to a deeper Christian life, Xavier also had an imagination which covered whole nations and peoples. He sought to raise the level of Christian living of the nominally Christian Portuguese adventurers and their mixed-blood children. He recruited members for his Society and made provision for training for the service of the Church converts from among the peoples of the East. He gave two years to the Paravas, a low-caste fishing folk in South-east India who in the hope of obtaining Portuguese help against the Moslem Arabs had recently accepted baptism. He learned enough of their language to put into their vernacular the Apostles' Creed, the Ten Commandments, and some prayers, including the Lord's Prayer, and appointed and trained catechists. To such effect did he labour that he prepared the way for the long process of Christian nurture which enabled the Paravas in the twentieth century to remain bulwarks of the Roman Catholic Church. In 1549 he went to Japan and there inaugurated what was to be one of the most successful and tragic missions of the period. He died on an island near the coast of China in an effort to gain access to that most populous nation of the world.

Following Xavier other missionaries, many of them Jesuits, went to South Asia and the fringing islands. Through their efforts small minorities of Christians arose in all the major and some of the smaller countries in the region. In Japan determined persecution drove them underground but did not exterminate them. After a few years of growth, the Christian communities in China remained stationary or declined, partly because of proscription by the State and partly because of a division in the missionary body over the degree of accommodation to the culture of the country. In Ceylon, under Portuguese rule of part of the island a substantial proportion of the population accepted the faith. When in the mid-seventeenth century the Dutch drove the Portuguese out of Ceylon, the new masters attempted to impose the Reformed faith on the inhabitants.

In their small African enclaves Portuguese missionaries won a few to their faith, but with only small continuing communities.

In the Portuguese possessions in Brazil, chiefly scattered as they were along the coast, Christianity was confronted by many of the challenges which it faced in Spanish America. The problem was difficult and acute of making the faith more than nominal among the professedly Catholic Europeans and of winning the non-Europeans. The callous exploitation of Indian and African labour was a challenge. As in Spanish America, missions were undertaken, mostly by religious orders which reflected the Catholic Reformation—Jesuits, Observant Franciscans, and Capuchins. Voices, both lay and clerical, were raised in behalf of Indians and Negroes and met with resistance from Europeans who profited by the enslavement of non-Europeans.

In the main, Christianity was weaker in Brazil than in the major centres of Spanish America and found even more formidable the recruiting and training of an indigenous clergy.

Until the nineteenth century the colonial empire of France did not approach the extent of the colonial possessions of Spain and Portugal. Before that century the largest area under the French flag was in North America in what was later embraced in Canada and in small holdings in the Mississippi Valley. At the outset the religious motive was prominent: Montreal was begun as an idealistic Christian community from which seculars could go to the French settlers and the Indians. As in the Spanish and Portuguese colonial empires missionaries were largely from bodies inspired by the Catholic Reformation—Jesuits, Recollects (Franciscans), Capuchins, Suplicians, and Ursulines. In North America all but a few small off-shore islands were lost to England in wars of the eighteenth century. However, an important French element remained and multiplied by a high birth rate. It held loyally to the Roman Catholic Church, in part because that church was a symbol and expression of French particularism.

In the vast region of Northern Asia the Russian Orthodox Church gained footholds from the Urals to the Pacific and, in the latter half of the eighteenth century, was represented across the Bering Straits in Alaska. The expansion came partly by settlement and partly by conversions of non-Christians. But population was sparse and widely scattered and only a minority called themselves Christian.

By the mid-eighteenth century the territorial expansion of Protestantism had only begun. Not until the nineteenth and twentieth centuries did it attain global dimensions. But before 1750 Pietists and Moravians had inaugurated missions among non-Christians in a few scattered places—Greenland, the West Indies, Surinam, North America, and India. To some extent through missions but mostly by white merchants and settlers, Dutch Protestantism was introduced to South Africa, Ceylon, and the East Indies. The tardiness of Protestant expansion was

due partly to a lack of missionary purpose, partly to the prolonged and often painful efforts to create constituencies in
Europe, and chiefly to the fact that Protestant peoples were
late in establishing contacts with non-European peoples and
until the nineteenth century did not acquire as wide territories outside Europe as did Roman Catholics.

The main foothold outside Europe established by Protestants
before the mid-eighteenth century was along the Atlantic seaboard of North America in the Thirteen Colonies which in the
1780's became the United States of America. Until after 1750
the frontier of white settlement had not extended beyond the
Appalachian Mountains. The settlers were chiefly from England, Scotland, and North Ireland but contained as well substantial elements from Germany and Holland and a smattering
of Swedes. In some of the settlements, notably in New England
and Pennsylvania, a major motive was escape from persecution on the other side of the Atlantic. Those dominated by
that motive were from the radical wing of Protestantism—chiefly
Puritans, Independents, Quakers, and Baptists—and from Reformed and Lutherans who were persecuted by Roman Catholic rulers, such as Huguenots from France and Germans from
the Archdiocese of Salzburg. They helped to shape the ideals
of the future United States. However, even in New England and
Pennsylvania only a minority had come from predominantly
religious motives. The overwhelming majority crossed the ocean
with the hope of improving their economic lot. With the exception of a very small minority of Roman Catholics, they were
Protestant by background, but at the mid-eighteenth century
probably only about five out of a hundred were church members. Although the Church of England was established in a few
of the colonies, notably Virginia, it had no resident bishop.
Some help came to the Anglican cause by literature from the
Society for Promoting Christian Knowledge (organized 1699)
and missionaries of the Society for the Propagation of the Gospel in Foreign Parts (founded in 1701); to the Lutherans from
the Continent of Europe, notably Henry M. Muhlenberg (1711–

1787, came to America in 1742), sent by the Halle Pietists; and to the German Reformed from Continental Europe, Michael Schlatter (1714–1790, came to America in 1746) making the deepest impression. But in the main such vitality as the churches displayed was prompted by indigenous leadership. In the second quarter of the eighteenth century what was called the Great Awakening broke out among the Reformed and Presbyterians in New Jersey and among the Congregationalists in the Connecticut Valley. In New England the chief figure was Jonathan Edwards (1703–1758). George Whitefield (1714–1770), of the Methodists, added impetus, but only one of his visits took place before 1750. Some missions to the Indians were conducted, but, partly because of the scattered population and the many tribes and languages, only minorities were won.

Retrospect, Summary, and Prospect

The two and a half centuries surveyed in the preceding pages witnessed fully as striking contrasts in the record of Christianity as had any of the preceding periods. Here was vigour in the peoples who called themselves Christian which broke out in many directions and through many channels. We have mentioned a few—in advancing the frontiers of human knowledge, in devising new instruments for that advance, in speculations about the nature of the universe and the validity and nature of human knowledge, and in creating nation-states ruled by absolute monarchs of rival dynastic families. Although they were no less notable, we have said little of the achievements in literature, painting, sculpture, architecture, and music. We have noted the fresh surges of life in Christianity, with the emergence and proliferation of Protestantism; in the Roman Catholic Church the much-needed moral reforms and the expression of Christian devotion through revitalization of old monastic orders and the creation of new kinds of monasticism; and lesser although important developments in the Orthodox Church in Russia. We have seen how professedly Christian European peoples be-

gan a geographic expansion unprecedented in extent. Although
at the beginning of the period these peoples occupied only the
western peninsula of Eurasia and even there were on the defensive against advancing Islam spear-headed by the Ottoman Turks,
by the mid-eighteenth century they had mastered a large portion of the Western Hemisphere and had ensconced themselves
on the fringes of Africa south of the Sahara and of South and
East Asia and had gained footholds in islands bordering on Asia.
Wherever they went, by political pressure, migration, and zealous
missionaries they planted the Christian faith. In the mid-
eighteenth century Christianity was more potent in the life of
mankind as a whole than it had ever been. Among the peoples
bearing the Christian name, although they were still far from
fully embodying the Gospel as set forth in the New Testament,
Christianity more nearly approximated that goal than at any
time since by the "conversion" of the Roman Empire it had
ceased to be the faith of a persecuted minority and become
a folk religion.

Yet much of the vigour in European civilization and the religion associated with it had expressions which were in striking
contradiction of the New Testament. As they had done long
before they were "converted," Europeans were chronically fighting. In several of the most devastating and exhausting of the
wars the combatants were nerved by fanatical loyalty to one or
another of the forms taken by Christianity. By drastic and
sanguinary persecutions Roman Catholics sought to eliminate
Protestantism, and Protestants endeavoured to hold back Roman
Catholicism and to erase rival branches of Protestantism. In
African slavery and in the exploitation or extermination of the
indigenous peoples of the Americas the inhumanity of man
to man assumed greater dimensions than at any previous period
in history.

On the other hand, men whose consciences were stirred and
whose resolution was sustained by the Christian faith sought
to counter and if possible to eliminate these evils. The Dutch
Protestant Hugo Grotius (1583–1645) and the Basque Domini-

can Francisco de Vitoria were only two of the many who endeavoured to put the relations between nations on the basis of
law rather than force. Here and there, as among the Quakers
and Anabaptists, were Christians who refused to participate
in any war. Bartolomé de Las Casas and Pedro Claver were
outstanding among thousands who were moved by their Christian faith to protest against the exploitation of non-Europeans
and to labour heroically on behalf of these victims of their fellow Europeans. Many Christians, Protestants and Roman Catholics tried to heal the divisions in the Church and to place the
relations among Christians on the basis of love. The Christian
faith inspired great literature, art, and music and contributed
to the daring of many in pushing forward the bounds of human knowledge. As always since the very beginnings of Christianity, thousands, the vast majority humble and obscure, were
transformed morally and spiritually, were radiant in the love
of God, and gave themselves unreservedly to the care of the
underprivileged, the sick, and the poor. Only a few of these
lives are remembered, yet they may well be among the most
significant and important fruits of Christianity.

If we are to understand the record of Christianity, to the contrast seen in these centuries two facts must be added. The first
will be evident as our narrative progresses: the contrast becomes
more striking in the nineteenth and twentieth centuries. The
second is that the contrast is more marked than in the history
of any other religion. The exploitation of the weak by the strong
and destructive wars have been chronic in history. Some wars
have wrought even more havoc, although not with as wide a
geographic extent or affecting as many millions, than those in
which professing Christians have been engaged. Into many wars
and in much of the exploitation non-Christian religions and
ideologies have entered. Among them, to give only a few examples, have been the devastation wrought by the fanatical Moslem,
Tamerlane, the African slave trade by Moslem Arabs for Moslem Arabs, domestic rebellions in China in which Taoism and
Confucianism have entered, and the enormous loss of life and

the forced labour imposed in the name of Communism in Europe and China. Yet not from any other religion or any ideology have as many movements emerged for the curbing and elimination of these evils. We saw a few in the European Middle Ages. More have emerged in the two and a half centuries covered by this chapter. We will see still more in the nineteenth and twentieth centuries.

CHAPTER IX

The Shock of Augmented Revolution,

A.D. 1750-1815

The decades of transition from the eighteenth to the nineteenth centuries were marked by an acute stage in the revolution which had begun to emerge in Western Europe in the fourteenth century. The new stage was a climax of movements and trends long present but now exploding in the intellectual, religious, political, and economic life of Western Europe. By processes already recounted, Christianity had become intertwined, seemingly inextricably, with that structure of Western European civilization which the new stage in the revolution undermined. Such apparent identification arose from inherent vitality in the faith and the ability to survive and to grow in potency in the successive eras of Western European civilization. But because of the close association of Christianity with that civilization as it existed at the mid-eighteenth century, the emerging stage in the revolution threatened the existence of Christianity. The challenge was the more thought-provoking because it arose in part from currents issuing from Christianity, and especially from its Protestant form.

An important aspect of the challenge was what was called the Enlightenment, with its strong emphasis on reason. A major contribution to the Enlightenment was Deism. Deism had many forms, but in the main it held to "natural religion." It maintained that a rational view of the universe and of man is that God exists, that He created the universe, that the universe is governed by laws inherent in its structure, and that these laws do not permit the departure from them which is seemingly implied in miracles and the Christian revelation. Deism held that God should be revered, that virtue and piety are essential to true worship, that men should repent of their sins, and that there is a future life with rewards and punishments for deeds done in this life. The more ardent Deists labelled revealed religion the product of self-interested priests. Deism was first formulated in England in the seventeenth century by laymen, members of the established church, but by the middle of the eighteenth century its influence in Britain had begun to wane. Deism had repercussions on the Continent, where its most popular advocate was Voltaire (1694–1778). By his pungent wit and caustic literary style he helped to give it wide circulation. The philosophers who produced the *Encyclopédie* (1751–1765) were mostly Deists or atheists and their seventeen volumes gave currency to their convictions. Rejecting the view of human nature which held to the depravity of man, they insisted that by experience and the use of reason men could achieve a perfect society. The emphasis on reason was widespread in Germany and Scandinavia and was popular in aristocratic circles in Russia. Deist views penetrated university circles in Germany, began a questioning, critical view of the Bible, and became influential in the erstwhile Pietist centre, the University of Halle. Deism spread to the English colonies in North America and had exponents in such influential figures as Benjamin Franklin and Thomas Jefferson. The trend in churches in Europe, both Protestant and Roman Catholic, was to emphasize reason and a morality based on reason. Warmth of religious experience and expression was decried as "enthusiasm."

Before the end of the eighteenth century trends in philosophy were beginning to discredit Deism, but not necessarily to the advantage of Christianity. Thus David Hume (1711–1776) challenged a basic conviction of Deism that natural religion and a belief in God can be supported by reason. Emmanuel Kant (1724–1804), who was to have an even greater influence in philosophy, argued that God must exist, said that Jesus Christ is the highest example of conformity to God's will, and held to immortality, but in his *Critique of Pure Reason* he maintained that the grounds on which the Deists sought to establish the existence and character of God were intellectually indefensible.

The churches were in poor condition to face the political phases of the revolution. For the most part they seemed inseparable from institutions that were either swept aside or profoundly altered. In France the bishops were from the aristocracy and spent much of their time at court. A social and economic gulf separated them from the parish clergy. As in France, so elsewhere, whether in Roman Catholic or Protestant states, the monarchs had succeeded in controlling the Church. Many of the intelligentsia were convinced that Christianity was outmoded and would soon disappear.

The political phases of the revolution had expression in the Thirteen Colonies in the War of Independence and the birth of the United States of America. In the agitation for independence and the formation of the new nation democratic ideas were nourished by the radical Protestantism prominent in New England and Pennsylvania and stimulated by the writings of John Locke. Locke, it will be recalled, was a child of Puritanism.

The first rumblings of a more spectacular explosion were heard in France in 1789. As the revolution mounted, the monarchy and the associated aristocracy were shattered and such of their representatives as escaped the guillotine fled to other countries. A republic was created. Ecclesiastical property was nationalized and some of it was sold to support the paper money of the State. Many monasteries and religious congregations were dissolved; monastic vows were declared to be no longer binding. By the Civil Constitution of the Clergy (1790) the Catholic Church was ordered reorganized, and that in spite of Papal condemnation. Pope Pius VI died as a prisoner of the French. At the height of the radical phase a young woman was enthroned in Paris in the Cathedral of Notre Dame as the Goddess of Reason. Napoleon Bonaparte claimed to be furthering the French Revolution. Catholic by profession but from political expediency, he sought to use the Church for his own ends, insisted on appointing the bishops, and brought Pope Pius VII to Paris for his coronation as Emperor—but placed the crown on his own head and that of his Empress. Napoleon declared the Papal States annexed to his empire. Because Pius VII excommunicated those who carried through the annexation, Napoleon ordered him taken captive. Partly before Napoleon came to power and partly under his rule drastic alterations were wrought in the Roman Catholic ecclesiastical structure in Germany. Among other changes, the princely archbishoprics in the Rhine Valley lost the status which had been theirs for eight centuries.

While the political face of Europe was being altered, what ultimately was fully as significant for the entire world was under way, but was not at first as spectacular. The Industrial Revolution was beginning. Its initial appearance was in Great Britain. From there it spread to the Continent, but not until after 1815. Even before that year its challenge to Christianity in Great Britain was becoming apparent.

Concurrently with the shocks to the old order in Europe and the threats to Christianity, on the geographic frontiers of the faith the gains of the preceding two centuries were shrinking. The waning of the vigour of Spain and Portugal affected adversely the missions in their possessions. The expulsion of the Jesuits from Portugal (1759), France (1764), and Spain (1767) and from their colonial possessions, followed by the Papal dissolution of the Society (1773), deprived the Roman Catholic Church of its chief missionary agency. In spite of the fact that other orders attempted to fill the gap, the enterprises once staffed by Jesuits suffered greatly, as in Paraguay, or expired, as in China. In China the persecution of Roman Catholics was accentuated. The French Revolution prevented all but a few reinforcements from being sent to any country, and the gaps in missionary staffs due to death were seldom filled.

While the blows being dealt by the Enlightenment, the French Revolution, and related movements were threatening the very existence of Christianity, here and there less spectacular developments were indications of a fresh tide of life which was to make that religion more potent in mankind as a whole than ever before. They were seen in the Roman Catholic Church but were more marked in Protestantism.

In the Roman Catholic Church evidence of continuing and renewed vitality appeared within a decade of the height of the climax of the anti-Christian tide in France. Most of them were in France, and it was in France that the anti-Christian trend was most pronounced and had its radiating centre. So resistant to attempts at de-Christianization did a loyal Catholic constituency prove to be that the necessity of some kind of accommodation to the Church became obvious. In July, 1801, a concordat with Rome was signed. Although the agreement gave the State fully as great control over the Church as had existed under the monarchy, one effect was to knit the Roman Catholic Church in France more firmly together and to increase its dependence on the Pope. In 1802 a book by Chateaubriand appeared which enjoyed a wide circulation. Of the nobility and a refugee, formerly infected with the scepticism which had been rife in his class, by a succession of personal experiences Chateaubriand had been led to return to the faith of his youth. Now, in the *Génie du Christianisme, ou Beautés de la Religion Chrétienne* (*The Genius of Christianity, or the Beauties of the Christian Religion*) he set forth a rhapsodic apologetic of the faith. His book was read by thousands, including numbers of the younger generation, and to many was convincing. In 1801 the Society of the Sacred Heart, a congregation of women, opened its first convent, in Amiens. Its purpose was, by teaching, to revive the faith by reaching the young. In 1800 the founder of the Picpus Fathers took the vows which dedicated him to the life of religion. The new congregation combined perpetual adoration of the Blessed Sacrament with missions at home and abroad.

Signs of awakening appeared in other countries. The indignities inflicted on the Popes aroused the sympathy of millions and tended to bring to the occupants of the Papal throne and to the office itself a loyalty which had been either dormant or lacking in the years when the popular image of the See of Peter had been one of luxurious impotence.

The year 1802 saw the founding of the Christian Brothers of Ireland to care for the destitute orphans in Waterford. Eventually it had a marked growth not only in Ireland but elsewhere as well. The Society of Jesus was restored. In 1801 the Pope approved its existence in Russia, where, since that country was not in the area where Papal bulls were binding, it had been continued after its dissolution had been ordered by Rome. In 1814 Pius VII authorized its full reconstitution. The United States witnessed the first stages of the growth of the hierarchy which in the nineteenth and twentieth centuries was to be one of the most striking developments in the history of Christianity. In 1784 John Carroll, a former Jesuit and member of an old and distinguished Maryland family, was appointed prefect apostolic for the new nation. In 1790 he was consecrated bishop and in 1804 he was made archibshop with jurisdiction over the entire country. He founded (1789) a college for the training of clergy and was indefatigable in travels to strengthen his church in the young republic. The cession of Canada to Great Britain (1763) and the toleration accorded by the new masters helped to make the Roman Catholic faith the symbol and tie of the incipient nationalism of the French inhabitants and so to keep the latter from being infected by the scepticism which was sapping the Church in France.

In Protestantism several movements were mounting. Not all were new, but those which dated from before the mid-eighteenth century were assuming larger dimensions. Pietism was putting forth fresh shoots in Germany and the Netherlands. Moravianism was having wide repercussions. For example, Friedrich Schleiermacher (1768–1834), whose writings were to be a milestone in Protestant theology, received part of his education in a Moravian school and in his later years declared himself still to be a Moravian. His first important book, *Über die Religion. Reden an die Gebildeten unter ihren Verächtern (Discourses on Religion to the Educated among Those Who Scorn It)*, was published in 1799. In it he sought to make Christianity intellectually respectable, especially to members of the younger generation. Hans Nielsen Hauge (1771–1824), a layman, during eight years of preaching (1796–1804) gave rise to an awakening in Norway which had a continuing and increasing effect.

The tides of life in Protestantism were running especially strong in England, and chiefly through Evangelicalism. Evangelicalism was spiritually akin to Pietism for, like the latter, it stressed the newness of life which comes through full commitment to the Gospel. From it issued efforts to give wider currency to the Gospel and to remove or at least combat some of the collective ills of mankind. Its roots were in Puritanism and in dissent from the established church. It gave rise to a new denomination, Methodism, quickened some of the dissenting bodies, and was potent in the Church of England. The phase of Evangelicalism which issued in Methodism had as its chief figure John Wesley (1703–1791) and was also deeply indebted to Charles Wesley (1707–1777), a younger brother of John, and George Whitefield (1714–1770).

The Wesleys were sons of a clergyman of the Church of England who had a difficult rural parish. They owed more to their mother than to their father. Both their father and their mother were from dissenting stock. John and Charles went to Oxford. There, with Whitefield, they were members of a deeply religious group whose members fasted twice a week, had frequent Communion, and sought to help prisoners in a local jail. In 1735 the two brothers went to the newly founded colony of Georgia as missionaries of the Society for the Propagation of the Gospel in Foreign Parts. On the outward voyage they came in contact with the Moravians and were impressed by their quiet peace and inward assurance of salvation through Christ.

In 1738 to both Charles and John, now back in London, came
the joy which they had seen in the Moravians. From their
earlier development and that experience came Methodism.
Charles made his chief contribution through hymns which
became part of the English-speaking Protestant tradition. John
travelled extensively through the British Isles preaching and
bringing converts together in societies. During his lifetime
the societies remained within Angelicanism, but to provide them
with clergy to administer the Communion where clergy were
not available, he, a presbyter and not a bishop, ordained some
of his preachers. By the time of his death the societies were
said to have about 71,000 members. They continued to grow
and eventually broke with the Church of England. By 1815
they had been planted in the West Indies and the United States.
In the latter country, under the leadership of Francis Asbury
(1745–1816) they began the remarkable growth which was to
make them one of the major religious bodies of that nation.

Both the Independents and the Baptists were stirred by the
surging Evangelicalism. Their numbers grew, new chapels were
erected, additional ministers were recruited and trained, and
lay preachers multiplied.

In the Church of England the Evangelical awakening had a
marked influence. That influence did not reach beyond a minority, but the minority grew. From it came notable preachers
and hymn-writers. Several wealthy Evangelicals clustered about
the parish church of Clapham, a suburb of London, and were
active in social reform. Chief among them was William Wilber-
force (1759–1833), who as a member of Parliament obtained
legislation (1807) abolishing the slave trade in the British
Empire. The Clapham group fought for long-overdue reforms
in elections to Parliament, for legislation to protect labourers
in the factories which were burgeoning as a result of the Industrial Revolution, for the relief of boys who swept chimneys, and
for more humane penal and game laws. Another of the Clapham
circle, Hannah More (1745–1833), helped by her sisters, initiated
and multiplied schools to counter the vice, poverty, and igno-

rance among miners and farm labourers. The Sunday School movement which in the nineteenth and twentieth centuries swelled to major proportions had as its chief pioneer Robert Raikes (1735–1811).

From Evangelical dissenters came other movements for improved social conditions. John Henry Howard (?1726–1790) early used his hereditary wealth to erect model cottages and to provide elementary education for children, but his chief contribution was in prison reform. At his initiative Parliament enacted legislation (1774) designed to remedy some of the worst features of the incredibly bad conditions in the jails. He extended his activities to the Continent.

The new life affected Scottish Christianity. As yet it was limited to small groups, some of whom broke with the established Church of Scotland.

The United States was the scene of awakenings closely akin to Evangelicalism. In the 1790's they rose to larger dimensions than in the Great Awakening. Camp-meetings, with highly emotional features, characterized the westward-advancing frontier. In the older states revivals took place. Methodism grew, and two bodies, the United Brethren in Christ and the Evangelical Association, Methodist in spirit and structure but centring on the Germans, came into being. A new denomination—the Disciples of Christ or Christians—arose on the frontier from Barton W. Stone (1772–1844) in Kentucky and Alexander Campbell (1788–1866) in Western Pennsylvania. Yet by 1815 less than one in ten of the population of the United States were church members.

Out of the Evangelical and Pietist awakenings came efforts to carry the Gospel to other lands. Although they had precursors, now for the first time the movements arose in Protestantism which in the nineteenth century swelled to major proportions. In 1792, from the vision and resolution of William Carey (1761–1834) the Baptist Missionary Society was organized. Under it Carey went to India, and there, in the Danish trading centre at Serampore, near Calcutta, he and his colleagues translated and printed part or all of the Bible into several languages and established a school which continued to be outstanding in the education of Indian clergy. In 1795 Evangelicals—Nonconformists, Methodists, and members of the Church of England—organized the London Missionary Society, later to draw its support chiefly from the Congregationalists. In 1799 Evangelicals in the Church of England founded what was eventually called the Church Missionary Society. The same year saw the formation of the Religious Tract Society. The year 1804 was marked by the beginning of the British and Foreign Bible Society, and in 1810 Evangelicals created the American Board of Commissioners for Foreign Missions. Partly inspired by the London Missionary Society, in 1797 the Netherlands Missionary Society was born. On the Continent Pietists were training missionaries, and in 1815, from Pietist circles, an institution for preparing missionaries was founded in Basel which was to have a long and distinguished history. Significantly, all these Protestant organizations for carrying the Gospel to other lands arose from small minorities while Europe was racked by the French Revolution and the Napoleonic Wars.

As we move into the nineteenth century we shall see the same contrast, but heightened, between forces which threatened Christianity in the geographic centre of its strength and movements which made that faith more a factor in mankind as a whole than in any earlier century.

CHAPTER X

The Nineteenth Century:

Mounting Western Domination, with Economic, Intellectual,

and Social Revolutions, A.D. 1815-1914

The nineteenth century, beginning in 1815 with the close of the Wars of the French Revolution and Napolean and terminated in 1914 by the outbreak of World War I, saw the heyday of Western imperialism and colonialism. One reason was the mounting industrialism, the technological inventions, and the associated intellectual revolution which gave Westerners the mastery of much of the world's natural resources. Another was the fact that only two major wars—the Civil War in the United States (1861–1865) and the Taiping Rebellion in China (1848–1865)—occurred, and these were not in Europe. Now and again wars *were* fought in Europe—the chief being the Crimean War (1854–1856) and the Franco-Prussian War (1870–1871)—but they did not draw all Europe into their vortex, as several earlier ones had done, and they were relatively brief. Here and there conflicts arose from imperial expansion, as in the Boer War (1899–1902) and the Russo-Japanese War (1904–1905). But only these two seriously challenged a European power. They were late in the century and in retrospect were seen to be the twilight of an era. By the year 1914 European peoples had made themselves the rulers of most of the planet.

The mastery of the planet was accomplished in part by gigantic migrations—from Europe to the Americas, in North America by the westward-moving population in Canada and the United States, in Australia and New Zealand by settlers from the British Isles, in South Africa by the north-eastward trek of the Afrikaners (or Boers, as they were often called), and in Siberia by the continued eastward expansion of the Russians. The mastery was also the result of comparatively peaceful occupation, as in the islands of the Pacific, Egypt, and Madagascar; by open conquest, as by the British in India, Burma, and Ceylon, by the French in North Africa and Indo-China, by the Russians in the trans-Caspian regions in Central Asia, and by the Dutch in Indonesia; and by exploration, as in Africa south of the Sahara, followed by peaceful partition, completed in the main in the 1880's.

By the year 1914 political independence from Western peoples was preserved only in the shrinking, badly weakened Turkish Empire; in Arabia, where encroachments had begun in Aden; in Ethiopia, with a precarious insecurity in its mountain fastnesses; in Persia, partly partitioned in Russian and British spheres of influence; in Afghanistan, a mountain buffer state between the British and Russian empires; in Thailand (Siam as it was then known), relatively safe because the British and the French, eyeing each other from Burma and Indo-China, would not permit either to annex it; in China, technically independent, but in fact occupied by Western powers who fixed the tariffs and whose citizens had extraterritorial status, and partially carved into spheres of influence; and in Japan, and from the 1850's into 1890's the independence of Japan had been compromised by the extraterritorial privileges of Westerners and the lack of full tariff autonomy.

Political domination was accompanied by a growing economic mastery as the European peoples sought raw materials and markets for the factories spawned by the Industrial Revolution.

In colonialism and imperialism Great Britain was outstanding. Politically, by the end of the nineteenth century Great Britain had erected an empire on which, so the boast was made, the sun never set. It embraced portions of each of the continents, some large and some small, and included many islands. The Russian Empire was next, with its grasp on Northern and Central Asia. By its extension across North America the United States, predominantly British in cultural tradition and in the ancestry of its citizens, was third in geographic area. Starting almost afresh after their losses in the eighteenth century, the French were fourth.

In economic imperialism Great Britian led by an ample margin. The British navy controlled the seas and the British merchant marine and British commerce were everywhere. Not until the eve of 1914 were the British seriously challenged. British predominance was due partly to the fact that Great Britain was the pioneer in the Industrial Revolution and for a time monopolized the machines through which the revolution was accomplished. British economic superiority was also an aftermath of the defeat of Napoleon, for that had been achieved largely through British mastery of the seas and through the wealth which "the nation of shop-keepers," as the English were derisively called, had accumulated by commerce, both in pre-industrial and in industrial years.

Through the colonialism and imperialism of European peoples the cultures of non-Europeans were here and there beginning to display the profound changes which in the twentieth century would quickly swell to major and often traumatic proportions. Those changes resulted from the impact of a civilization itself in revolution. By the close of the nineteenth century the revolution in Western civilization was mounting. In the twentieth century it, too, was rapidly to attain much larger dimensions.

The revolution in Western civilization—it had begun at least as far back as the Renaissance and had shaken much of Europe in the last decades of the eighteenth and the opening decades of the nineteenth century—had several aspects. Each aspect increased in the ten decades between 1815 and 1914.

Politically the American and French revolutions were an introduction to movements towards democracy which undermined the inherited monarchical structures and substituted for them legislative and administrative institutions chosen by popular suffrage. For a time after 1815 the elements which had subdued Napoleon attempted to turn the clock back and to restore political Europe as it had been in 1789. But the forces which had sent Louis XVI and his Queen to the guillotine and had introduced the first French republic could not be suppressed. In 1830 they broke out in France and had repercussions elsewhere. In 1848 they exploded much more violently, again first in France, where they issued in the Second Republic, soon followed by the Second Empire. In other lands the reverberations shook but did not completely overthrow the existing order.

The "liberal" political movements were closely associated with a rising tide of nationalism. Nationalism, as the nineteenth and twentieth centuries knew it, was of recent and Western origin. It had been quickened by the French Revolution and further roused through resistance to Napoleon. In the revolutionary year of 1830 it was largely responsible for the creation of an independent Belgium. In 1848 it appeared for a time to be uniting Germany. It contributed to the unification of Italy, finally achieved in 1870 through a "liberal" monarchy. It was a factor in the emergence of Greece, Serbia, Rumania, and Bulgaria from the decaying Ottoman Empire. In 1870 it found expression in the proclamation of the German Empire—with the defeat and collapse of the Second Empire in France and the coming of the Third Republic of that country.

The Industrial Revolution spread from Great Britain to the Continent of Europe and the United States. It was made possible by technological inventions—the application of power (water and steam) to machines, at first in textiles and soon to mining, metals, and many manufactures; the steam-boat; the steam railway; the electric telegraph and cable; electric lights; the telephone; the electric railway; and on the eve of 1914 the automobile, the beginnings of "wireless telegraphy," and the first airplanes. The Industrial Revolution brought new urban centres and the rapid growth of existing cities. The technological inventions were furthered by developments in science and man's rapidly expanding knowledge of the physical universe. These in turn were associated with intellectual movements and a temper of mind which magnified the "scientific" approach making that knowledge obtainable.

As in the eighteenth century, many aspects of the revolution appeared first in Great Britain, where an extreme form of Protestantism was potent. That was true of the Industrial Revolution, the early technological inventions, many of the intellectual currents, and much of democracy. To what extent, if at all, radical Protestantism was responsible would be impossible to determine.

THE CHALLENGE TO CHRISTIANITY

The mounting revolution challenged Christianity. It had its origin and its radiating centre in Western European peoples, among whom it had had the nearest approach over a longer time to relatively unhampered freedom in moulding an emerging civilization than had occurred anywhere else on the planet. As we have seen, beginning in the eighth century advancing Islam had reduced Christians in Western Asia and the Eastern Mediterranean to dwindling minorities. Among the "barbarians" who dominated Western Europe and whose inherited cultures were disintegrating in their contact with Greco-Roman civilization, Christianity, from the fifth century onward an integral part of that civilization, had the opportunity to shape the ideals and the emerging patterns of life. Long before the nineteenth century these peoples had become ostensibly Christian. That the official faith had made a deeper impress on them than it had on the Greco-Roman world before their irruption into that world is clear. That it was far from bringing them even to an approximation to the standards set forth in the New Testament is also obvious. In the nineteenth century and still more in the twentieth century, the revolution reshaping these peoples threatened the existence of the religion which had become identified with them. In this new revolution could European civilization, now in a state of flux, more nearly than previously approach the ideals presented in the Gospel? Could Christianity be effective in the impact of that civilization upon the rest of mankind? Or, weakened by the forces it had helped to evoke, would it wane and eventually disappear?

That Christianity was challenged is undebatable. The challenge was partly directed to the institutions with which Christianity had been closely associated, and the churches seemed inextricably bound to the form of society which was being openly attacked or which was being eroded. In seeking to replace absolute monarchy with "democracy," or at least to "liberalize" it, the Church was attacked as a support of the existing order. Anti-clericalism was rife, especially in lands in Europe and the Americas where the Roman Catholic form of the faith was the prevailing representative of Christianity, but also where Protestant churches were subject to the State, notably in Germany and Scandinavia. In Italy the Papal States were an obstacle to the nationalistic demand for political unification.

The Industrial Revolution was giving rise to a new social structure. In place of the prevailingly rural economy to which, through the parish system, the Church had adapted itself, mining and manufacturing towns were rapidly emerging and the populations of existing cities were mounting and were outgrowing or making anachronistic the ecclesiastical structures of earlier days. The Industrial Revolution gave rise to a ruthless exploitation of labour. Long working hours, poverty accentuated by low wages, wretched housing, periodic unemployment, the menace to health and physical safety, intolerable conditions in crowded jails and prisons, and the deterioration of morals in festering slums evoked angry assaults on the system of which they were a feature and on the failure of the Church to remedy them. The various forms of socialism that arose dismissed Christianity as irrelevant and the Church as an enemy supporting the existing order. What became the most widely spread form of socialism was formulated by Karl Marx (1818–1883) aided by Friedrich Engels (1820–1895). Both were reared as Protestants but attacked all religion as "the opiate of the people" and intellectually untenable in a scientific age. Their *Communist Manifesto* was issued in the revolutionary year of 1848, and the first volume of *Das Kapital (Capital)*, which was to be the accepted formulation of Communism, was published in 1867.

The challenge to Christianity was partly on intellectual grounds. The account of creation as given in the Bible was considered discredited by the theory of evolution as first set forth by Charles Darwin (1809–1882) in *On the Origin of Species* (1859) and popularized by Thomas Henry Huxley (1825–1895). Associated with the theory of evolution was the work of geologists, of whom a notable pioneer was Charles Lyell (1797–1875). Lyell's *Principles of Geology* was first published in 1830 and was issued in successively revised editions, the last in 1872. Herbert Spencer (1820–1903), reared in Evangelical surroundings, popularized evolution and applied it to society and religion. Although he rejected atheism and pantheism, he would not accept theism and regarded himself as an agnostic.

Widely read intellectuals openly attacked Christianity. Auguste Comte (1798–1857) sought to substitute for it a new religion, Positivism. Arthur Schopenhauer (1788–1860), a thoroughgoing pessimist, denied personal immortality and regarded happiness as an illusion. Ludwig Feuerbach (1804–1872) maintained that God has no objective reality but is a projection of what man conceives to be his needs. Friedrich Wilhelm Nietzsche (1844–1900), descended from Protestant clergymen, declared that God does not exist and that Christianity fostered a slave mentality and the mental and physical deterioration of Europeans. The egotistical musician Richard Wilhelm Wagner (1813–1883) held that Christianity had effected a Jewish corruption of the German spirit and sought to exalt pre-Christian German paganism. Although he retained a belief in God, Thomas Carlyle (1795–1881) abandoned the Christian faith. The Utilitarians, founded by Jeremy Bentham (1748–1832), were anti-clerical and sought to discredit dogmatic Christianity. John Stuart Mill (1806–1873), educated according to Bentham's counsel, believed in God, supported the ethical teachings of Jesus, but disavowed supernatural support for them. The novelist whose pen name was George Eliot (1819–1880) rebelled against the Evangelicalism in which she had been brought up but kept a sympathetic understanding of Evangelicals. Thomas Hardy (1840–1928), in his later years hailed as the outstanding living man of letters in the English-speaking world, in his youth a believing Christian, in his maturity held that men's lives are governed by blind, unconscious, purposeless cosmic forces. Johann Wolfgang von Goethe (1749–1832), esteemed by Germans as their greatest poet, was deeply religious but not in a Christian sense. Georg Wilhelm Friedrich Hegel (1770–1831), who left the stamp of his philosophy on much of Western thought of the nineteenth and twentieth centuries, declared Christianity to be the perfect religion, employed Christian terminology in such fashion that he appeared to endorse it, but was in fact a pantheist.

Scholars applied current scholarly methods to the Bible and formulated theories which seemed to discredit Christianity. David Friedrich Strauss (1808–1874), at first a Protestant but in his later years giving up belief in a personal God and immortality, cast doubt on the accuracy of the records of the sayings and deeds of Jesus and rejected the virgin birth of Jesus. Joseph Ernest Renan (1823–1892), who had prepared for the Roman Catholic priesthood but later left the church of his boyhood, in his readable *Vie de Jésus (Life of Jesus)*, published in 1863, portrayed Jesus as attractive, but unpractical and futile, a son of Joseph and Mary, and held that He did not rise from the dead.

THE ROMAN CATHOLIC RESPONSE

The response of the Roman Catholic Church to the forces which were shaping the new day was mixed. On the one hand were serious losses. On the other hand was vitality which expressed itself in striking movements and knit that church more closely under the direction of a succession of strong Popes than at any time since the thirteenth century.

The losses were multiform and in many countries. In France urban populations, some of the rural districts, and labourers in mines and factories tended to drift away from the Church. Anticlericalism increased. Shortly after 1901 many congregations of the religious were suppressed and thousands of schools conducted by members of congregations were closed. In 1905 the tie between Church and State was severed and most of the church edifices were declared to belong to the State. The use of the churches was permitted but under terms which were denounced by the Pope. French Roman Catholics presented no common front to the challenge but were divided. Many refused to coöperate with the Third Republic.

In Italy the rising nationalism expelled foreign, chiefly Austrian, rule, unified the country politically, erased the Papal States, and (1870) took possession of Rome. The Pope was unreconciled to the loss of his temporal domain, refused the compensation proffered by the State, and regarded himself as a prisoner in the Vatican. He forbade the faithful to participate in the civil government. The Kingdom of Italy confiscated many of the properties of orders and congregations.

In Spain the tide ebbed and flowed. In 1820 "liberals" obtained control of the State, dissolved nearly half the monasteries, and cancelled the State support of the clergy. But in 1823 the régime which had taken these measures was crushed and the monasteries were restored. In the ensuing long years of civil strife mobs killed many priests and monks; in 1846 more than half the bishoprics were vacant. In the latter part of the century a stable government was achieved. It placed public instruction under the inspection of ecclesiastical authorities and gave financial support to some benevolent institutions of the Church. In 1910–1911 an anti-clerical prime minister took action against several congregations, and diplomatic relations with the Vatican were broken. With measures against the Church relaxed, in 1912 diplomatic relations with the Vatican were resumed.

Something of the same record marked the course of the Roman Catholic Church in Portugal. In 1833, after an exhausting civil war, "liberals" came into power, abolished tithes, closed a number of monasteries and convents, and nationalized their properties. In the latter half of the century restrictions on the Church were somewhat eased. Soon after 1900 a fresh anti-clerical wave suppressed a number of orders and congregations; under a newly created republic, Church and State were separated (1911).

Throughout Spanish America the Catholic Church suffered severely. In that vast region, as we have seen, under the impulse of the Catholic Reformation the major territorial expansion of that form of the faith in the sixteenth, seventeenth, and eighteenth centuries had been achieved. In the fore part of the nineteenth century all Spanish America except Cuba and Puerto Rico obtained their political independence, but during the course of the struggle the Church was dealt crippling blows. Some of the blows were from the scepticism engendered by the Enlightenment and the anti-Christian philosophies of the nineteenth century, especially the Positivism of Comte. Only minorities among the upper classes were seriously affected. However, many of the missions, staffed as they had been from Europe, were turned over to the secular clergy and disintegrated. The major embarrassment came from the conflict between the Spanish Crown and the emerging governments over the control of ecclesiastical appointments, especially to bishoprics. The Spanish Crown was slow to recognize the independence of the revolting colonies and insisted upon retaining command of the appointments. The régimes set up in the new republics claimed the same authority. The Popes, faced with anti-clericalism in Spain, hesitated to weaken the Church in that country by acceding to the demands of the new governments. As a result, many bishoprics were left unfilled. In 1826 only ten of the episcopal sees had occupants, and of them two were incapacitated and two left within the year. Deprived of ecclesiastical leadership in a period of political strife, the clergy suffered in morale and few priests could be recruited. Not for several years did Rome yield to the demand of the new governments. Moreover, in each of the

Spanish American countries a chronic struggle ensued between anti-clericals and those who favoured maintaining the tie between Church and State. The overwhelming majority of the population regarded themselves as Roman Catholics, but the degree of their conformity to the standards of the faith, already low, dropped further. The number and quality of the indigenous clergy were insufficient even to maintain the existing level of faith and morals. The deficiency was partly made up by clergy from Europe, mostly regulars. Such missions to the non-Christian tribes as existed were undertaken by members of European orders and congregations. As it had been from the beginning, the Christianity of Spanish America was parasitic, dependent for what life it contained on transfusions from the parent church in the Old World.

The Roman Catholic Church was fully as weak in Brazil as in Spanish America. The political tie with Portugal was severed without the fighting which marked the separation of Spanish America from the mother country. Nor was the strain between Church and State as acute as in Spanish America. But Positivism gained a wide following among the intelligentsia and was chiefly responsible for the separation of the Church from the State (1890). The quality of the clergy during much of the century is indicated by the fact that many, including bishops, were Free Masons, in spite of the Papal prohibition to Catholics of membership in that order. As in Spanish America, the indigenous clergy were too few to give adequate spiritual care to those who called themselves Catholics and the deficiency was only partly corrected from Europe. From Europe, too, came almost all the missionaries to the non-Christian Indians in the vast interior.

Serious as were the losses suffered by the Roman Catholic Church, inherent vitality was displayed in a variety of responses to the challenge.

One of the responses was in the heightening of the quality and effective power of the Papacy. Several factors were responsible for that development. One was the need felt by bishops

for support against the mounting tide of anti-clericalism. Another arose from intellectuals who were leaders in the revival
of the Catholic faith of which Chateaubriand had been a symptom and an agent. Outstanding were Joseph Marie, Comte de
Maistre (1754–1821) and Félicité Robert de Lamennais (1782–
1854). In a book, *Du Pape*, published in 1819, Maistre argued
that true liberty could be achieved, not through the popular
sovereignty advocated by the "liberals" who had manned the
French Revolution, but through stern self-discipline, and that
this could be accomplished only by a sovereignty superior to
all others—the Papacy. *Du Pape* had an enormous circulation.
In more voluminous and also widely read writings Lamennais
presented a fresh apologetic for the Christian faith as against
eighteenth-century rationalism, criticized Gallicanism (the traditional belittling of Papal authority in the French Church),
and stood for the Papacy as a safeguard of the faith. Many
thoughtful spirits, reacting against the near-anarchy of the revolutionary movements and moved by the Romanticism which
glorified the Middle Ages, enthusiastically endorsed the Papacy
as a bulwark against the "liberalism" which to their mind was
threatening civilization. The movement was known as ultramontanism—looking beyond the mountains (the Alps) to Rome.
To millions the Papacy symbolized the values of European culture which were menaced by the forces reshaping the Western
world.

Ultramontanism grew and with it the Papacy achieved dominance in the Roman Catholic Church under the leadership of
three extraordinarily able men who occupied the See of Peter
in the seventy-eight years immediately preceding World War I.
They were Pius IX, Leo XIII, and Pius X.

Pius IX, who had the longest tenure on the throne of Peter,
from 1846 to 1878, since the hypothetical one by the Prince of
the Apostles, on his election was hailed by many as a "liberal,"
hopefully a champion of the unification of Italy. The events of
the revolutionary year of 1848 cured him of any leanings he
may have had towards the surging currents of the day which

were threatening the established order, and he became a staunch conservative. In 1854 he proclaimed the immaculate conception of the Virgin Mary as dogma revealed by God to be believed by all the faithful. He thus gave the support of his office to the conviction that Mary had been born without original sin—a theological position on which Roman Catholic scholars had not been agreed—and by implication denounced views recently put forth by Strauss and held in many circles which denied the virgin birth of Jesus. In 1864, at the decennial of the proclamation of the immaculate conception, Pius IX issued the lengthy *Syllabus of Errors*. In eighty succinct paragraphs he listed contemporary beliefs and trends of which he disapproved. Among them were pantheism and the positions that human reason is the sole arbiter of truth and falsehood and good and evil; that Christian faith contradicts reason; that Christ is a myth; that philosophy must be treated without reference to supernatural revelation; that every man is free to embrace the religion which, guided by the light of reason, he believes to be true; that Protestantism is another form of the Christian religion in which it is possible to be as pleasing to God as in the Catholic Church; that the civil power can determine the limits within which the Catholic Church may exercise authority; that Roman Pontiffs and Ecumenical Councils have erred in defining matters of faith and morals; that the Church does not have direct or indirect temporal power or the right to invoke force; that in a conflict between Church and State the civil law should prevail; that the civil power has the right to appoint and depose bishops; that the entire direction of public schools in which the youth of Christian states are educated must be by the civil power; that the Church should be separated from the State and the State from the Church; that moral laws do not need divine sanction; that it is permissible to rebel against legitimate princes; that a civil contract may among Christians constitute true marriage; that the Catholic religion should no longer be the religion of the State to the exclusion of all other forms of worship; and "that the Roman Pontiff can and should reconcile himself to and agree with progress, liberalism and modern civilization."

Pius IX called the first council recognized by his church as ecumenical since that of Trent. It met in the Vatican in 1869–1870, and its most notable decrees, later promulgated by the Pope, declared "that the Roman Pontiff, when he speaks *ex cathedra*, that is, when in discharge of the office of pastor and doctor of all Christians, by virtue of his supreme apostolic authority, he defines a doctrine of faith and morals to be held by the universal Church, by the divine assistance promised to him in blessed Peter, is possessed of that infallibility with which the Divine Redeemer willed that His Church should be possessed for defining doctrine regarding faith or morals; and that therefore such definitions of the Roman Pontiff are irreformable of themselves, and not from the consent of the Church"; and that the Roman Pontiff has "full and supreme power of jurisdiction over the universal Church, not only in things which belong to faith and morals, but also in those which relate to the discipline and government of the Church spread throughout the world."

Significant of the growing power of the Papacy is the fact that, although a minority of the Council did not vote for these findings, after they were approved by the Pope every bishop submitted. Only a small minority of Roman Catholics, led by an eminent historian, Johann Josef Ignaz von Döllinger (1799-1890), declared that the Vatican decrees were untrue to history and, excommunicated by the Pope, constituted themselves the Old Catholic Church.

Significant of the growing power of "liberal" nationalism was the fact that the Vatican Council did not officially adjourn but dispersed because of the seizure of Rome by the Kingdom of Italy and the extinction of the Papal States. To that, as we have said, the Popes would not assent. Eventually (1929) the Papacy won a token approval of its position by the Lateran Treaty in which the Kingdom of Italy consented to the creation of Vatican City, a small domain of 109 acres, mostly centring about St. Peter's, and to the recognition of the Supreme Pontiff's status as a sovereign prince.

Leo XIII, who reigned from 1878 to 1903, did not openly dissent from the positions taken by his predecessor, but he was more inclined to come to an accommodation with the new age than Pius IX had been. Like the latter he was impeccable in his private life, and was free from the nepotism which had tainted the reigns of some even of the Popes who had been brought to their office by the Catholic Reformation. He had diplomatic skill in adjusting certain of the conflicts of his see with the forces of the age. He constrained Bismarck, the leading European statesman of the day, the creator of the German Empire, to yield in the *Kulturkampf* in which the latter had attempted to control the Catholic Church in Germany as many monarchs had done in preceding centuries. Leo XIII endeavoured, without compromising his church's basic convictions, to establish friendly relations with governments in which anti-clericalism was strong. In the encyclical *Rerum Novarum* (1891) he frankly recognized the economic and social conditions brought by the Industrial Revolution and attempted to formulate constructively his church's policy towards them. To meet the intellectual currents of the day he encouraged the study of Aquinas and other schoolmen of the Middle Ages.

In Pius X, who reigned from 1903 to 1914, the Papal throne had an incumbent who had had experience as a parish priest and was at heart a pastor. Essentially conservative, he early came into collision with the separation of Church and State in France and Portugal. He formally condemned what was known as "modernism," a trend among some of the clergy to conform the faith to the scholarship of the age. Positively, he concerned himself with the education of priests in Italy, exhorted clergy the world over to aspire to what he set forth as the standard for the perfect parish priest, encouraged frequent, even daily Communion by the laity, urged that children be admitted to that sacrament as soon as they understood the simple doctrines of the Church, stressed Christian marriage and family life, had the breviary reworked to make it more useful and to ensure the recitation of the whole Psalter each week, and enjoined devotion to Mary. He felt acutely the sufferings of both individuals and multitudes. World War I brought him deep agony of soul and is said to have hastened his death. Even in his lifetime miracles of healing by his prayers were reported. Within half a century after his death he was canonized, the first Pope since the sixteenth century and the second since the thirteenth century to be accorded that recognition.

In other ways the vigour inherent in the Roman Catholic Church made itself felt. Significantly, its most striking expressions occurred in France, the country where the anti-Christian, anti-clerical movements had been most pronounced and the secularism most corrosive. In the nineteenth century more new congregations came into being, entailing in their members complete dedication to God through the vows of poverty, chastity, and obedience, than in any preceding century, and the majority had their birth in France. In the reviving effort to spread the faith among non-Christian peoples, more Roman Catholic missionaries went from France than from all the rest of the Roman Catholic Church. Here was begun (1822) the Society for the Propagation of the Faith, which in the following century was to become the chief agency of the entire Church for raising money to support foreign missions. In 1881, in Lille, the first of the Eucharistic Congresses was held; in the remainder of the century and in the twentieth century such congresses were employed to nourish among the faithful devotion to Christ and His sacrifice. To a Frenchman, Prosper Louis Pasqual Guéranger (1805-1875), is attributed the beginnings of the Liturgical Movement. In the next century it was to attain world-wide proportions as a means of stimulating the laity to intelligent participation in the central rite of the Church. In France were reported the most famous of the appearances of the Virgin Mary of the nineteenth century—in 1846, to two young shepherds on the plateau of La Salette in Savoy, and in 1858 to Bernadette Soubirous, a peasant girl, in a grotto near Lourdes, which became a shrine where miracles of healing were reported. Normandy was the home of Thérèse of Lisieux (1873-1897), who as the Little Flower was believed through her intercession after her death to have been responsible for many miracles and who was canonized in 1925.

Jean Baptiste Marie Vianney (1786-1859), the Curé of Ars, wrought a moral transformation in the village where he was priest, was sought by high and low from far and wide for spiritual counsel, and was also canonized in 1925. France saw the development too of profound theology and of movements to solve the social problems brought by the revolutionary age.

Vitality was apparent in other countries. Germany was the home of distinguished scholarship. Wilhelm Emmanuel von Ketteler (1811-1877), in 1850 created Archbishop of Mainz, greatly improved the quality of his clergy and formulated programmes for social reform in a land where the Industrial Revolution was beginning to be felt. English Roman Catholics were emancipated from centuries-long legal disabilities (by various steps, culminating in unconditional emancipation in 1829). The English hierarchy was reëstablished (1850), and many notable English converts were made, outstanding among them John Henry Newman (1801-1890). Through a high birth rate Roman Catholics multiplied in Canada, dominated the province of Quebec, and spread to other parts of the country. Roman Catholics poured into the United States by the millions, at first chiefly from poverty-stricken Ireland, then from Germany, and later from Italy and other parts of Europe. A nation-wide ecclesiastical structure was rapidly erected for them and an extensive school system was created to nurture youth in the faith. In Australia a large immigration, mainly from Ireland, was provided with clergy and a hierarchy. As never before the Roman Catholic Church became world-wide. In spite of the forces which appeared to be threatening its existence, its loyal adherents, although in some former Catholic lands a minority in a majority of nominal Catholics, were more numerous than ever before.

THE PROTESTANT RESPONSE

Even more than the Roman Catholic Church, Protestantism rose to the challenge and came to the year 1914 with improved morale in Western Europe, with a mounting effect on civilization, and with relatively a more extensive geographic expansion than any other branch of Christianity.

On the Continent of Europe the record was impressive. In Germany vigorous scholarship endeavoured to examine theology and the Bible through the new approaches of the period. Schleiermacher lived until 1834 and inaugurated a new era in Protestant theology. He not only wrote but also lectured, preached, and concerned himself with the active affairs of the Church. Ernst Wilhelm Hengstenberg (1802-1869) was a staunch advocate of a revival of strict Lutheran orthodoxy. The nineteenth-century German theologian whose influence was second only to that of Schleiermacher was Albrecht Ritschl (1822–1889). Ritschl was intent on helping to bring in the Kingdom of God on earth and reflected and influenced the optimistic belief in progress which characterized much of the Occident of that day. A galaxy of theologians and church historians are usually classed as Ritschlians. Eminent among them was Adolf von Harnack (1851-1930), whose major writing was in the history of dogma. He maintained that the core of the primitive Gospel was "eternal life in the midst of time, by the strength and under the eyes of God," but that it had been obscured and distorted by its early contact with Greek thought. Another historian who came under the influence of Ritschl but might better be considered as in the tradition of Schleiermacher was Ernst Troeltsch (1865-1923). His chief interest was the history of religion. He wished Christianity to be brought into harmony with the rapidly changing Occident.

Much of German scholarship was devoted to the study of the Bible. A major approach, known as the "higher criticism," sought to apply to the Scriptures the methods employed in the study of other ancient documents. Heinrich Ewald (1803-1875), enormously erudite and possessing the fervour of a prophet, was for a generation esteemed the outstanding expert on the Old Testament. Julius Wellhausen (1844-1918), a pupil of Ewald, was even more famous than his teacher. He popularized an hypothesis which was already being put forward—that the religion of the Hebrews had developed from a primitive stage centring in Yahweh as a tribal deity to a belief in Yahweh as the God of righteousness and of the whole earth.

The controversy precipitated by Strauss's *Leben Jesu* stimulated a fresh approach to the New Testament. Especially outstanding was Ferdinand Christian Baur (1792-1860). He was influenced by Hegel and the latter's dialectic, in accordance with which he held that the primitive Church as seen in Jerusalem was distinctly Jewish, that Pauline Christianity was its antithesis, and that the conflict between the two was resolved in a synthesis, the Catholic Church. He maintained that the real essence of Christianity as it came from Jesus is in the Sermon on the Mount, the parables, and the various discourses of Jesus. Later in the century what was known as the eschatological interpretation of Jesus developed. Its classic expression was called, in its English translation, published in 1910, *The Quest of the Historical Jesus, a Critical Study of Its Progress from Reimarus to Wrede*. Its author was Albert Schweitzer (1875——), who later acquired another kind of fame by going to Africa (1913) as a medical missionary. Schweitzer maintained that much of the effort to discover the Jesus of history had ended in a blind alley, for it had attempted to clothe Him in modern dress. Jesus, so Schweitzer said, was a child of His age and of His Jewish environment, expected the Kingdom of God to come in the lifetime of Himself and His disciples, but was disappointed.

German theological and Biblical scholarship created a stir in both Protestant and Roman Catholic circles in Germany and many other lands. It stimulated discussion, gave rise to controversy, and attracted scholars from other countries to German universities.

German nineteenth-century Protestantism was characterized not only by scholarship but also by many awakenings. Some were in Reformed and others in Lutheran churches. A reaction against the emotionally sterile rationalism of the eighteenth century and akin to the prevailing Romanticism and philosophic Idealism, they led to a warm and deep religious life. Some were part of a swelling tide of Pietism. Others were a revival of Lutheran orthodoxy with emphasis upon the historic confessions —statements of Lutheran beliefs. Many combined orthodoxy and Pietism.

Partly from Pietism and partly from the Enlightenment came a movement for church unity. In Prussia and several other states into which Germany was divided unions of Reformed and Lutherans were effected. The unions were resented by many strict Lutherans, who viewed them as a departure from the faith. Efforts were also made at coöperation among the many *Landeskirchen*, or territorial churches, which reflected the political structure of the country.

As a fruit of the awakenings came efforts to provide adequate clerical care for the mounting population and especially for the rapidly growing cities. The *Landeskirchen* were controlled by the State. Although legally individuals could withdraw from them, few did so. Most of the traditionally Protestant population was baptized, and an increasing proportion, although usually less than half, were confirmed. But parishes, especially in the cities, were too large to permit much congregational life. Pastors could do little more than preach, baptize, give pre-confirmation instruction, confirm, celebrate the Communion, officiate at marriages and funerals, and supervise the religious instruction which was given in the state schools. Some new church buildings were erected, but not enough to keep pace with the increase in population. Attendance at church services seems to have declined. Yet improvement was registered in the character and the training of the clergy.

Another outcome of the awakenings in German Protestantism was a spate of movements to deepen the life of Christians and to rise to the challenges brought by the Industrial Revolution. By contagion from abroad came Sunday Schools and Young Men's Christian Associations. Out of the Protestant conscience arose many efforts to meet the needs of the new Germany. Thus Theodor Fliedner (1800-1854) developed at Kaiserswerth, where he was pastor, an institution for training deaconesses in which women were prepared to staff hospitals and orphanages. To it came Florence Nightingale (1829-1910), an Englishwoman who did much to develop nursing as a profession. After its pattern similar institutions were created in several countries. Johann Hinrich Wichern (1808-1881), a Pietist of Lutheran background, was the creator of the Inner Mission. At the outset, in a suburb of Hamburg he trained young men, largely artisans and peasants, to form a kind of Protestant order to serve in orphanages, hospitals, and asylums for the feeble-minded and epileptics. The Inner Mission as such was launched in the revolutionary year of 1848. Wichern's purpose was to recruit missionaries to win to a living faith the baptized and nominally Christian masses. He gathered laymen in voluntary associations to minister to men's material needs. From the Inner Mission sprang many charitable institutions and movements. They and others like them were brought into a national federation. One of the most notable institutions connected with the Inner Mission was at Bethel, near Bielefeld. Its founder was a Pietist pastor, Friedrich von Bodelschwingh (1831-1910). At Bethel were created a home for epileptics and feeble-minded, a workers' colony, a church, a house for deaconesses, another house for training men nurses, and a seminary in which, while preparing for the ministry, young men could have practical experience with unfortunates in the Bethel institutions.

Scandinavia was also the scene of impressive awakenings. In Denmark eighteenth-century rationalism was challenged. Pietism grew and prompted many to form circles and maintain institutions within the Lutheran state church. The Danish Inner Mission differed from the German Inner Mission. Thanks in part to Vilhelm Beck (1829-1901), an able preacher and organizer, the country was divided into districts, and colporteurs and home missionaries systematically distributed Bibles and other literature and by personal contacts endeavoured to win the nominal Christians to an earnest Christian commitment. Through the Inner Mission new churches were erected in Copenhagen, Sunday Schools multiplied, books and periodicals were published, and schools for various purposes were conducted.

Quite apart from the Inner Mission, Nikolaj Frederik Severin Grundtvig (1783-1872) by a prolonged spiritual pilgrimmage became the prophet of a varied movement. Grundtvig wished a spiritual rebirth of the nation from the depths into which it had been cast by siding with Napoleon. He reminded Danes of their great historic heritage and held that they and the age in which they were set could be saved only by repentance and a return to the Christian faith. He made much of the sacraments, through which he believed the new life in Christ is created and maintained. In connexion with them he stressed the Apostles' Creed and the Lord's Prayer. He promoted adult education, with emphasis on the rights and duties of a citizen in a modern democratic state. From the movements which he inspired came folk high schools.

Very different was Sören Aabye Kierkegaard (1813-1955). From a traumatic experience which included association with a gloomy, deeply religious father and the rupture of an engagement for marriage came a stream of writings which in the next century contributed to the existentialism of those who were oppressed by the tragedy in the Western world. Kierkegaard was intense, painfully honest, extremely sensitive, melancholy by temperament, and tortured by questions which have troubled men since they began to think and which were aggravated by the intellectual challenges of the age. He knew profound despair, sought to face it squarely, and rejected the Danish state church from the conviction that it was an enemy of true Christianity.

Yet the Inner Mission, Grundtvig, and Kierkegaard did not fully transform Denmark. Also potent was the mounting tide of secularism, reënforced by intellectuals, such as the Jew Georg Morris Cohen Brandes (1842-1906), literary critic and historian, who were out of line with the Christian tradition.

In Norway, too, was a contrast—between, on the one hand, a secularist indifference to religion and caustic critics of contemporary conventional Christianity such as Henrik Johan Ibsen (1826-1906) and Bjornstjerne Björnson (1832-1910) and, on the other hand, religious awakenings which profoundly stirred thousands. The awakenings had as outstanding figures Hauge, whom

we have already met and who inspired a succession of lay preachers and Gisle Johnson (1822-1894), a distinguished scholar associated with the Inner Mission. The Inner Mission endeavoured
to bring nominal Christians to a full commitment and gave
rise to prayer houses and folk schools for the quickening and
nourishing of the faith.

Sweden was the scene of a surge of revivals which moved away
from the cold rationalism of the Enlightenment and the chronic
alcoholism that gave to the fore part of the century the designation "the brandy age." In the South-west was Henric Schartau
(1757-1825), who mingled easily with all classes and who by
his preaching had a profound effect which continued after his
death. In the North groups of "New Readers" emerged from
contacts with the Moravians. From them also sprang free churches
which, in contrast with the Inner Mission in Denmark and Norway, separated from the state church. Towards the end of the
century Ritschlianism and the historical criticism of the Bible
entered from Germany, but in the person of Nathan Söderblom
(1866-1931), who combined scholarship with a radiant faith,
to some degree they were constructive. First as a professor in
the University of Uppsala and then (1914-1931) as the Archbishop of Uppsala and so as the Primate of the Church of
Sweden, Söderblom had an influence which, as we are to see,
extended far beyond his native land.

In Sweden, in spite of the revivals, the labourers in the growing industries were drifting away from the faith. The leaders
and many of the members of the labour unions were hostile to
the Church and the religion for which it stood. By the end of
the century clergy were declining in numbers, illegitimacy had
increased, alcohol was still a problem, church attendance was
falling off, and, although confirmation was required by law, many
had not presented themselves for it.

Finland, culturally and formerly politically tied to Sweden
and with a Lutheran state church, also experienced awakenings.
Some were continuations of the Pietist movements of the
Eighteenth century. Others had little connexion with them. They

were strongest in the North but spread through the nation. The new capital, Helsinki (Helsingfors), became a centre of them. Yet with industrialization organized labour made its appearance and in 1903 adopted a programme which had Marxist, anti-Christian implications.

Estonia and Latvia, where traditionally German landlords had been dominant and Lutheranism was the prevailing religion, when the nineteenth century opened were under Russian rule. Because of the Russian connexion some of the peasants moved into the Russian Orthodox Church, but the majority remained Lutheran. Some revivals were experienced and a body of clergy of Estonian and Latvian stock was slowly developed.

In Hungary, as a phase of the revolutionary year of 1848, the Protestant minorities who had survived the persecution accompanying the Counter-Reformation were relieved of some of the legal disabilities from which they had suffered. Fresh life entered through contacts with Protestantism in other lands.

Swiss Protestantism had suffered from the benumbing effects of the Enlightenment. Early in the nineteenth century, in common with Protestantism in several other countries, it experienced an awakening, with warm personal commitment. In the French-speaking cantons it was known as the *réveil*. The *réveil* contributed decisively to a movement which was to acquire world-wide dimensions, the Red Cross. The Red Cross arose from the initiative of Henri Dunant (1828-1910). From an old, respected, well-to-do family in Geneva, Dunant was reared in the atmosphere of the *réveil* and was inspired by it. He was active in bringing into being the World's Alliance of the Young Men's Christian Associations (in Paris in 1855). Present at the Battle of Solferino (in Italy, in 1859, as an incident of a war between France and Sardinia on the one hand and Austria on the other), he was appalled by the lack of care of the sick and wounded. His book issued in 1862 which depicted what he had seen created a European sensation. From his determination that an international effort must be made to prevent a similar tragedy in future wars the International Red Cross was organized (1863).

Dunant persuaded the Swiss Government to call a conference (1864) in which representatives of sixteen nations drew up the Geneva Convention—eventually ratified by a large proportion of the world's governments.

In most of Latin Europe—notably in Italy, Spain, and Portugal —Protestantism won only slight footholds. In Italy in the revolutionary year 1848 the Waldenses were accorded permanent civil rights and, although a minority of only about twenty thousand, adopted an ambitious programme for the evangelization of the country. But in Spain and Portugal such numerically feeble Protestant groups as emerged arose out of missionary effort from other countries. In France Protestantism had survived the persecutions and emigrations of the seventeenth and eighteenth centuries and was quickened by contacts with awakenings in other countries, notably the Swiss *réveil*. By successive steps it was accorded toleration. In 1872 a national synod was convened, the first since 1659. From the Protestant minority came notable statesmen and thinkers.

The Netherlands, with a large Roman Catholic minority, chiefly in the South, was predominantly Protestant. Most Protestants were in the Dutch Reformed Church, a church that had suffered from the Enlightenment. Now came an awakening which paralleled that in Switzerland. Indeed, it was often called the *réveil*. Many in the Dutch Reformed Church were critical of the *réveil*, and partly as a result, some of the most earnest supporters of the *réveil* seceded and formed the Christian Reformed Church. Theological discussion and controversy over the historical study of the Scriptures waxed warm. Abraham Kuyper (1837-1920), a pastor in the Reformed Church, had a profound experience which moved him to a firm emphasis on Calvinism as, in his judgment, the completed evolution of Protestantism. Convinced that the principle of the sovereignty of the people embodied in the French Revolution rather than the sovereignty of God leads to disaster, he headed a political party and from 1901 to 1905 was prime minister. In that office he altered the colonial policy in the East Indies in the direction of the interests of the native peoples rather than the profits of the Dutch. He was the first rector of the Free University of Amsterdam, founded in 1880 to uphold the theology he advocated. From the movement led by Kuyper came another secession from the Dutch Reformed Church which united with the majority of the Christian Reformed Church to form the Reformed Churches in the Netherlands.

Paralleling the leadership of the British Isles in the Industrial Revolution, the world's commerce, and the rapid expansion of the British Empire, surges of life in the churches made Protestant Christianity more widely vital in Britain than at any earlier time. The Evangelicalism of the eighteenth century quickened many of the population. It made its effect felt in the Church of England, in Nonconforming Protestantism, in Scottish Presbyterianism, and in Wales and Ireland.

In England Nonconformity grew, chiefly in several Methodist bodies, now fully severed from the Church of England, and in the Congregational and Baptist churches. It was also seen in smaller denominations, some old, like the Quakers, and some new, like the "Plymouth Brethren" (who preferred the simple designation of "Brethren"). The Presbyterianism inherited from Commonwealth days for the most part became Unitarian. In the course of the century, a variety of steps removed most of the legal disabilities which had hampered Nonconformists. Nonconformists came chiefly from the middle class. With the rising industrialization, commerce, and prosperity of the country that element in the population grew and with it Nonconformity flourished. Although only a minority of the population, Nonconformists were proportionately a larger minority than were dissenters from the Protestant state churches on the Continent, except possibly in the Netherlands.

The Church of England was aroused from its somnolence and the Deistic infection of the eighteenth century. Part of the fresh vigour came through the Evangelicals. Much was through a renewed emphasis upon the Catholic heritage which found expression in a revival that had its radiating centre in Oxford and is variously known as the Oxford or Tractarian Movement. The latter designation is derived from a succession of papers, or tracts, in which the convictions of the leaders were expressed. Dating from a sermon preached by John Keble in the university church in 1833, the Oxford Movement boldly asserted the right of the Church of England to a life of its own associated with but not dominated by the State. Its outstanding figures included John Keble (1792-1866), John Henry Newman (1801-1890), and Edward Bouverie Pusey (1800-1882). It stressed the heritage from the undivided Catholic Church of the early centuries and was accompanied by the enrichment of individual and collective worship, the re-appearance of some Catholic features in public worship, with crucifixes, candles, incense, auricular confession, frequent Communion, the reserved sacrament, the invocation of the saints, and the veneration of the Virgin Mary, and the appearance of orders of men and women. Some of the clergy and laity made their peace with Rome. Much opposition was aroused, chiefly by the innovations in ritual, and at times had violent expressions.

As a result of the Evangelical and Oxford movements and of other currents marked improvements were seen in the Church of England. Pluralism (holding two or more posts and drawing the revenues from them) and absenteeism were terminated. Sinecures were abolished. "Simony"—the purchase and sale of livings—was dealt a severe blow. Incomes of some of the wealthier episcopal sees were reduced and added to those of poorer sees. New bishoprics were created to care for the shifts and growth in population. Diocesan conferences of laity and clergy were held and convocations of the archiepiscopal provinces of Canterbury and York convened regularly, thus providing for more responsibility of the Church for its own affairs. The laity took an increasing part in church life. The quality of bishops and clergy rose and was never as high as on the eve of World War I. New church buildings were erected to take care of the expanding population, especially in the cities. Old church fabrics were restored, notably of the cathedrals, and the dignity of public worship was improved.

With the growth of the British Empire, the huge emigration to the colonies, and missions among non-Europeans the Anglican communion became world-wide. Beginning in 1867, usually every ten years, conferences of all Anglican bishops were convened in Lambeth Palace, the London residence of the Archbishop of Canterbury, and under the chairmanship of that prelate.

Cognizance was taken by both Anglicans and Nonconformists of the current intellectual movements, especially in theology and the study of the Scriptures. In general, in accord with the English temperament, such study did not go to the extremes it reached in some quarters in Germany. Opposition was aroused in conservative circles, but so much of what was written was obviously from reverent scholars, constructive rather than negative, completely devoted to Christ and His Church, that in time general assent was given by the majority of thoughtful churchmen to the more moderate conclusions. Between the Evangelicals and the High Church-men was a large and diversified element called Broad Church. It sought to re-state the historic faith in such fashion that whatever was true in the new intellectual currents would be accepted and interpreted in the light of the Gospel.

A variety of movements arose to meet the challenges of the social changes brought by the growth of cities and the Industrial Revolution. In 1878 the Salvation Army was begun by William Booth (1829-1912) in an effort to reach the dregs in the slums of London and quickly spread to other cities and countries. In 1844 the Young Men's Christian Association was founded by George Williams (1821-1905), then a draper's clerk who like many other young men had come from a farm to seek his fortune in London. A product of Evangelicalism, it sought "the improvement of the spiritual condition of young men engaged in the drapery and other trades, by the introduction of religious services among them." The Young Men's Christian Association soon expanded its programme to meet the social, physical, and intellectual as well as the religious needs of young men in the lower- and middle-income groups. It was rapidly reproduced, both in England and abroad, and had its largest development in the United States. Most of the labourers in the factories and mines which were major products of the Industrial Revolution drifted away from the churches. However, many were reached and some of the outstanding leaders in the emerging labour organizations had their initial training in Nonconformist circles, notably as Methodist lay preachers. Yet, while exact statistics are lacking, by the end of the century the percentage of the population attending public worship, although larger than in Germany, appears to have declined from the level of the mid-century.

What was often called the Nonconformist conscience, supplemented by Evangelicals in the Church of England, addressed itself to remedying the appalling conditions from which labourers suffered, whether servile or free. In 1833 through pressure from Evangelicals, both Nonconformist and Anglican, an act of Parliament abolished slavery in the British Empire, with monetary compensation to the slave-owners. Legislation to shorten hours of labour and improve sanitary conditions for men, women, and children employed in mines and factories was indebted chiefly to Evangelicals. Outstanding in obtaining its enactment and in helping in voluntary measures to remedy conditions which damaged human lives was Anthony Ashley Cooper (1801-1885), the seventh Earl of Shaftesbury. He was a loyal Evangelical who owed his Christian nurture to a devout nurse. The temperance movement brought a reduction in the heavy drinking of the eighteenth and the fore part of the nineteenth century.

Clergy and laity, both of the Church of England and of the Nonconformists, were active in adjusting disputes between labourers and employers and in seeking to improve housing and other labour conditions. What was known as Christian Socialism appeared and won advocates. Although he was not strictly a Christian Socialist, John Frederick Denison Maurice (1805-1872) gave impetus to the movement. In 1889 the Christian Social Union was founded. It sought the application of Christian truths and principles to social and economic conditions.

Partly because of the quickened Christian conscience, the administrators of the widely extended colonial empire endeavoured to make British rule serve the welfare of the peoples whom they governed and not simply to increase British wealth. A high degree of integrity characterized the top echelons and the rank and file of the civil service and the Colonial Office. A certain aloofness from the "natives" and a social life apart from the latter provoked irritation. But many of the governed were willing to say that those who constituted the contact between the governed and the governing sought even-handed justice and, while somewhat scornfully regarding the rank and file of the subject populations as "half devil and half child" and "lesser breeds without the law," spent themselves unstintedly in their behalf.

Although many of the British intelligentsia felt that in view of the advance of human knowledge they could no longer be Christians and, as we have seen, much of literature and thought was religiously sceptical, some widely influential figures in prose and poetry remained unashamedly Christian. Prominent among them were Charles Dickens (1812-1870), Alfred Tennyson (1809-1892), and Robert Browning (1812-1889).

English Protestantism made major contributions to education. The old universities, Oxford and Cambridge, Anglican foundations, were progressively secularized. In the eighteenth and the early decades of the nineteenth century Nonconformists had "academies" which, while not granting degrees, gave fully as good higher education as did the universities at Oxford and on the Cam. Secondary schools, usually called "public," were mostly Anglican. Although the moral and intellectual tone of many left much to be desired, in the course of the nineteenth century under the inspiration of clerical headmasters marked improvement was seen. With the growth of an industrial and democratic society, education for the rank and file became imperative. Most of it was long in private hands, chiefly Anglican, but before the end of the century the State undertook elementary education.

Scotland had a state church, the Church of Scotland, Presbyterian. At the outset of the century some independent small Presbyterian and other Protestant bodies existed, and Episcopalians constituted an influential minority. In the course of the nineteenth century awakenings stirred the Church of Scotland, bringing major divisions. In 1843 what was known as the Disruption, led by Thomas Chalmers (1780-1847), brought into being the Free Church of Scotland. The Disruption was ostensibly a protest against the control of the parish clergy by the lay proprietors and the constraints on the Church by the State as a concomitant of the establishment. But it embodied other sources of friction. The Free Church was warmly Evangelical and was strongest in the middle classes in the cities and in the Highlands. By withdrawing from the Church of Scotland, the Free Church lost any share in the ancient endowments and the existing church fabrics. Since an even larger proportion of the laity than of the clergy went with it, with their assistance the Free Church erected new church buildings, founded theological schools to prepare its ministers, and was active in foreign missions. Smaller groups who had seceded from the Church of Scotland in the eighteenth century joined it. In 1900 the United Presbyterians and the large majority in the Free Church came together in the United Free Church of Scotland. The United Presbyterians had come into being in 1847 by the union of two previously dissenting groups. It was heartily Evangelical and was especially active in foreign missions. A small conservative minority of the Free Church, mostly in the Highlands and known humorously as the Wee Frees, did not go into the United Free Church but kept vigorously aloof from it.

The Church of Scotland retained the theological moderates and the political conservatives. It enrolled the well-to-do farmers, the local gentry (not the nobility, for most of the latter adhered to the Episcopal Church), and many of the officials. Undiscouraged by the secession of the Free Church, it created new parishes to meet the needs of the growing urban population and recruited and trained a body of clergy to replace those who went with the Free Church. It introduced organs and made other innovations in public worship. In 1874 by an act of Parliament the choice of ministers to existing benefices was taken from the landlords and vested in the communicants and such adherents as the church might admit to the parish rolls. But the connexion with the State was not severed. In 1929 the Church of Scotland and the United Free Church came together under the designation "the Church of Scotland" and free from any control by the State.

The theological and Biblical issues brought by the intellectual currents of the age troubled the Scottish Presbyterians as they did Protestants in other countries. From the Scottish Presbyterians came many scholars whose writings were widely read in the English-speaking world. In the main, as in England, the best-known works of scholarship were accepted by large numbers and no major division was occasioned by them.

In the nineteenth century the religious life of the principality of Wales rose considerably in quality. The Church of Wales was in communion with the Church of England and was established by law. At the dawn of the century the non-residence of clergy was notorious, church fabrics had fallen into disrepair, and many of the resident clergy were poorly trained. In the course of the century a striking improvement was seen, and disestablishment (in 1914) hastened rather than retarded the advance. Nonconformity flourished and advanced in quality as well as numbers. The denominations having the most adherents were the Congregationalists, the Calvinistic Methodists, the Wesleyan Methodists, and the Baptists. Nationalism was rising, and in the minds of many Nonconformity was associated with it. Nonconformity was stimulated by notable revivals in 1828-1830, in 1859, and especially in 1904-1905.

The Church of Ireland, in communion with the Church of England, was disestablished in 1869. It survived the shock and in 1911 enrolled a slightly larger proportion of the population than at the time of separation from the State. But it was the church of only a minority. Roman Catholics, closely associated with ardent Irish nationalism, were in the overwhelming majority. In the North of Ireland, where a substantial proportion of the population was of Scottish ancestry, Presbyterianism was prominent. It reflected the Protestant awakenings of the century but in general remained more Calvinistic than did the Presbyterianism of Scotland. Methodism enrolled increasing numbers but still a minority. Congregationalists and Baptists included smaller numbers.

The Response of the Eastern Churches

The nineteenth century witnessed a substantial growth of the Eastern Churches in Europe due to developments in the Turkish Empire and Russia.

The progressive disintegration of the Ottoman Empire had as a major feature the regaining of independence by Greece, Rumania, Bulgaria, Serbia, Montenegro, Bosnia, and Herzegovina. Each of these countries was prevailingly Orthodox. Under Turkish rule their bishops had been largely Greeks appointed by the Ecumenical Patriarch from the Phanar district of Constantinople. When Turkish rule was thrown off, the churches became administratively independent of the Ecumenical Patriarch. In some instances, notably in Bulgaria, friction with that office was acute, chiefly over autonomy. In the main, with independence, especially in Greece, ecclesiastical and political autonomy was followed by some recovery from the ebb in the quality of Christian living during Turkish rule.

The Russian Orthodox Church, largest of the Eastern Churches, was, as we have seen, tied closely to the State and subordinate to it. Its faith was threatened by sceptical movements from Western Europe, especially among the intelligentsia. Through Western influence, mainly contacts with Pietism and Quakerism, Alexander I, who ruled from 1801 to 1825, experienced a conversion. Among other acts he encouraged Bible societies, patterned after the British and Foreign Bible Society. In the course of the century Slavophiles, who wished Russia to free itself from the cultural influence of the West, were devoted to the Russian Orthodox Church as a bulwark against the alien currents. In general, conservatives, whether or not they were Slavophiles, looked to the Russian Orthodox Church as a mainstay against revolution.

Parallel with the effort to use the Russian Orthodox Church to counter revolution was an awakening in the inner life of the Church. The awakening came partly through *startsi*, or elders, who gave themselves to the ascetic life and to prayer, and were a continuation of the kenoticism, or emptying of self, which we saw early characterized Russian monasticism.

The Russian Orthodox Church also experienced an awakening in its intellectual life. Outstanding was the contribution of Vladimir Sergeyevich Solovyev (1853-1900). In his teens Solovyev had rejected the faith in which he had been reared, but by the time he was twenty he had returned to it. He was a mystic, a prophet, a moral teacher, a philosopher, and a theologian. To him may be attributed at least part of a revival of the Christian faith which was seen on the eve of World War I. Some of the novelists of the century, notably Dostoyevsky, reflected the influence of the Christian faith. Leo Nikolayevich Tolstoy (1828-1910) also was profoundly stirred.

Some religious movements of Christian origin existed but were not contained in the Russian Orthodox Church. Most of them were of pre-nineteenth-century origin.

PROTESTANTISM IN THE LARGER EUROPE: THE UNITED STATES

In the larger Europe which arose from emigration, Protestantism was increasingly important, particularly, of course, in areas peopled chiefly from the British Isles and the Protestant countries of the Continent. Outstanding was the United States.

Throughout the nineteenth century, religiously the United States was prevailingly Protestant in ethos, and of the British tradition. At the outset of the century its population was descended chiefly from immigrants from Great Britain and North Ireland, with substantial minorities from the Protestant portions of Germany and the Netherlands and slight contingents of Huguenots and Swedes. As the years passed, the Protestant elements were substantially augmented by accessions from Germany and Scandinavia, and with some from the British Isles. By the end of the century Roman Catholics grew by several millions from Ireland and Germany and latterly from Italy and Central Europe.

Although the United States by tradition was prevailingly Protestant, at the beginning of the nineteenth century only a small proportion, said to have been about seven in a hundred, were members of churches. Presumably the percentage who had been baptized was not much larger. Here was an obvious challenge. Could the proportion be increased? Growth was threatened by the mobility of the population. A vast movement from the older settlements on the Atlantic seaboard to the rapidly westward-advancing frontier was a major feature in the young nation. Would the small minority of these migrants who were already baptized retain their church connexions? Would those without these connexions be adequately reached? Such traditions of the union of Church and State has had existed in colonial days were early officially dissipated. The Federal Constitution forbade the Congress to establish any religion. In 1833 the last remnant of an earlier establishment in individual colonies was erased. The absence of formal establishment lessened the danger of the anti-clericalism which was marked on the other side of the Atlantic but did not entirely remove it. Financially the churches were dependent on voluntary contributions and not taxes, as in Europe. Would the constituencies respond? Most of the sceptical currents which were eroding the faith of many in Europe were present in the United States. Industrialization and the rapid growth of cities brought problems similar to those in Europe. In addition were several million Negro slaves, having no Christian heritage, and thousands of Indians, non-Christian, widely scattered in many tribes.

A striking feature of the Protestantism of the United States was the fashion in which the challenge was met. The percentage of the population having church membership rose decade by decade. It is said to have been 15.5 in 1850, 35.7 in 1900, and 43.5 in 1910. Part of the growth came through the Roman Catholic Church, but most of it was in Protestant churches.

The growth took place by processes which were chiefly indigenous. On the frontier it was due partly to camp-meetings, partly to the activity of slightly educated preachers who could speak the language of the settlers and often were itinerant. The Methodists developed a system of circuit riders, supervised by district superintendents and bishops. With their loose form of organization in autonomous churches grouped in regional associations and state conventions, Baptists fitted into the democratic pattern of the frontier. Denominations with higher educational standards, such as the Presbyterians, the Congregationalists, and the Baptists of the eastern seaboard organized societies which sent missionaries to the western settlements but did not gather as many converts as did the men who were sprung from the frontier and spoke its language. Later, as towns and cities grew, preachers who were called evangelists travelled through them, holding meetings which might last for several days or even weeks and calling for open decision for the Christian life. Outstanding among the evangelists were Charles Grandison Finney (1792-1875) in the middle of the century and Dwight Lyman Moody (1837-1899) in the second half of the century. Both extended their activities to the British Isles. They were only two of hundreds who were less well known. From Europe came missionaries to German and Scandinavian settlers. In general the European missionaries were of Pietist background and theologically conservative. Sunday Schools for the nurture of children and youth were extensively employed, especially by the churches which appealed to the older American stock—those whose ancestors had come to the Thirteen Colonies before independence. The American Bible Society, begun in 1816 partly through the example of the British and Foreign Bible Society, sought to place a copy of the Scriptures in every home in the United States as well as helping in the distribution in other countries.

Out of these methods of propagating the faith and with immigration came a Protestantism which, though rooted in Europe, was in many respects different from that on the other side of the Atlantic. In it denominations which were very much in the minority or were non-existent in Europe enrolled the majority of the Protestant church members. The largest bodies were Baptists (in several national or regional conventions, some of them Negro, for the majority of such Negroes as became Christians were Baptists), Methodists (in more than one ecclesiastical structure, some of them also Negro), the Disciples of Christ (of American origin), the Church of Latter Day Saints of Jesus Christ (Mormons, also sprung from the soil), Christian Scientists (likewise indigenous), and the Seventh Day Adventists (born in the United States). The total membership of the Protestant churches which were established in Europe and represented in the United States—Episcopalian, Lutheran, Reformed, and Presbyterian—did not equal that of bodies on the other side of the Atlantic regarded as dissenters.

In the Protestantism of the United States financial self-support was universal. The lay element was more prominent than in Europe; it was evident in the Young Men's and Young Women's Christian Associations and it also characterized the ecclesiastical bodies. In the second half of the century organizations came into being to enlist the younger generation, among them the Young People's Society of Christian Endeavour and the student divisions of the YMCA and the YWCA. They proved contagious and gave rise to world-wide movements. From the student YMCA, through John Randolph Mott (1865-1955), came the World's Student Christian Federation (1896), which united on a global scale similar movements in other lands.

The intellectual currents that challenged Christianity in Europe were also present in the United States. Militant scepticism made itself heard. The voice which had the widest hearing was that of Robert G. Ingersoll (1833-1899). Son of an itinerant evangelist, spotless in his family life, loyal to his friends, a superb orator, a lawyer and politician, Ingersoll rejoiced in pointing out what he believed to be the evils sanctioned in the Old Testament and was an enthusiastic Darwinian. In every major denomination were those who wrestled with the problems presented to Christianity by the philosophy, historical methods, and science of the age. In doing so, some became Unitarians. Unitarianism centred in Boston, where the eighteenth century had seen departure from the inherited Calvinism. As a phase of the religious ferment which found expression in Unitarianism, and influenced by Carlyle and much of current German thought, Transcendentalism arose, also in Massachusetts, partly as a protest against the spreading materialism. Its direct influence was confined to a small circle, but it had wide repercussions. Those who, like the Congregationalists and Presbyterians, had been reared on Calvinism and the Westminster Confession endeavoured to defend that system or adjust it to the new conditions. The issues raised by German scholarship in the study of the Bible created discussions. Towards the end of the century an extreme reaction against any accomodation to higher criticism gave rise to the beginnings of Fundamentalism—stressing what its adherents believed were the basic tenets of the Gospel—a movement which was to assume larger dimensions after 1914.

Protestantism had many profound effects on the life of the United States. It was the source of the "American dream"—achieving an ideal society in the New World, free from the contamination of the Old World and from the evils which chronically beset mankind. From it issued the movement that eventually brought about the emancipation of the Negro slaves. In the same breath we must hasten to say that it was by whites of Protestant ethos that the Negroes had been enslaved. Emancipation did not solve the problem of the freedmen. Though Protestants, white and coloured, strove in many ways, especially through schools, to help the Negroes make a successful adjustment to their new status, progress was slow. From Protestantism came agitation for peace and the crusade for temperance. In several states the temperance movement brought about the prohibition of the manufacture and sale of alcoholic beverages, and in 1919 prohibition was written into the national Constitution. From Protestantism sprang also a widening stream of philanthropy. Not all private munificence had Christianity as the direct cause, but in much the Christian faith was the impelling motive.

The most notable of philanthropists of the nineteenth century was John Davison Rockefeller (1839-1937). His extensive gifts sprang from his Christian conviction that his wealth was a trust from God. In the latter part of the nineteenth century what was known as the "social gospel" endeavoured to realize fully the Kingdom of God on earth by remedying the chronic ills of mankind. Its best-known exponent was Walter Rauschenbusch (1861-1918), whose social convictions stemmed from a Pietist background.

Protestantism had a profound influence on education in the United States. All but one of the earliest colleges issued from it, and out of them came the oldest universities—Harvard, Yale, Columbia, and Princeton. Protestantism fathered scores of colleges and universities on the westward-advancing frontier. It was responsible for most of the early secondary education. In several states universal primary education was initiated by Protestants who were moved by their Christian faith.

Some of the men who did most to shape public life and national policies owed much of their ideals and resolution to Christianity. Outstanding was Abraham Lincoln (1809-1865). Not a church member, he was a diligent student of the Bible and as President during the agony of the Civil War meditated profoundly on the bearing upon it of the purposes of God. His second inaugural address, delivered shortly before an assassin's bullet killed him summarized his conclusions and called for reconciliation between the warring sections, "with malice towards none, with charity for all."

PROTESTANTISM IN THE LARGER EUROPE: LATIN AMERICA

Protestantism could not gain a foothold in Latin America so long as Spain and Portugal were in power. Following independence, relaxation of the ban on that form of the faith began. Before 1914 Protestantism made its chief numerical gains through immigration, chiefly of Germans in Brazil and of Waldenses in Uruguay and Argentina, but these were small minorities. Missions from the British Isles and the United States gathered a few converts among pagan Indians and nominal Roman Catholics. Not until after 1914 did Protestantism have a substantial growth.

PROTESTANTISM IN THE LARGER EUROPE: THE BRITISH DOMINIONS

By the end of the nineteenth century Protestantism was represented by growing constituencies in new nations which were arising from immigration and which by 1914 were self-governing dominions within the British Empire.

The most populous of the British dominions and the largest in area was Canada. As we have seen, Canada had a strong and relatively compact French Roman Catholic element. In the nineteenth century to the French were added substantial numbers of Roman Catholic Irish. The large majority of the nineteenth-century immigrants were Protestant by heritage, most of them from England, Scotland, and North Ireland. As a consequence the largest Protestant bodies were the Church of England in Canada, the Presbyterians, and the Methodists. Baptists constituted a minority and still smaller minorities were in other denominations. In 1914 by far the greatest part of Canada's population called itself Christian and of this group a majority expressed either direct affiliation with or preference for one or another of the Protestant bodies. Missions won many of the aborigines—Indians and Eskimos—to the Christian faith, and white occupation was not accompanied by as extensive wars and exploitation of non-whites as took place in the United States.

In Australia, next in size and population and more recently settled than Canada, the initial immigration was by penal transportation, unpromising material for a new nation. The majority of the immigrants came voluntarily, however, mostly from the British Isles. Roman Catholicism, chiefly of Irish origin, was strong, but more than half the population were Protestants by ethos or membership, with Angelicans leading and with important Presbyterian and Methodist minorities.

New Zealand was more recently occupied by Europeans than

was either Canada or Australia. Its population was predominantly from Great Britain, with the Church of England and Presbyterianism numerically the main forms of Protestantism.

In South Africa the majority of the European stock were Afrikaners, of Dutch ancestry. With very few exceptions Afrikaners were members of one or another of the Dutch Reformed Churches. A large minority of the Europeans were from the British Isles and included Roman Catholics (from Ireland), Anglicans, Presbyterians, and some of other Protestant denominations. An increasing proportion of the Africans bore the Christian name and overwhelmingly as Protestants.

THE SPREAD OF CHRISTIANITY OUTSIDE THE EUROPEAN WORLD

A feature of the religious history of the nineteenth century was the diffusion of Christianity among non-Christians. Most of it was by missionaries inspired by the awakenings in Christianity. The spread was associated with the imperialism and colonialism of European peoples, achieved as these were by aggression and followed by the exploitation of non-Europeans. Through its expansion Christianity registered the most widely extended geographic footholds that it or any other religion had attained. Associated though the expansion was with Western imperialism and colonialism, it had less support from governments than at any time since the adoption of the faith by Constantine. Often, in spite of the fact that it was increasingly anti-clerical, the French Government gave assistance as a means of extending its political and commercial ambitions. The British administrators did not use missions as a tool for conquest. Such support as they gave was chiefly through subsidies to mission schools, maintaining order, and seeing that British missionaries were protected. The aid was given not because the schools were under Christian auspices but because they were assisting in the education which the government was promoting as a means of fulfilling what it deemed its obligation to subject peoples. Protection was accorded missionaries not because they were missionaries but because the maintenance of order was one of the objectives of the government; protection was given all foreigners and especially British citizens, regardless of their occupation. The Tsarist regime helped Russian Orthodox missions, but these were not extensive and with a few exceptions were within Russian domains.

The nineteenth-century expansion of Christianity among non-Western peoples was brought about almost entirely by Roman Catholics and Protestants, with Protestants doing the larger part.

Roman Catholic missions were maintained through existing orders—chiefly the Society of Jesus and the Brothers Minor, with important Dominican contingents—and also, to a lesser degree, through newly organized societies and congregations. Among the agencies of nineteenth-century origin were the *Société des Missionnaires de Notre Dame d'Afrique,* usually known as the White Fathers, an outgrowth of the attempt to use the extension of the French Empire in North Africa as an opportunity to spread the faith; the Congregation of the Immaculate Heart of Mary, a Belgian organization with headquarters at Scheutveld, a suburb of Brussels; the Society of the Divine Word, made up of Germans from Steyl, in Holland, not far from the German border; St. Joseph's Society of Mill Hill, with its centre near London, but with predominantly Dutch personnel. As we have seen, the majority of the Roman Catholic missionaries were French.

Protestant missionaries came from almost all countries where Protestants were a substantial proportion of the population—Germany, the Scandinavian countries, Switzerland, the Netherlands, the British Isles, the United States, Canada, Australia, and New Zealand. The majority were from the British Isles and the United States. Until 1900 the British Isles provided the larger contingents, but in later decades the churches of the United States assumed an increasing role in the enterprise and in 1914 were contributing more money than were the British Churches.

The mounting participation of the Protestants of the United States was given a major impulse by the Student Volunteer Movement for Foreign Missions. It dated from a student conference held in 1886 with Dwight L. Moody as host and the chief speaker. It was there that John R. Mott, for years the chairman of the executive committee of the Movement, dedicated himself to missions. Under the slogan "The Evangelization of the World in This Generation" the Student Volunteer Movement enlisted thousands from colleges, universities, and theological seminaries and spread to the British Isles and the Continent of Europe. Evidences of the growing share of the United States in the foreign missionary movement were the holding in New York in 1900 of what was called the Ecumenical Missionary Conference and the fact that the epoch-making World Missionary Conference convened in Edinburgh in 1910 had Mott as its presiding officer and chief organizer and made him chairman of the Continuation Committee from which emerged (1921) the International Missionary Council as a means of coördinating Protestant missions of all nations.

The outpouring of life by Roman Catholics and Protestants led to the planting or strengthening of Christianity in every continent and in the majority of countries. More and more, the purpose was to bring into being churches which would not be dependent on foreign personnel and funds. Except in a few small islands in the Pacific, until 1914 the Christian communities which arose from missions from the West were small minorities, Christian enclaves in overwhelming non-Christian populations, dependent on continued infusions from Europe and America and regarded by the non-Christian neighbours as aliens, the religious phase of Western imperialism and colonialism.

In North Africa and Western Asia, traditionally Moslem, very few converts were won, and such as came were predominantly from the Eastern Churches, themselves encysted minorities. In Africa south of the Sahara European explorations were spearheaded chiefly by Protestants, of whom the earnest and courageous David Livingstone (1813–1873), a Scottish missionary, was outstanding, followed by Henry Morton Stanley (1841–1904), British born but a citizen of the United States. By the year 1914, from the Roman Catholic and Protestant missionaries who followed these and other pioneers small Christian communities were appearing, harbingers of the remarkable and accelerating growth of the next fifty years.

India, shortly after the mid-century brought completely under British rule, was the scene of increasing Roman Catholic and Protestant missionary effort. Christianity was already represented by the ancient Syrian Church and Roman Catholic contingents partly controlled by the Portuguese. The numbers of Christians grew, mainly in the South where the earlier communities were strong. But by the outbreak of World War I they totalled less than one per cent. of the population.

Dating from the Portuguese occupation, the Christians of Ceylon were about ten in a hundred, overwhelmingly Roman Catholic. Burma and Siam had small Christian groups, most numerous among the animistic peoples of Burma. In Indo-China, under French protection, Roman Catholics experienced a substantial growth but were still a small minority. The Dutch East Indies had growing Christian communities, mainly Protestant and among former animists.

On reluctant China, opened to Westerners by cannon, predominantly British, Roman Catholics and Protestants expended much effort, chiefly in the second half of the century and mostly after 1900. By 1914 less than one-half of one per cent. of the population called themselves Christians. In Korea, helpless victim of her large neighbours, China, Japan, and Russia. Christians were not tolerated until the 1880's. Beginning in the 1880's they grew rapidly, most of them Protestants and from missions from the United States. Japan did not permit the re-entrance of missionaries until 1859, and then only grudgingly. Protestants, Roman Catholics, and a small contingent of Russian Orthodox were active. By 1914 fewer than one in five hundred of the population professed Christianity.

The Philippines, mostly Roman Catholic as the result of the Spanish occupation, were somnolent until nationalism stirred early in the 1890's and annexation by the United States occurred (1899). Adjustment of the Roman Catholic Church to the changed situation was painful. In protest against the refusal of

Rome to appoint Filipino bishops a secession into an independent church carried away several hundred thousand. Protestant missionaries entered and quickly won growing numbers. The islands of the Pacific, widely scattered over a vast expanse, were the scene of extensive Protestant and some Roman Catholic missions. As a result the populations of several of the islands, mostly in the east and all previously animist, were converted.

Missionaries, especially Protestant missionaries, were pioneers in helping non-European peoples adjust to the invading European culture. They opened schools, where necessary reduced the languages to writing, in the effort to further physical health brought in Western medicine and surgery, and fought famine. Protestants translated all or part of the Bible into hundreds of tongues and distributed it widely.

A Look Backward and Forward

In a century which saw mounting threats in the centre of its greatest strength, Christianity suffered losses. But it also displayed a vigour in striking contrast with its langour on the eve of the revolutions which ushered in the nineteenth century. That renewed strength was seen in all major branches of the faith—Roman Catholics, Protestant, and Orthodox. Vigour was displayed in a variety of ways. It reduced the compromises by the churches of the preceding century and gave rise to new movements which made Christianity more nearly in accord with the Gospel than it had been since its earliest centuries. It succeeded in holding to the faith or winning back millions of emigrants or descendants of emigrants in North America and Australasia. The chief losses were in Roman Catholic constituencies in Latin Europe and Latin America. The main, but not the only, advances were through Protestantism. Missions planted Christianity, still insecurely, among more peoples than it or any other religion had yet reached.

Now followed a stage in the revolution which threatened all the gains of the past. Spectacular losses were seen, chiefly in

Europe, the historic centre of what had been called Christendom. But, as we should by now expect, the vitality inherent in the Gospel found expression in ways which, if mankind be viewed as a whole, made Christ more influential in the human scene than He or any other born of woman had ever been.

CHAPTER XI

Christianity, Challenged and Expanding:

The Half-Century Which Followed A.D. 1914

The summer of 1914 was marked by the inception of a fresh stage in the revolution to which we have repeatedly called attention and which began at least as far back as the Renaissance. During the half-century between 1914 and the time when these lines were penned, it continued to mount with increasing rapidity. We must first outline the main features of that stage of the revolution, next describe, also succinctly, the fashion in which it threatened Christianity, both by open attack and by less open but subtle and more dangerous erosion, and then call attention to how the challenge was faced—with the result of a greater impact of Christianity upon mankind as a whole than at any earlier time.

THE MAIN FEATURES OF THE REVOLUTION

The feature of the augmented revolution to be mentioned first is that, as in its earlier stages, it originated in and radiated from what was formerly called Christendom—Europe, and especially Western Europe, where Christianity had longest had its best opportunity to make itself effective in the life of man. As we have earlier hinted, the question emerges as to how far, if at all, the revolution is attributable to Christianity. Had Christianity set in motion forces which it could not control and which were inherently destructive, not only of Christianity, but of all human civilization and even of mankind itself? Had Christianity unwittingly created and opened a Pandora's box? We can venture no conclusive answer. We can simply remind ourselves what he have repeatedly noted: that on this planet God seems to be intent on developing children and not robots and that in doing so He has deliberately taken the risk, as in the incarnation and the crucifixion, of having His freely offered gifts abused by the evils to which mankind is heir; but that here are also a challenge and God's offer of power to overcome the evil in such fashion as to augment man's welfare—that where sin abounded grace might much more abound.

The second and most spectacular feature was war. In contrast with the preceding century of relative peace, two major world wars engulfed all mankind. The major theatre of both was Europe. The first (1914-1918) began in Europe, and the second, while having its initial rumblings in the invasion of China by Japan (1931), is usually reckoned as breaking out in Europe in 1939. Even if September 1939, is counted as the inception, World War II was more prolonged than World War I, for it lasted almost six years, until August, 1945. It was more widely destructive and exhausting than its predecessor. Other wars, mostly local, were born of forces released by the revolution—notably the civil war in Spain in the 1930's, war in Korea in the 1950's, and the prolonged struggles in what was once called Indo-China in the 1950's and 1960's. Overshadowing them all was the menace of thermonuclear war. The major accumulation of atomic weapons was in countries once counted as Christian. The order for the first use of the atomic bomb was given by a President of the United States who was a communicant in good standing in a Protestant church and had declared—although not specifically in that connexion—that he endeavoured to be guided by the Sermon on the Mount.

A third feature was closely associated with war: the emergence of totalitarian régimes out of the wreckage wrought by war—the most prominent being Communism in Russia and China led by Stalin and his successors and Mao Tse-tung, the Nazis and Hitler in Germany, the Fascists and Mussolini in Italy, and the Falange and Franco in Spain. Most of them professed to be democratic but all departed far from the Anglo-Saxon democracy sprung from radical Protestantism.

A fourth feature was the triumph of anti-religious (not just anti-Christian) Communism in large and growing segments of the world and the confidence expressed by its spokesmen that it would eventually be adopted by all mankind.

A fifth feature, more dangerous than Communism, was secularism. Secularism threatened to undermine the foundations not only of Christianity but also of all religion. It, too, was due to factors within the erstwhile Christendom and spread to other parts of the world. One source was intellectual. The scientific discoveries and the philosophies of the age appeared to many to make Christianity and every religion untenable by informed and honest minds. Another factor was the absorption of men's interests in obtaining what they deemed the good things of life—the physical comforts and aesthetic values which seemed to be independent of religion. Still another factor was the disintegration of the social structure with which religion had been associated and the consequent weakening or disappearance of customs that ordinarily accompanied religion. Contributing to secularism was the surging tide of nationalism which made religion ancillary to patriotism and supported it only as it reinforced loyalty to the State. Thus conservative, anti-Communist forces in the United States invoked Christianity as a bulwark of "the American way of life." Islam, Hinduism, and Buddhism were reviving, but they were valued chiefly because they were identified with particular nationalisms—Arab, Indian, Singhalese, or Burmese. One keen Chinese intellectual, Hu Shih, not a Communist, declared that the Chinese, because of a long tradition of agnosticism, would be the first people to outgrow religion—suggesting that religion is a stage through which mankind passes on its pilgrimage from infancy to maturity. Nationalism, like the other sources of secularism, had its first appearance in "Christendom."

A sixth feature of the mounting revolution was the surging tide of revolt against Western imperialism and colonialism. It was in part a fruit of nationalism and in part the almost inevitable reaction against the nineteenth-century domination by Western European peoples of most of the non-Western world. To no small degree it could be ascribed to the former Christendom, for one of its major causes was a burning and formerly impotent resentment against the assumption by the European that he was of a superior race and civilization and so had an inborn right to rule.

Even before World War I sensitive observers discerned the writing on the wall. Indians, Chinese, and Japanese were seething with indignation and were seeking ways of forcing respect from the Westerners and gaining full independence. In a very real sense the two world wars were Occidental civil wars, reciprocally destructive to the combatants. Western European powers were so badly weakened that demands for independence could not be ignored. After World War I in several lands concessions looking towards autonomy were forced on reluctant Western governments. After World War II independence progressed apace. Before the 1960's most of Asia and Africa had been freed from the Westerner's yoke.

The situation was complicated by the fact that in large sections of the globe a new imperialism, that of Communist Russia and China, succeeded Western imperialism. Communist Russia dominated much of Central Europe, the Balkans, and Mongolia, was seeking to penetrate the Americas through a puppet régime in Cuba, and was aspiring to control much of the Middle East and Africa. The Chinese Communists, from their capital in Peking, had mastered Tibet, were reaching their tentacles into South-east Asia, and were endeavouring to make their weight felt in Latin America and Africa.

Associated with revolt against imperialism and colonialism was a seventh feature: conflicts over race. The legal emancipation

of Negroes brought by the Protestant conscience in the British
Empire and the United States did not immediately solve the
problems born of slavery. If anything, for a time it aggravated
them. In many countries inter-racial tensions existed and
mounted—in Africa, especially South Africa, between peoples
of African habitat or ancestry and "Christian" peoples of European ancestry, in the West Indies, and in the United States.
Conflict arose in Assam from the demand of hill tribes, recently
become Christian, for a degree of autonomy as against Indian
nationalism, which insisted on their integration with the predominantly Hindu Republic of India.

An eighth aspect of the revolution was a further stage in the
industrial and technological revolution. This, too, had its radiating centre in the former Christendom. It made vast strides in
Europe, the Americas, and Australasia and spread throughout
the non-Western world. It was a means to material wealth and
as such was eagerly sought by industrially "backward" peoples,
for to them it appeared to be a way of freeing themselves from
their chronic poverty and acquiring the wealth and the power
which they envied in Western European peoples.

The industrial and technological revolution was made possible
by advances in science. Men now seemed about to eliminate poverty and disease and aspired to reach beyond the planet into the
other members of the solar system. All peoples sought to equip
themselves with science and its tools.

From the industrial and technological revolution came a ninth
aspect of the revolution. Vast changes were wrought in the life
of mankind. Rapid communication and travel—by radio, television, and the automobile and airplane—made the planet a
shrinking world and brought men into a neighbourhood. The
neighbourhood was quarrelsome, all the more dangerously so
because of its narrowing physical dimensions and the tools of
destruction with which industries and technology had equipped
it. Cities burgeoned. In several countries in Europe, the Americas,
Asia, and even Africa, lately brought into the zone of the revolution, great urban centres and clusters of urban centres appeared,

almost before men were aware of them. They became aggrega-
tions of deracinated individuals and small family units. The
older rural communities dwindled, and with the new means of
communication their collective life was threatened or disappeared. Through the improvement in public health brought by
science, populations mounted. Few parts of the world escaped
the population explosion brought by the reduction of the death
rate.

THE THREATS TO CHRISTIANITY BROUGHT BY THE REVOLUTION

In each of its features the revolution was a threat to Christianity. The menace brought by war is obvious. The toll of life
in the twentieth-century wars was numerically larger than that
of their predecessors. Among the losses were young men who
held promise of constructive contributions had they lived to
maturity, even more millions of non-combatants, and other
millions of deracinated refugees. Still more serious from the
standpoint of Christian morals were the inevitable concomitants
of dishonesty, cruelty, and hate.

The totalitarism régimes were accompanied by the loss of
that respect for the individual which is inherent in Christianity
and the callous liquidation of minorities who stood in the way
of the dictator. Among the mass atrocities were the executions of
those who were obstacles to Stalin and the starvation of millions
in Russia through the deliberate neglect of the Communist
rulers, and the execution of thousands in the accomplishment
of "land reform" by the Communist Party of China, and the
virtual enslavement of other thousands in forced labour by that
party. Especially sobering was the fate of the Jews in Nazi
Germany and the lands overrun by the Nazis, for Germany had
been the original source of the Protestant Reformation and was
the home of some of the most vital movements in both Protestantism and the Roman Catholic Church. Hitler, Mussolini, and
Franco were nominally Roman Catholics. Was Christianity
powerless to prevent the horrors wrought by the descendants of

generations who for centuries had been nurtured in a civilization which was ostensibly Christian?

The threat of Communism was sobering too, for it had been formulated in "Christendom," by men reared as Protestants, and had its first triumphs in "Holy Russia," whose capital, Moscow, had been acclaimed by Russian Orthodox as the third Rome, the seat of true Christianity. As we shall see, the Communists did not succeed in fully eliminating Christianity in the Union of Soviet Socialist Republics, but one of their early acts was to sever the tie between the Russian Orthodox Church and the State and they waged a persistent anti-Christian—and anti-religious—campaign. In the Soviet satellites in Central Europe and the Balkans the Roman Catholic, Protestant, and Orthodox Churches were curtailed. In China, during the latter half of the nineteenth and the first five decades of the twentieth century, as much Christian missionary effort, Roman Catholic and Protestant, had been expended as in any other one section of the non-European world. By the mid-1960's the (Communist) People's Democratic Republic was slowly tightening the noose about such Christian churches as survived on the mainland—the area under its domination.

Secularism, more dangerous to Christianity and all religion than Communism, was taking heavy toll in lands where either the Roman Catholic Church or Protestantism had long had its chief strength. In Latin Europe, Eire, and much of Germany, historically Roman Catholic, the overwhelming majority were baptized. The same was true in the Protestant portions of Europe, including Great Britain and North Ireland. But Roman Catholic authorities sorrowfully said that only a minority of their baptized, even in almost solidly Catholic Spain and Portugal, were practising their faith. In the 1950's two French Roman Catholic priests, Henri Godin and Yvan Daniel, wrote a book, *La France, Pays de Mission?* in which they spoke of their native land as a mission field. In the Protestant sections of Western Europe after 1914 church attendance in both cities and rural districts drastically declined and recruits for the ministry fell off: Christian conviction was confined to minorities. In Latin America secularism and scepticism continued to penetrate the nominally Roman Catholic majority, of whatever class. For example, in Uruguay Christmas was re-named "Family Day" and Easter "Tourist Day," and the leading newspaper in Montevideo printed the name of God in small letters. In Brazil the vacuum left by the decay of the Roman Catholic faith was partly filled by spiritualism, much of it a crude animism derived from Africa and some a more sophisticated form inspired by Hinduism. In the United States the proportion of church members to the population fairly steadily increased, until it was nearly two-thirds. But the complaint was repeatedly voiced that the growth was more from social convention than religious conviction and that actually among professed Christians much indifferentism existed. In French Canada the Roman Catholic Church was vigorous, but much of the loyalty could be ascribed to a French Canadian particularism as against the Anglo-Saxon majority—as could that in Eire of Irish nationalism against the long-standing tie with Great Britain, recently dissolved. Of the Protestant elements in Canada, Australia, and New Zealand, in the census returns almost all continued to express a church preference, but church attendance, while large, was only of a minority, and the numbers of indigenous clergy did not keep pace with the demand. In Protestantism and among non-practising Roman Catholics in both Europe and the Americas much religious relativism existed. The opinion was widely held that truth and error in all religions were equal, that religion was a symptom of man's effort to penetrate the mystery of his existence and of the universe, and that none of the many answers which had issued from the quest had ultimate validity. Significance may be seen in the fact that most of the comprehensive studies of the religions of mankind had been made in Christendom rather than by adherents of the non-Christian religions.

The revolt among non-European peoples against Western imperialism and colonialism often heightened the denunciation of Christianity because of its association with the Occidental expansion of the nineteenth and earlier centuries. Presumably the mounting nationalism and resentment against the white man would erase the footholds won by missionaries from the Occident.

The industrial and technological revolution augmented secularism, in whatever part of the world it was found. The vast increase in population which arose from that phase of the revolution multiplied the numbers of non-Christians. Since the most spectacular growth was in Asia, overwhelmingly non-Christian, by the mid-1960's the earth contained more outside the Christian fold than when Christ died—or even at the outset of the twentieth century. Although the numbers whom religious statistics labelled Christian—at best a doubtful and superficial classification—were increasing, the proportion of mankind listed in that category was declining.

THE RESPONSE OF CHRISTIANITY

Serious as was the threat, and sobering as were the losses, the response in the fifty years which succeeded the summer of 1914 shows that far from being moribund, Christianity was rising to meet the challenge. More than in any preceding age, the contrast to which we have repeatedly called attention was striking. On the one hand were the mounting dimensions of the chronic ills of mankind—the outcome of man's ignorance, folly, self-interest, and pride—reaching their most colossal expressions in an ostensible Christendom; on the other hand was the power issuing from what Christians believe to have come from the incarnation, the cross, the resurrection, and the Holy Spirit. As always, much of that power was seen in humble persons who were remembered only by a few and of whom a later generation and the historian would be unaware. But some was displayed in ways which the historian could detect.

Part of the response was directed to the challenge of war. In World War I, fought almost entirely between professed Christians, most of the belligerents invoked the aid of God and declared that they were fighting for justice. In the case of the United States, late to come into the war, its President, Woodrow

Wilson, summoned the nation to enter the struggle as a war to end war. Himself earnestly Christian, from a long Protestant heritage and from a commitment made in impressionable adolescence, Woodrow Wilson was inspired and sustained by his faith. From that faith arose his championship of the League of Nations. For many years the dream of such an international organization to bring all mankind into coöperation, to seek the welfare of non-European peoples ruled by Westerners, to solve international tensions through international action and without war had been cherished in Christendom. Since the Napoleonic Wars it had become more insistent and had taken the form of concrete proposals. Woodrow Wilson insisted that the Covenant of the League of Nations be written into the peace treaties which terminated World War I. The League of Nations did not prevent the outbreak of World War II. Although technically it survived until 1946, actually it had been proved impotent before 1939.

The dream did not die. Chiefly through the determined labours of Protestants, it was embodied in the United Nations, through the Charter framed in 1945. No one strove more earnestly to make the United Nations an effective instrument than its Secretary General, Dag Hammarskjöld, who, reared in the Lutheran household of Nathan Söderblom, in his later years returned with deepened convictions to the faith which for a time he had felt himself intellectually constrained to surrender. Through Protestant leadership the United Nations adopted the Declaration of Human Rights. Because of the Christian convictions of a Protestant, John Foster Dulles, the treaty of peace between the victorious United States and the defeated Japan was not made punitive but gave the vanquished an opportunity for recovery. During and after each of the two world wars measures for the relief of suffering by combatants and non-combatants on both sides of the warring front were undertaken by Christians, Roman Catholic and Protestant, on a scale greater than in any previous war, and far larger than any in wars waged by non-Christians—such as those of Moslem Arabs, animist Mongols, Hindu and Buddhist conquerors, and the Moslem Timur (Tamerlane).

In 1964, when these lines were penned, in no country, except possibly North Korea and North Vietnam, had Communism succeeded in fully liquidating Christianity. In the U.S.S.R. the Russian Orthodox Church, the Armenian (Gregorian) Church, and Protestantism not only persisted but as well recruited members and clergy from the younger generation. Much the same record was seen in Rumania, Bulgaria, Poland, Hungary, Czechoslovakia, and East Germany. In the People's Republic of China both the Catholic Church and Protestantism survived, and Protestantism had some adult conversions and trained clergy. The possible disappearance of Christianity in North Korea and North Vietnam—for in 1964 no dependable religious news came from either—was partly due to mass migrations of Christians to South Korea or South Vietnam.

The erosion by secularism in Western Europe, the Eastern Churches outside Communist domains, the Americas, and Australasia was countered by vigorous movements, some of them new, in all branches of Christianity.

In Western Europe the Papacy saw the continuation of the succession of able and devoted Pontiffs which had marked the second half of the nineteenth century. Benedict XV (reigned 1914-1922) spanned the years of World War I and the first quadrennium of the uneasy peace. He worked tirelessly to relieve suffering and put forward proposals for terminating the agonizing struggle. Pius XI (reigned 1922-1939) was an able administrator of vision, determination, and sterling character. He entered into an arrangement with Mussolini which eased the longstanding tension between the Church and the State, partly through the creation of Vatican City and partly in decreased control of the Church by the Italian Government. He also aided the expansion of the Church and its deeper planting in the non-European world. In the encyclical *Quadragesimo Anno* (1931) he renewed and adapted to the changing times the principles put forward by Leo XIII in *Rerum Novarum*. Pius XII (reigned 1939-1958), at the outset of his pontificate was faced by World War II. As had Benedict XV, he endeavoured to put before the world suggestions for ending the struggle. Like Benedict, he gave himself unsparingly to the relief of the suffering. He stoutly denounced Communism when that ideology was sweeping across much of Eurasia. As was to be expected from his deeply religious nature, he issued (1943) the encyclical *Mystici Corporis Christi*, dealing with the Church as the mystical body of Christ and identifying it with the Roman Catholic Church. While warning against rash deviations from current practice, he somewhat guardedly endorsed the Liturgical Movement, with its emphasis on the intelligent participation of the laity in the mass. He encouraged Biblical scholarship but deplored Modernism, Neo-Kantianism, Marxism, and rationalism. He promulgated (1950) as a doctrine to be held by all the faithful the bodily assumption of Mary into heaven. In the world mission, he stressed an indigenous clergy and episcopate among non-European peoples. John XXIII (reigned 1958-1963) came of peasant stock and rejoiced in his humble parentage. As pastor, administrator, and diplomat he had had extensive experience before ascending the throne of Peter. Although seventy-eight years of age when installed, he brought to his post imagination and energy. In his encyclical *Mater et Magistra* he supported in terms of his day what Leo XIII had formulated in *Rerum Novarum* and Pius XI had reiterated in *Quadragesimo Anno*. His encyclical *Pacem in Terris*, issued a few weeks before his death, bravely called all men of goodwill, Christians and non-Christians, to comprehensive efforts for peace. In a generation near despair because of the threat of atomic holocaust it inspired hope and renewed determination. John XXIII endeavoured to establish friendly personal relations with leading Communists. His crowning achievement was the Ecumenical Council of which we are to speak later. Paul VI (1963– ––) followed John XXIII and continued much of the latter's programme. The Ecumenical Council resumed its sessions (1963). Friendly relations with non-Roman Catholic Christians were cultivated—partly by inviting accredited observers to the Council and appointing observers to meetings of the Divisions of the World Council of Churches, and partly by a visit to Jerusalem and a friendly conference with the Ecumenical Patriarch. Paul

VI also authorized courteous approaches to non-Christian religions.

In other ways the Roman Catholic Church displayed great vigour, especially but by no means only in parts of France, Belgium, the Netherlands, Germany, Switzerland, and North Italy where the forces making for secularism were particularly potent. That vigour had several expressions. One was the continuation of the Liturgical Movement, accentuating the participation of the laity in the central rite of the Church, aided by the dialogue mass and putting all but the heart of the Communion into the vernacular. Another was the multiplication of Eucharistic Congresses, some of them on a world scale and some national. Much stress was placed on Catholic Action, for the coöperation of the laity in making Christianity effective in every phase of life, in deepening the devotion of the rank and file of the Church's constituency, and in winning others to the faith. Lay movements of many kinds proliferated—among youth, students, workers in various occupations, and women, and in efforts to strengthen the Christian family. Christian Democratic parties emerged, made up chiefly of Roman Catholics, particularly after World War II. They were potent in several countries. Bible study was promoted, partly by fresh translations of the Scriptures into the vernacular. So prominent were the lay movements that at times the age was described as the century of the laity. "The priesthood of the laity" became almost a cliché—not in the Protestant sense of the priesthood of all believers, but with the inference that, although the functions of the laity did not supplant those of the clergy, the role of the laity was quite as important as that of the priests. Much scholarly activity was seen, in the professional study of the Bible and in theology and philosophy, the latter to take account of contemporary currents in thought.

In Protestant Europe and the British Isles, although church attendance fell off sharply and candidates for the ministry declined in numbers, many new movements appeared—in what might be called creative minorities—and enlisted hundreds and in some cases thousands. Among them were the Evangelical

Academies, chiefly of post-World War II origin and centring in Germany. They paralleled the emphasis on the laity in the Roman Catholic Church, for their purpose was to gather laymen and lay women of various professions and occupations into centres for free discussion of what the Christian faith demanded in daily life. Under the leadership of Reinhold von Thadden-Trieglaff (1891—), a scion of the East German Pietist nobility and a former prisoner of war in Russia, beginning in 1949 great assemblies of German Protestants were held, under an old name, *Kirchentag,* but with a new programme, to promote worship, Bible study, and the Christian life and to give a sense of community to what had been the sadly beleaguered anti-Nazi Protestants and those who sympathized with them. In Germany much of the vigour of the post-World War II years came from the Confessing Church (*bekennende Kirche*). As a result of World War I the territorial churches (*Landeskirchen*) of Germany had been disestablished, but strong ties with the community as a whole remained and there was a temptation to perpetuate under the Nazis the submission of the Church to the State which had existed from the time of the Protestant Reformation. Hitler attempted to bring into being a Protestant church which would support his régime. However, a substantial minority would not conform and constituted the *bekennende Kirche*. Many persons were imprisoned and some were liquidated. Among the latter was Dietrich Bonhoeffer (1906-1945). Of a scholarly, cultured family, Bonhoeffer could have been secure in a pastorate in London or the United States, but he chose to return to Germany, took his place with the Confessing Church, was incarcerated, and was executed shortly before the Nazi collapse. His writings, several of them composed in prison, had a wide influence on post-World War II youth, both in Germany and elsewhere.

In the Netherlands in World War II numbers of Protestants, especially among the clergy, courageously spoke out against inhuman measures of the Nazis who were occupying the country. After the war a movement akin to the Evangelical Academies—

Kerk en Wereld—was initiated to train youth among the laity in theology and methods of evangelism. Conferences on a variety of subjects were convened and workers were prepared for leadership in social and cultural relations and for the promotion of good relations in industry. To coördinate the various centres the Federation of Lay Training Centres in Holland was organized. Regional *Kerkdagen* were held, inspired by the *Kirchentagen* of Germany.

Sweden had the Sigtuna Foundation, organized in 1917 in a town not far from Stockholm. Its purpose was to provide an opportunity for intellectuals, not all of whom might be committed to the faith, to work in a Christian environment and thus to penetrate Swedish culture with Christianity and make possible conferences for the discussion of social and cultural problems.

The Iona Community, the creation of George Fielden Mac-Leod (1895—), later Sir George MacLeod, centred on the island off the West Coast from which much of the conversion of the country had been accomplished, endeavoured to create and nourish a fellowship which would bring renewed life to the Church of Scotland, especially in urban depressed areas.

The English scene was varied. The free churches were handicapped, partly by the blows dealt the middle class by the two world wars and the economic and social changes. They had drawn most of their strength from the middle class, but although they lost in membership, they persisted. The Church of England also suffered in attendance and from a shortage of clergy. It continued to display a great variety in churchmanship—from these with an extreme emphasis on the Catholic tradition, through Evangelicalism (some of it very conservative in its attitude to modern scholarship), to what was formerly called Broad Church, sometimes self-styled as Modern Church, whose extreme representatives denied the virgin birth and many of the miracles of Jesus. In accord with trends which we have seen in the Roman Catholic Church and Protestantism on the Continent, the Church of England provided for an enlarged participation by the laity. To the Church of England came bishops of outstanding devotion and ability. The most notable was William Temple (1881-1944), the brilliant son of an Archbishop of Canterbury and successively rector in a London parish, Bishop of Manchester, Archbishop of York, and Archbishop of Canterbury. He was eager to have Christians address themselves to the problems presented by industrialized society. Bishops were no longer great lords but lived simply and for the most part gave themselves devotedly to their flocks. Incomes of clergy declined. But in many pulpits were courageous voices, and both parish priests and bishops undertook to deal with the personal and collective problems of the times. Retreat centres multiplied, with opportunities for withdrawal for brief periods from the rush of contemporary life for quiet meditation and prayer.

Protestant theological and Biblical scholarship in Europe flourished and had many expressions, evidence that, as in the Roman Catholic Church, efforts were not lacking to keep Christian thought creatively abreast of the changing currents. In theology the Swiss pastor and teacher Karl Barth (1888——) was the most widely influential. Reacting from the liberalism of the pre-1914 decades, with its confident trust in the human intellect and will, he caught the attention of many of the more thoughtful, disillusioned by the gulfs in Western civilization revealed by the two world wars. He did not yield to the despair of many of the sceptical existentialists but, recognizing the weaknesses of man in his search for truth and taking account of nineteenth-century scholarship, stressed the initiative and action of God in the progressive revelation of Himself in the ancient Jewish prophets culminating in the incarnation and work of Christ. He became one of the formulators of what was known as neo-orthodoxy.

In Biblical studies the most discussed scholar in the post-World War II years was the German Rudolf Bultmann (1884-——). Bultmann employed the methods of *Formgeschichte* (form criticism), which had emerged in Germany on the eve of World War II. In the effort to make the Gospel relevant to contemporary man, bemused by science, the application of current historical methods to the Bible, and existentialism, Bultmann furthered "de-mythologizing," endeavouring to free the Gospel from the integuments of the first-century culture of the Mediterranean world and showing its eternal relevance, including especially its message to twentieth-century man. He provoked much controversy and did not win general agreement among scholars, whether Roman Catholic or Protestant.

In the Eastern Churches, long resisting change in their efforts to preserve their existence in the face of the encompassing aggressive Islam, some fresh currents made their appearance. In the Orthodox Church in Greece the Zoë Brotherhood of theologians, begun shortly after World War I, although having a small membership, helped to bring new vitality to the faith with application to the contemporary scene. Through Zoë the Bible was widely circulated and the education of the clergy was improved. In the ancient Coptic Church great reverence was still paid to the monastic life in which the Christians of Egypt had been pioneers. Seeking to counter the inroads of secularism, some of the laity strove to raise the cultural level of members and to make preaching and the liturgy more pertinent to the life of both the educated and the rank and file. Sunday Schools multiplied and the Bible was studied. In Ethiopia the Emperor Haile Selassie endeavoured to make the Church more nearly autonomous as against the Coptic Church, for the latter had long appointed the leading ecclesiastic. He also furthered the education of the clergy.

Although seemingly moribund, the Christianity of Latin America gave indications of fresh life. After World War II Catholic Action began to spread. In 1955 a world Eucharistic Congress was held in Buenos Aires, out of which came the Latin American Bishops Conference, known by the initials CELAM. From headquarters at Bogotá, through several departments it sought to improve the quality of the professing Roman Catholics. Now that Europe was unable to supply as many clergy as formerly, increasing help in personnel came from Roman Catholics in the United States. After World War I Protestantism grew rapidly, in part through immigration, chiefly Lutherans from Germany to Brazil. Until World War II most of the Lutheran clergy came from Germany, but after that war an indigenous supply of clergy emerged. Several major denominations of the United States had missions. Their converts were mostly from the middle class. Fastest growing of Protestant bodies were the several Pentecostal groups. They drew chiefly from lower income and educational levels and were most numerous in Brazil and Chile. Increasingly they were self-supporting and had indigenous leadership.

The United States forged to the head of the non-Communist world and therefore of what was historically Christendom. It was religiously pluralistic. Roman Catholics increased in numbers, chiefly by birth. With the exception of Louisiana, they were still strongest in the inner-city metropolitan areas, mostly in the North and West. Originally predominantly unskilled labourers, their educational and economic level rose. Many had only a nominal connexion with their church and were subjected to secularizing currents. Difficulty was encountered in recruiting clergy, and numbers were imported from Ireland, where the supply was ample and where no language barrier existed to service in the United States. Jews multiplied but were largely secularized. Most of them conserved their heredity ties in special social centres and in a few ritual observances inherited from their ghetto status in Europe. In 1928, on the initiative of a Protestant, E. Clinchy, the National Conference of Christians and Jews was begun to promote sympathetic understanding among Roman Catholics, Protestants, and Jews.

In its denominational proportions, the complexion of Protestantism in the United States remained substantially as it had been in 1914. Except for the Lutherans, Protestantism had its core chiefly in descendants of those who had come to the country in colonial days. However, millions of the offspring of more recent arrivals were incorporated in its churches. In general, except for the Negroes, Protestants were from middle and upper income levels. Although they were still strong in the dwindling rural communities, increasingly they moved to the suburbs of the growing cities and were characterized by the attitudes common to suburbia. Here was much fluidity, for changes of residence became characteristic of a larger proportion of the population. Denominational affiliation was determined as much by geography and social status as by distinctive religious convictions. As the educational and economic levels rose of denominations which had traditionally been recruited from the lower economic strata— such as Methodists, Baptists, and Disciples of Christ—other denominations and movements grew by their appeal to elements, largely of the older American stock, who remained on the level from which these proletarian denominations had once drawn most of their constituencies. So far as they were church members, Negroes were still chiefly Baptists and to a lesser degree Methodists. Many Negroes, especially among the educated, were subject to the prevailing secularism and if they had a church connexion it tended to be purely nominal. Increasing difficulty was experienced in recruiting a Negro ministry, especially from men of better than average educational training.

So multiform was the Protestantism of the United States that if an attempt is made to suggest other general trends, many exceptions can at once be named. We can merely note a few which would have to be given a place in a complete picture. To one we have already called attention—the increasing percentage of the population who had church membership in Protestant churches. Within the Protestant membership a general drift, varying from denomination to denomination, occurred from a firm adherence to earlier Evangelical theology and the inerrancy of the Scriptures to a modification of these convictions arising from adjustment to the intellectual currents of the day. Conservatives enrolled a larger proportion from the lower than from the higher intellectual and economic levels. Soon after World War I conservatism found expression in a militant Fundamentalism formulating what were esteemed as the minimum bases of Evangelical belief: the deity and virgin birth of Christ, the bodily resurrection of Christ, salvation through faith in His substitutionary sacrifice on the cross, the inerrancy of the Scriptures, and the visible return of Christ, in judgment, to set up His Kingdom. Soon after World War I Harry Emerson Fosdick (1878––), a Baptist clergyman, became a focus of the Fundamentalist attack. He was supported by large elements of Evangelical heritage who held to what they believed to be the heart of that heritage, but with attempts to take account of the intellectual, economic, and social currents of the revolutionary age. Through the radio he had a nation-wide audience. Fosdick was also pastor of the new interdenominational Riverside Church whose building, as a kind of symbol, loomed high above the Hudson in a district in New York City in which were several institutions of higher education. Across a street from the Riverside Church was eventually erected the Interchurch Centre, which housed the national and international headquarters of a large proportion of the Protestantism of the country. The kind of evangelism represented in the nineteenth century by men like Charles G. Finney and Dwight L. Moody persisted, with an appeal to many in the strata which had been moved by these and less famous men. In the 1950's and 1960's its outstanding representative was William Franklin (more familiarly "Billy") Graham (1918––). Graham held meetings in most of the major cities, had millions of listeners through radio and television, and presented his message in all the continents. Transparently sincere, humble, and forthright, with a simple Evangelical message which was not unaware of contemporary theological and Biblical scholarship, Graham was acclaimed by millions, generally of the background which had been reached by his great predecessors but now only a minority of the population.

As in Western Europe, in the United States a major theological trend came from the disillusionment born of World War I and the burgeoning industrial society. For countless persons the hope was shattered of achieving the Kingdom of God in the United States and in the world which had long been cherished, especially in the latter part of the nineteenth century. Instead, man was regarded as basically sinful; though if repentant he could be forgiven, he and his fellows could never attain perfection.

The most widely heard exponent of this conviction was Reinhold Niebuhr (1892——). He spoke of Christ as setting forth "impossible possibilities," but, undespairing, laboured indefatigably to promote measures which would keep society from complete deterioration. After World War II his friend and colleague Paul Tillich (1886——) had a wide hearing among intellectuals. A refugee from the Hitler régime and a sensitive, highly intelligent, and painfully honest soul into whom the iron of the revolutionary age with its two world wars had deeply entered, Tillich wrestled with the issues faced by mankind and especially by Christians, both collectively and individually, and was listened to wistfully but not always with understanding.

A growing feature of the religiously pluralistic United States was the mounting number of Orthodox. They came, by immigration, from several of the national bodies. They continued to suffer from the divisions of their Old World background but trained indigenous clerical leadership and groped towards a united front.

The members of the British Commonwealth peopled predominantly by Western European stock—Canada, Australia, and New Zealand—showed the effects of the revolutionary age in much the same way as did the British Isles and the Protestantism of the United States. Indigenous leadership developed, more rapidly in Canada and New Zealand than in Australia. Partly because of the tradition created by the convict beginnings and not entirely displaced by the free immigration from which the majority were recruited, and partly because of the tropical and semi-tropical climate which favoured outdoor sports and recreation, Australia was more nearly secular than were its sister commonwealths.

By the mid-1960's what had been another British commonwealth, the Union of South Africa, had completely broken away (1961) from its imperial ties. Now, as the Republic of South Africa, dominated by the Afrikaners who constituted the majority of the European elements, it attempted to solve its pressing race problem by *apartheid*. As in the nineteenth century, the overwhelming majority of the Afrikaners were members of one or another of the Dutch Reformed Churches. A courageous minority in these bodies endeavoured to modify *apartheid* in a fashion which they deemed more equitable to the Africans and were assisted by some of British background.

The revolt among non-Europeans against imperialism and colonialism was accompanied by the deepened rootage of Christianity. Because Christianity had been associated with that imperialism and colonialism, the revolt might have been expected to lead to the waning of the Christian communities as alien enclaves. As we have suggested, that was the case on the mainland of China. But elsewhere the result was the exact opposite. In land after land the Christian churches grew and were increasingly self-governing, self-supporting, and self-propagating—as a long-cherished dream of Western missionaries had envisioned them.

In most of Africa south of the Sahara the proportion of Christians—Roman Catholic and Protestant—rapidly mounted and received more and more African leadership, lay and clerical. The increase was particularly marked after World War II. In the Roman Catholic Church African priests multiplied and were rapidly placed under African bishops. By the early 1960's an African had been elevated to the cardinalate. In 1962 the Roman Catholic bishops of Africa formed a continuing organization to deal comprehensively with the problems of the continent. More and more Protestant churches were autonomous and independent of foreign control. Protestants had difficulty in developing a highly trained African ministry and were troubled as the newly independent governments took over the schools, which had long been staffed by African Christians and partly subsidized by foreign funds. Many individuals had combined the functions of teacher and pastor. As the two became separated, the pastor had less social recognition and a smaller salary than the teacher— to the detriment of the pastoral functions. African Protestants came together across political and denominational lines. In 1963 an all-Africa youth conference was held in Kenya and a continuing all-Africa (Protestant) Christian council was set up by a delegated conference in Nigeria.

In India, in spite of the mounting population, between 1914 and 1963 the proportion of Christians grew from about one in a hundred to between three and four in a hundred. Indian leadership emerged in both the Roman Catholic Church and the Protestant Churches. In Indonesia, when, during World War II, all missionary personnel were expelled or imprisoned, Batak Christians increased by about 100,000. The Bataks were a vigorous, formerly animistic folk in the highlands of Sumatra. In the second half of the nineteenth century German Protestants had planted the faith among them. So thoroughly rooted had it become that after foreign personnel was withdrawn Batak leaders continued to spread it. After World War II some help came from abroad, but only as the Bataks asked for it, and chiefly for assistance in preparing clergy. In the Republic of Korea, with the achievement of independence Christians, both Roman Catholic and Protestant, multiplied and Korean leadership mounted. Much the same happened on Taiwan under the Republic of China. In the Philippines the Roman Catholic Church was more and more staffed by Filipino clergy and bishops, and Protestants grew in numbers and Filipino initiative. In 1959 the East Asia Christian Conference was inaugurated. It had as its purpose coöperation among the Protestants of East Asia in spreading the Gospel in that part of the world. In other words, the Protestants, most of them small minorities, were not willing to lead self-enclosed ghetto existences but were helping one another in witnessing to the faith.

To the growing Christian communities among non-European peoples aid continued to be given by Christians in Europe and the larger Europe. Most of the assistance to the Roman Catholics outside the Occident came from Europe. From France still went more missionaries than from any other country—although not, as in the nineteenth century, more than from all the rest of the Roman Catholic Church. Belgium and the Netherlands ranked next after France. Roman Catholics gave more support in personnel than did Protestants. In 1958 the latter's foreign staff numbered 34,181. While that total had doubled since the eve of

World War I, in 1950 Roman Catholic missionaries were said to be 42,689. In money the cost of Protestant missions was much larger than that of Roman Catholic missions. In the Protestant enterprise an increasing proportion of personnel and finances came from the United States and Canada. In 1911, 7,239 Protestant missionaries were sent out from North America and 14,068 from other regions, predominantly the British Isles and the Continent of Europe. In 1958 the corresponding figures were 25,058 from North America and 13,548 from the rest of the world. The changing proportions were presumably a reflection of the growing wealth of Canada and the United States and the impoverishment of Western Europe by the two world wars. But they may be ascribable in part to more rapid progress of secularization on the eastern than on the western shore of the Atlantic.

In meeting the challenge of industrialization and of the mounting divorce of labourers in factories and mines from Christianity, no striking progress could be reported. Many earnest efforts were made. They included worker-priests in France in the 1930's and especially in the 1940's and 1950's. Under various names and auspices the worker-priests attempted to reach the de-Christianized labourers by joining with them in their daily toil and ministering to them at night and at odd hours. However, some phases of the enterprise came under the censure of ecclesiastical authorities. In Great Britain, Germany, and the United States, Protestants had other experiments, but without making any considerable dent on the problem as a whole.

A striking development, most of it after 1914 and rapidly mounting with the years, was the movement towards the unity of all Christians. From the very beginning the dream was inherent in Christianity. Jesus was remembered to have commanded His disciples to love one another as He had loved them and to have prayed that all who believed in Him might be one as He and the Father were one. Yet never had all who believed in Him been in a single fellowship. Rifts had always been present. They multiplied! Christians became more divided than the adherents of any other high religion. During the nineteenth century and notably in the twentieth century the trend was reversed—and chiefly through Protestantism, by its genius the most fissiparous form of Christianity.

Movements towards unity had several expressions. (1) Christians of many denominations came together as individuals and not as officially representative of their respective churches, as in the Young Men's and Young Women's Christian Associations. (2) Unions of severed branches of one denomination took place —as Methodists in Britain and in the United States. (3) There were unions of different denominations—as the United Church of Canada, a fusion in 1925 of the Methodists, the Congregationalists, and a majority of the Presbyterians in that country; the Church of Christ in Japan (in 1941), principally of Methodists, Presbyterians, and Congregationalists, but also including some smaller bodies; the Church of South India (1947), made up of Anglicans, Presbyterians, Methodists, and Congregationalists; and in the United States the United Church of Christ (1957-1961), composed of Congregationalists, Christians, Evangelicals, and Reformed. (4) Regional or national councils of churches were formed in which several denominations joined. Among them were the Federal Council of the Churches of Christ in America, organized in 1908, in which churches of the United States and Canada joined, enlarged in 1950 to the National Council of the Churches of Christ in the United States of America; the British Council of Churches, brought into being in 1942; *Die Evangelische Kirch in Deutschland* (the Evangelical Church in Germany), in 1945, usually called EKD or EKiD for short; and several national Christian councils in Asia, formed after World War I. All were parts of what Protestants called the Ecumenical Movement.

The Ecumenical Movement had its global expression in the World Council of Churches, originally a fusion of the World Conference on Faith and Order and the Universal Christian Council for Life and Work. Both had come into being after 1914 and the latter was at the outset due to the vision and will of Nathan Söderblom. The two authorized a meeting of representatives of member bodies at Utrecht (1938) under the chairmanship of William Temple to draw up a provisional constitution for the World Council of Churches. During World War II that body was described as "in process of formation." From its headquarters in Geneva in neutral Switzerland it served effectively in many ways. In 1954 it was formally constituted in a gathering in Amsterdam. In 1961 at a meeting in New Delhi the International Missionary Council was integrated with it as the Division on World Mission and Evangelism. By 1963 the member churches embraced the overwhelming majority of the Protestants in Europe, the majority of the Protestants in North America, and almost all the Eastern Churches, including the Russian Orthodox Church, which included the large majority of the membership of that divided wing of Christianity. In 1961 the Pope sent official observers to the New Delhi meeting.

In the meantime many Roman Catholics, especially in France, Belgium, the Netherlands, and Germany, developed an eager interest in the Ecumenical Movement. Paul Couturier (1881-1953), a priest in Lyons, promoted a prayer for unity in which Roman Catholics, Orthodox, Anglicans, and Protestants joined. It sought God's guidance in achieving unity but did not attempt to dictate the method by which it should be attained. When, in 1962, the twenty-first Ecumenical Council, called by Pope John XXIII, met in the Vatican, at his invitation official observers were present from several Anglican and Protestant churches and from the Russian Orthodox Church. The council had as its announced objective the renewal of the Church to meet the challenge of the changing times. It also sought to promote the unity of all who bore the Christian name. One of the first utterances of Paul VI, elected in June, 1963, to succeed John XXIII on the latter's death, promised the resumption of the Council, which had been adjourned in December, 1962.

In the Ecumenical Movement, very much in its infancy, but in one form and another embracing the large majority of Christians, was an attempt to bear a united witness in the rapidly shrinking and dangerously quarrelsome world.

THE MOUNTING WORLD-WIDE INFLUENCE OF CHRISTIANITY

In the twentieth century more nearly on a world-wide scale than ever before, Christianity made itself felt far beyond the formal borders of the churches. That influence was seen in a variety of ways. Among them was the United Nations, sprung from Christian faith but with a membership embracing predominantly non-Christian nations whose total populations exceeded those of the members from the former Christendom. The Red Cross, with a symbol giving evidence of its Christian origin and doing a service which encompassed all the non-Communist world, had become quite thoroughly secularized, but owed its beginning to the Christian faith—and, ultimately, to Christ. Gandhi would not call himself a Christian. In his younger days while in South Africa he had been urged to identify himself with Christ but had decided not to do so. Yet he was a warm admirer of Christ both as a person and for His teachings and used Christian hymns in his entrance into some of his fasts and when, feeling his object attained, he resumed eating. Through him something of the influence of Christ had an effect on millions of Indians. When he fell at an assassin's hand thousands of Indians said that he had died a Christ-like death. Thus, perhaps without realizing the full significance of what they were saying, they acknowledged Christ as the ideal by whom to measure their national hero.

In the mid-twentieth century Christ was by no means dominant and of the minority—although a large one—of mankind who statistically were Christians only a portion could be said to have made a full commitment to Christ. Indeed, with the population explosion even the nominal Christians were a smaller minority than fifty years earlier. Nevertheless, it is safe to say that no other being who has lived on the planet was as influential as Christ and that that influence, far from fading, was growing.

CHAPTER XII

An Attempt at an Appraisal and Forecast

We have brought our story to the date when, because the scroll
has unrolled to a point where to attempt to peer into what
it next contains would be to pass from history to prophecy, we
must pause. Inevitably the question arises: what of the future?
Does the record justify any confident predictions? At the outset
we noted that the nineteen and a half centuries we have covered
are only a small fragment of the course of *Homo sapiens* and
even of what we call civilization; when viewed against cosmic
time they constitute only a fraction of a second and embrace
a small planet which is a mere speck in the vast universe. We
have seen that Christianity is a religion having as its heart
Jesus and what His early followers remembered of His life,
teachings, death, resurrection, and ascension. We have called
attention to the fact that Christianity has never fully embodied
what came from Jesus, that it has repeatedly been modified by
its cultural environment, and that through the centuries some
of its aspects have contradicted much that was at the very core
of the early Christians' memories of Jesus. Again and again we
have remarked that some of the chronic evil seemingly inseparably associated with mankind has displayed several of its
colossal dimensions among peoples who have called themselves

Christian, but that repeatedly efforts to counter this evil, some of them at least partly successful, have been put forth by men and women inspired and sustained by Christian faith.

We have suggested that this contrast was to be expected from what Christians believe to have been the incarnation of the Eternal God. The Eternal God, so they maintain, coming in weakness in Christ so provoked the evil in man that the official representatives of as high a religion and of as good a government as the world had known committed the greatest crime in history, the crucifixion of the Son of God. We have reminded ourselves that Paul saw in the cross both the weakness and the power of God and the seeming foolishness and yet the wisdom of God. We have given as a possible explanation that God's purpose in creating man has been, not to produce automata, with no freedom to do other than what is determined by their heredity and environment, but to give birth to sons. To do this He has granted men a degree of free will, limited but authentic, and by respecting that free will in the apparent weakness of the incarnation and the cross and by a combination of judgement and love which has accompanied men, both as individuals and in human society, He has sought to win their willing repentance and love. To those who do "receive Him," He has given "power to become the sons of God." But that "power" always works within individuals who still suffer from the limitations inherited from man's long past. The greatest of those who most nearly approximate to the ideal seen in Christ are not perfect. Often, as we have noted in those whom the Church regards as saints, contradictions are vividly seen of what God wishes them to be. They are *in via* towards the "high calling of God in Christ Jesus" and, as Paul humbly recognized in himself, have not yet "attained" but are pressing "toward the mark for the prize of the high calling of God in Christ Jesus." This, as at least this author sees it, is the Christian understanding of the human record. Non-Christians and many Christians would not view it in this fashion. Here is, frankly, the conviction from which the preceding pages have been written. We have attempted to limit ourselves to facts which are there for all to see, but our choice and presentation of facts have been governed, consciously or unconsciously, by this basic conviction.

In the course of our story we have seen that Christianity has never been even nominally accepted by more than a minority of mankind. In the first five centuries that minority was almost entirely in a small portion of the earth's surface, embraced by the shores and islands of the Mediterranean and some outlying districts and containing only a minority of even civilized mankind. When what was then "Christendom" disintegrated from internal weaknesses which Christianity did not fully remedy, and by pressures from invaders, it shrank to about half its former size. It was then slowly enlarged by the "conversion" of rough barbarians from the North. For several centuries "Christendom" embraced only the western tip of a peninsula of Eurasia and a few dwindling fragments in Western and Central Asia and North Africa which had not fully succumbed to Islam. Although "Christendom" was partly moulded by what came from Christ and His apostles, much of its pre-Christian past was painfully evident, and neutral observers would not have adjudged its civilization to be as high as that in some sections of Asia. In the fourteenth and fifteenth centuries even that "Christendom" was further reduced by fresh advances of Islam and by internal corruption. But beginning in the last decades of the fifteenth century a vast expansion began, partly through attempts of minorities to bring "Christendom" to a nearer approximation to the standards seen in Christ and partly by explorations, conquests, and migrations which within the brief course of four centuries brought all the earth's surface under the control of "Christian" peoples. Much of that expansion, both internal and external, was marked by heightened contradictions of what was set forth in the Gospel. Yet efforts emerging from the Christian faith were conspicuous and were partly successful in resolving those contradictions in such fashion as to bring individuals and the nascent world community more nearly to conformity to the demands of Christ. In the twentieth century the contradictions were heightened. Within "Christendom" emerged forces, notably war, Communism, and secularism, which threatened to erase whatever remained of its Christian faith, to make the mounting impact of its culture on the rest of mankind destructive of all religion, and, through devices created by "Christians," either to erase life on the planet or to plunge such of mankind as survived back into pre-civilized barbarism. Yet Christianity became more widely represented and more deeply rooted in more peoples than it or any other religion had ever been, and Christians tried to counter the evils of the era made more colossal by forces which were a perversion of the energy released by the Gospel.

What would the future hold? Was the dominance of Western "Christian" civilization a passing phase of mankind's long pilgrimage? Would Christianity, closely associated with that dominance, continue to spread, be brought nearer to the standards and the hope set forth in Christ, and ultimately prevail? To the last question individual Christians throughout the centuries and especially in the nineteenth century would have given a confident affirmative. Even in the twentieth century, when many in "Christendom" talked of the "post-Christian era," suffered from a loss of nerve, and were under a dark cloud of pessimism, a Pope dedicated the entire human race to Christ and some Roman Catholics and Protestants still took seriously the early Christian dream of making disciples of all nations, baptizing them, and teaching them to observe all that Christ commanded.

The historian as a historian makes no prediction. He can simply point out the contrasting trends. As a Christian he finds no certain answer in the Bible. He remembers that the Old and New Testaments speak of a climactic end of human history, that much in the New Testament identifies the end with the second coming of Christ, and that an early Christian prayer was "even so come, Lord Jesus." As a Christian he also recalls that again and again in the Scriptures, in one form of words or another, confidence is expressed that it is God's purpose to sum up all things in Christ, both in heaven and on earth. By faith he is confident that we live in a universe created by God through the Word become flesh in Christ, and that God is pursuing elsewhere as well as on this planet the methods which He has employed with man. He believes that God's might and love as seen in the incarnation, the cross, and the resurrection infill the entire universe, both that small fragment of it dimly seen by men through their science, a science most extensively developed in "Christendom," and the vast world where those who have passed beyond our present sight and entered, by His grace, eternal life continue to grow in their knowledge of and fellowship with the Triune God. The Christian recalls the hope that in one of his inspired moments Paul declared: "the creation waits with eager longing for the revealing of the sons of God . . . because the creation [and that must mean the entire universe] will be set free from its bondage to decay and obtain the liberty of the children of God." The Christian also recalls the varied ways that many of his predecessors have envisioned the forms which that consummation will take. He remembers that even those with whom Jesus talked in the forty days after His resurrection could think of the Kingdom of God—the burden of His discourse—only as the restoration of the kingdom to Israel. Jesus by-passed that interpretation, saying that it was not for them to know "times or seasons which the Father has fixed by His own authority," but that they were to receive power and were to be His witnesses to the ends of the earth. Elsewhere, we are told, Jesus promised those who sought to obey His breath-taking commission that He would be with them "to the close of the age."

That age may seem evil and the close be either at hand or far off, but we as Christians must continue to witness, seeking to bring all men to discipleship and to lead them to obedience to what Jesus taught His disciples. We must do it humbly, recognizing the congenital sin from which we are not yet fully freed, but determined to abound in the work of the Lord, confident that our labour is not in vain if it be in the Lord.

Bibliography

This little book does not call for an extended bibliography. That can be found in three much larger works by the same author, from which much of the material in the preceding pages is drawn: *A History of Christianity* (New York, Harper & Brothers, 1953, pp. xxvii, 1516) covers the entire story from the beginning to 1945. *A History of the Expansion of Christianity* (New York, Harper & Brothers, 7 vols., 1937–1945) embraces the centuries from the beginning to 1945. *Christianity in a Revolutionary Age. A History of Christianity in the Nineteenth and Twentieth Centuries* (New York, Harper & Row, 5 vols., 1958–1962) deals with the period indicated by the title.

If more detailed but semi-popular accounts on particular periods and subjects are desired, the following may be suggested:

For the first four centuries, H. Lietzmann, *A History of the Early Church,* translated by B. L. Woolf (New York, Charles Scribner's Sons, Vols. 1, 2, 1937, 1938; London, Lutterworth Press, Vol. 3, 1950).

On monasticism, H. B. Workman, *The Evolution of the Monastic Ideal from the Earliest Times to the Coming of the Friars* (London, The Epworth Press, 1913, pp. xxi, 368).

On the Protestant Reformation, R. H. Bainton, *The Reformation of the Sixteenth Century* (Boston, The Beacon Press, 1952, pp. xi, 276); R. H. Bainton, *Here I Stand. A Life of Martin Luther* (New York, Abingdon-Cokesbury Press, 1950, pp. 422); W. Walker, *John Calvin, the Organizer of Reformed Protestantism,* 1509-1564 (New York, G. P. Putnam's Sons, 1906, pp. xviii, 456); R. H. Bainton, *The Travail of Religious Liberty* (Philadelphia, The Westminster Press, 1951); J. G. Ridley, *Thomas Cranmer* (Oxford, Clarendon Press, 1962, pp. 450).

On the Catholic Reformation: P: Janelle, *The Catholic Reformation* (Milwaukee, The Bruce Publishing Company, 1941, pp. xiv, 397).

On the United States: W. W. Sweet, *Religion in Colonial America* (New York, Charles Scribner's Sons, 1942, pp. xiii, 367); W. W. Sweet, *The Story of Religion in America* (New York, Harper & Brothers, 1950, pp. ix, 493).

Index